ALSO BY LISA JOHNSON

Don't Think Pink: What Really Makes Women Buy—
And How to Increase Your Share of This Crucial Market
with Andrea Learned

MIND YOUR
X's and Y's

Satisfying the 10 Cravings
of a New Generation of Consumers

Lisa Johnson

With Cheri Hanson

FREE PRESS
New York   London   Toronto   Sydney

FREE PRESS
A Division of Simon & Schuster, Inc.
1230 Avenue of the Americas
New York, NY 10020

FREE PRESS and colophon are trademarks of Simon & Schuster, Inc.

For information about special discounts for bulk purchases,
please contact Simon & Schuster Special Sales at
1-800-456-6798 or business@simonandschuster.com

DESIGNED BY ERICH HOBBING

Manufactured in the United States of America

1   3   5   7   9   10   8   6   4   2

The Library of Congress Cataloging-in-Publication Data is available.

ISBN-13: 978-0-7432-7750-1
ISBN-10: 0-7432-7750-3

For my incredible husband, Dave

CONTENTS

Mind Your
X's and Y's

THE RISE OF
THE CONNECTED GENERATION

I had one foot planted in the established marketplace and the other in the new consumer playground before I realized that something big was happening. As a marketing and research specialist by day, I work with top companies across the nation to help them build more compelling brands.

On weekends and weeknights, our home becomes the adult equivalent of the neighborhood Kool-Aid house, filled with college students and twenty- or thirtysomethings watching football games, making dinner, and sitting around the outdoor fire pit (my husband and I have informally mentored groups of twentysomethings for years, and we love having people over to our home). My client work didn't seem to indicate that the marketplace was dramatically shifting, but the conversations I was having with my student interns and our large network of young friends clearly indicated that something was afoot.

Cassie told me that University of Oregon students were obsessed with a new online community called Facebook, which had quickly become the procrastination tool of choice. She e-mailed me her pass code and I got a wide-eyed glimpse behind the college curtain.

Josh, a talented singer-songwriter, was not just dreaming of a music career anymore. He had built a personal page on MySpace.com and quickly landed two experienced music promoters who were already booking regional concerts on his behalf.

Nearly a dozen of my young friends skipped the traditional summer internship routine and left for overseas service projects that included working in orphanages, rebuilding tsunami-devastated homes, and helping in other areas of need. I had never seen so many people acting on their hunger to give back.

Then Kalen and Rachel went skydiving, Brook bungee jumped in New Zealand, and our friend Dave's thirty-eighth birthday party was an adrenaline-filled adaptation of *The Amazing Race*. Everyone seemed eager for a little adventure.

Even popular media was shifting and reinventing itself. Friends and colleagues started blogging to express their opinions and build their businesses. While wandering among the bookstore shelves one afternoon, I discovered a new magazine that explored popular culture through a spiritual lens.

During one of my weekly regrouping sessions at my favorite coffee shop, I began scribbling on a napkin. Iced Americano in hand, I started to put the pieces together. What emerged were ten major cravings that are driving this Connected Generation of twenty- and thirtysomethings and reshaping the marketplace into a veritable playground for consumers.

My curiosity piqued, I began searching for more examples of this new market—a place where people were embracing technology, creativity, and their own power with a childlike zeal. Suddenly, the cravings that I had outlined on my coffee shop napkin were apparent all around me. I made a list of companies, large and small, that have hit a nerve and tapped into these powerful desires.

I spent the next year talking to the owners and marketers leading these maverick brands, the people who love them, and sometimes even their critics. Smart and savvy, the minds behind these fascinating organizations had great insights to share. They were also hungry for the big picture. Many were aware that they held one piece of a much bigger puzzle and they, like me, were eager for a bird's-eye view of how the market has shifted, creating massive opportunities for quick-witted newcomers and leaving many established companies, and even whole industries, scratching their heads.

Working systematically with Cheri Hanson—a leading journalist and content strategist—I unpacked the new marketplace. We developed consumer profiles, built a detailed understanding of the ten market cravings, and learned a great deal from the brands that are leading the way. The patterns emerged quickly and clearly. Brands that attract loyal customers from Generations X and Y are not just lucky. These organizations are instinctively following an innovative set of guideposts that inform their products, services, and market strategies. While it's certainly not formulaic, there is a clear market code.

THE NEW CONSUMER PLAYGROUND

Imagine for a moment that the market has always been a playground—a place where people go to buy, sell, learn, engage, share, and socialize. In the past, this playground had few toys and lots of rules. There was always someone carrying a whistle, ready to stop the fun. Corporations developed and marketed products. Consumers decided whether or not to buy them. It was hierarchical and formally structured.

Today, a new model is infusing this stagnant market with life, and in many cases creating new opportunities that no one imagined were possible. The people who sparked this revolution have developed a fresh set of criteria. When they live the five essential criteria—experience, transparency, reinvention, connection, and expression—it naturally reshapes the market, which is living, breathing, and constantly evolving. There are very few rules, and everyone is invited. The structures are loose, and anyone is free to reshape the process, launch a new category, and join the fun.

It began with some underground rumblings: Napster developed free file-sharing software; eBay offered the first online auction service; Apple put a premium on design; blog writers gained full media credentials at political conferences. These developments all sprang from individuals' desire to create change. As these new ways of operating built momentum and gained mainstream acceptance (often raking in mammoth profits to boot), they fundamentally altered the way business is conducted. These Web sites, services, and products were the first signs of a new market language—a code that now pervades everything from health care to auto sales.

In this book, you'll learn to crack the code of the new market. You'll learn what drives young, connected consumers and how their unspoken code of behavior has given way to ten essential market cravings. Regardless of whether you're a marketer, an ad exec, a student, the head of a nonprofit, or an artist, you need to understand this colossal shift. It's critical to realize that these market changes are not just a trend. The hierarchical structure of business has collapsed, giving way to a world that, in its best form, is more honest, accepting, engaging, and fun. One era in business has ended and a new one has begun. The fire is spreading and we're not going back.

INTRODUCING THE CONNECTED GENERATION

You might be inclined to think that computer nerds or pierced-and-tattooed punk bands changed the rules, and in many ways you'd be right. But the people who dismantled the marketplace share more than age or image—they share the same worldview. They share a common DNA that crosses traditional demographics and fuels a subsequent set of cravings.

To a large extent, this worldview belongs to Generation X (1965–1979) and Generation Y (1980–1997), a powerful group collectively known as the "Connected Generation." As a technology-fluent generation embraced cell phones, texting, and other forms of communication, a new generation of "always on" individuals emerged. For example, *Business Week* online posted a July 2004 article entitled "Reaching the Connected Generation." At the same time, educators working with Gen Y began to write about effectively teaching this "Connected Generation" in articles and books. In 2006, there are an estimated 62.1 million Americans ages twenty-seven to forty-one who fall under the Gen X umbrella. Approximately 74.2 million Americans ages nine to twenty-six are known as Generation Y. For marketing purposes, at the moment Gen Y usually excludes those younger than "tweens," that is, anyone younger than age nine (as of 2006).[1]

The Connected Generation covers a huge blanket of ages (nine to forty-one) and life stages (from teenagers to new moms to college students and high-powered executives). Again, what links them as the Connected Generation is their attitude—a worldview that informs their education, careers, choices, and lifestyles. This generation is radically restructuring the way we all live and behave in the market. Empowered with new tools and highly networked communities, these young consumers are not content to watch from the sidelines. They're actively reinventing the market.

X AND Y LEAD THE CHARGE

Growing up amid rapid technological growth requires learning how to multitask. It requires absorbing and integrating several forms of media every day, and knowing how to receive and process an enormous number of advertising messages.

Whether we like it or not, recent technologies have changed how our brains operate. They have altered the way today's consumers think—not just what they buy, but how they buy, how they act and react, and which products and services they find compelling.

Technology, in other words, is reshaping the marketplace because it is reshaping consumers from the inside out. This shift has left thousands of companies scrambling to keep up. They copy what's already out there, or they produce a bunch of one-offs that don't work and cost a lot of money. In the end, most businesses have not been able to reach their target consumers. Businesses need to understand how to reach the multitasking, constantly upgrading customers who grew up in the Internet era—the Connected Generation.

It's increasingly urgent for businesses to understand Generations X and Y. In five years, this group will render many traditional business and marketing practices obsolete.

Baby Boomers have a tremendous amount of cash, but the Connected Generation is radically changing the rules of engagement and setting the pace for how companies and organizations of every kind will interact with consumers.

In the next ten years, many members of Generation X will turn forty. Historically, these are the peak earning and spending years. This generation, joined by members of Gen Y, will soon be filling higher executive positions as Boomers retire, while Gen X's smaller overall numbers will catapult even younger workers high up the promotion chain. With a higher percentage of the Connected Generation in the role of decision-makers for companies, businesses will need to focus not only on Business to Consumer principles, but on Business to Business as well. The Connected Generation is set to become corporate-level decision-makers, wielding important influence over a wide range of products and services. Moreover, they'll be earning more than ever before, and they'll spend their money on their kids, spouses, and aging parents, as well as themselves.

Gen Y, despite their young age, is proving to be a crucial demographic, thanks to its large numbers and proven brand loyalty. It's the next megasized population that everyone hopes will stimulate the economy in years to come. Advertisers have also found that Gen Y's brand choices hold great sway with the generation above them. If companies portray a younger age group in their advertisements, they also draw in Gen Xers who don't want to be left behind.

According to a recent study published in the *Harvard Business Review,* this younger generation of proactive consumers now has the ability to make or break new brand-name products only a few months after they hit the market, thanks to the Internet and other connected information technologies. Today's consumers self-organize online chat rooms, conventions, and meet-ups to celebrate their favorite products without any efforts from the companies that create them. Today's consumers are more empowered—indeed, more powerful—than consumers past. Consumer word of mouth and loyalty have never been so crucial.

Unfortunately, this group is not easy to reach. Now that they have outgrown their favorite "young" brands (such as MTV), Gen Xers are becoming even more difficult to categorize. While a few companies are succeeding (Starbucks, Apple, Target), most are not. Generation X is fragmented because it has an antagonistic relationship with the media and with overt brand labeling. Inundated with hundreds of thousands of advertisements over the years, Gen X has been called cynical, independent minded, and difficult to reach with products, services, or forms of entertainment. As a result, Gen X has received very little attention over the past ten to fifteen years, and marketers and advertisers have made a raft of incorrect assumptions about what they want. This generation, however, pioneered today's most widespread technologies, both at home and in the workplace (laptops, BlackBerries, cell phones, e-mail, the Internet, etc.). Marketing to them needs to be equally technologically savvy.

Generation Y, on the other hand, embraces the marketing process but presents a different yet equally important challenge—they have been studied only as teenagers, so we understand their attitudes and behaviors through a very small brand spectrum, including fashion, entertainment, and food. We still don't know how Gen Y will interact with a range of high-end products such as real estate or insurance, and we have yet to determine or understand their adult buying behavior.

Together, the Connected Generation has grown to expect an accelerated innovation cycle of fresh, compelling, well-designed, and customized quality products, as opposed to Boomers, who get exhausted by this cycle. But these tech-savvy adventurers are simply the early adopters who alert us that something is about to happen.

THE FIVE ESSENTIAL CRITERIA
OF THE NEW MARKET CODE

Before outlining the ten consumer cravings, it's important to understand those five essential criteria (experience, transparency, reinvention, connection, and expression) that underlie each craving. With the Connected Generation, all the previous markers—age, income, location—go out the window, and instead these eighteen-to-forty-year-olds seek these five criteria in everything they do and buy. Regardless of your industry or the products or services you are selling, you should always keep these five qualities in mind.

Experience

Today's consumers have a desire to get out there and try new activities, explore, test personal limits, and see what's possible. Splashier examples include ESPN's X-Games and the rising popularity of sports such as snowboarding, surfing, skim boarding, mountain biking, and rock climbing. Now the desire to feel alive and adventurous is seeping into the veins of older, less traditionally daredevil consumers. Middle-age women are taking kayaking trips into Alaska and seniors are embarking on African safaris. The company picnic means cleaning litter from the river basin or a competitive game of Frisbee golf. The push for adrenaline is reaching beyond the fringes.

Twenty- and thirtysomethings also seek specific, firsthand experience. They want to explore wine from a certain geographical region or to volunteer at the local soup kitchen instead of sending checks to faceless charities. The quest for experience could even mean something as small but satisfying as learning how to use a digital camera. There is a longing to feel alive and to shake up a stale routine. There's also a deeper push to engage the senses. Life is often so scripted and structured that it can feel wonderful and special to cook a meal from scratch, attend a live concert, arrange fresh flowers on your desk, or sink your hands into the garden.

In the new playground, experience is currency. It's more valuable and prized than any material belonging. Unusual experiences spark conversations and help people understand each other. They provide a vehicle for exploring passions, for developing a stronger sense of self, and for giving back to the community. The longing for experience also encompasses a desire to tell your own stories and to create your own content—to shoot the Grand Canyon footage and mix it with some favorite music instead of buying a souvenir DVD.

In their drive for experience, these people want to be able to say to themselves:

- I am actively participating (versus passively consuming). Pursuing quirky activities (some new, some retro)—dodgeball, knitting circles, make-your-own-stiletto classes, tae kwon do, boccie on the beach, Moroccan cooking, hang gliding, coaching a fantasy sports team.
- I am testing my abilities. Proving things to myself through solo international travel, NASCAR driving school, launching a business, writing a screenplay, starting a nonprofit.
- I am exploring my edges. Calling out dormant parts of my personality—confirming I'm sexy at pole-dancing lessons, declaring my courage during stand-up comedy night, learning to sing my heart out at Rock Camp, freeing my inner badass at Harley-Davidson driving school.

Transparency

Consider the new market an antispin zone. Forget about slick, forget about overpackaging, and forget about faking *anything*. There's a new spirit of transparency in the air. Companies and consumers alike need to get comfortable with full disclosure. That means being accountable for choices and decisions. Everyone makes mistakes, but the key is to take responsibility, address the damage fairly, and move on.

For years, the market has functioned with a push model. It's the idea that screaming louder will raise a message above the chaos and show people why they simply can't live without that new product. This model is tiring and it's broken. There's a swelling desire for authenticity and substance. Take Martha Stewart's triumphant emergence from prison. Whereas most people might consider a prison stint the ultimate public fall, Stewart took the opportunity to convey an air of greater self-awareness, subtlety, and kindness.

Transparency can be a tricky trait to understand. Traditional wisdom holds that you show only your good side and hide anything that's less than camera ready. But today, people are looking for access, clarity, and authenticity. It's okay to be flawed. What's not okay is to pretend that you're perfect and deny even the tiniest blemish.

According to Jackie Huba, a well-known blogger, word-of-mouth expert, and coauthor of *Creating Customer Evangelists,* the rise of blogging has directly paralleled this new demand for transparency. Organizations large and small are beginning to understand the need to pay attention to A-list bloggers. Yet the blogosphere has become so intricately connected that even small bloggers have major power because other, more influential bloggers will quickly pick up their compelling posts. This new tribe of online writers constantly references mainstream media and research, and links back and forth to each other. They are talking about brands and sharing their ideas and opinions. Smart companies need to listen and respond.

The new market has sharp watchdogs that work to protect the integrity and authenticity of the playground. Bullies, liars, fakes, and dictators are quickly exposed. Accountability is key, and decisions are consensual. People want the truth, and will be satisfied only when they can assert the following (even if it's just to themselves):

- I am exposing shortcomings and half-truths. Embracing my role as a marketplace watchdog—Googling people's history, blogging about Dell Computer Hell (and getting a full refund), driving a giant recall/refund by videotaping how to pick Kryptonite bike locks with a ballpoint pen.
- I am helping to create a new level of consumer due diligence.

Writing detailed product reviews on Epinions, warning fellow travelers about which motels have cockroaches on Tripadvisor.com, filtering through the clutter and providing personal bestseller lists, offering context by hyperlinking and sourcing information, giving behind-the-scenes information.

- I am helping the community. Taking a leadership position in an online peer review community, monitoring and removing slanderous comments on Wikipedia's online encyclopedia, sharing my links and folders on del.icio.us.

Reinvention

It's the shift that has brought entire industries to their knees. When people can forgo the video store for a home DVD service, and download their favorite songs (both legally and illegally) at the click of a mouse, the old rules just don't apply anymore.

There's a rumbling hunger for what's new, better, faster, and more efficient. When something clicks—such as buying only your favorite singles from a full album on iTunes—the new way will rule. Some might chalk up this phenomenon to a short attention span or lack of loyalty, but there's a deeper truth. The market is now a place of constant change. Thriving brands, people, and organizations understand how to handle this lightning pace and learn to evolve with each new shift. It's a matter of basic math. Why keep a home phone line if you're rarely at home and unlimited cell phone coverage is cheaper? Why stand in line at the grocery store if an affordable delivery service can bring milk and eggs while the baby sleeps?

Market hierarchies have crumbled as individual people gain access to production and distribution channels. Self-publishing, for example, is a viable possibility when there's a global market waiting online and a reader in Switzerland can download your poetry book. The new market is open to everyone, and as more smart people create fun ways to play, the possibilities grow exponentially.

If something doesn't work, consumers will turn on a dime, 180 degrees, and do it a new way. The new market is horizontal and everyone has different needs. It's time to embrace change and stay flexible.

Consumers want to be able to make these claims:

- I am seeing new possibilities. Noticing opportunities instead of barriers—publishing an online magazine, launching my garage band through the Internet, choosing a great indie film over a hyped Hollywood blockbuster.
- I am changing channels. Punishing pushy brands and exiting mass media—turning off the television and tuning into podcasts and playlists, skipping television ads with TiVo, buying new music I heard through a video game, making free long-distance calls over the Internet.
- I am changing the rules. Turning traditional business models inside out—modifying my favorite video game, writing a new ending to the latest installment of *Harry Potter* on fanfiction.net, making video ads for Converse instead of watching their versions, creating iPod accessories in my garage and selling them on CaféPress.com.

Connection

The new market runs on cooperation. It's about people blending their talents and perspectives to improve the experience for everyone. There's a spirit of dialogue, sharing, volunteering, and connections. The hottest sites on the Internet—such as eBay, Amazon, Match, and Craigslist—connect users to each other for many different purposes.

People also want greater connections to the market. They're eager to interact with companies and brands, and to share their ideas. When consumers love a company, such as Apple, they often have a true desire to help them improve their products and make them even more lovable.

Information is valuable in the new market, and influence comes not from hoarding information, but from sharing it. Knowing what's cool, how something works, what's happening underground, or what the experts are saying has major cachet. People are coming together to rally around causes or to talk about their favorite topics. They are buying each other's antiques, finding employees for job openings, sharing music, talking about political issues, and finding an incredible variety of ways to connect.

Connections equal power, and when groups of people gather, cultural shifts occur. Even individual connections can spark change. The community rules. It's a place to play, to learn, to talk, to help, and always to share.

Today, we are not happy unless we can say:

- We are sharing who we are. Expressing opinions and personalities— blogging our love of Luna Bars, posting online photo albums for friends to browse, creating shopping profiles on Yub.com.
- We are sharing what we know. Joining the massive share-a-thon online—writing up Grandma's famous cranberry sauce recipe on all recipes.com, creating a tutorial on how to build a better online dating profile, pointing people to natural remedies for common ailments.
- We are gathering. Staying close to the people we love and creating loose connections—Flickr photo sites, meeting new friends on JDate.com, rallying fellow Democrats at moveon.org, texting to create a spontaneous pillow fight in the university commons, staying in touch over the summer through facebook.com.

Expression

Anything is possible. This credo drives the new market and inspires people to sing, dance, or even diet on reality television shows. It's a desire to customize existing items—such as adding covers, trinkets, ring tones, and screen photos to a standard-issue cell phone—and to express the layered facets of your personality.

No one minds if the results feel raw or amateur. Today, people believe that everyone has something to say, and it builds street credibility to raise your voice and to create something obscure, alive, or simply authentic. There's a yearning to dream big—and to feel that people understand and applaud those big dreams. Talents should be revealed and quirks are endearing.

People are searching for novel ways to express themselves. Creativity is honored, but it's not limited to traditionally "artistic" pursuits such as drawing, painting, or singing. Personal expression also emerges in small choices, such as the songs you put on your iPod or the skull-and-crossbones collar on a pet Chihuahua. It lives in activities, careers, recreational pursuits, and spirituality. The new market values self-expression and has little interest in anything standard or homogenized. Even celebrities mix their designer labels with "mass" brands such as Gap or H&M.

It's all about expressing individuality. Each of us wants to be able to say:

- I am trying it myself. Getting more hands-on—test-driving a new career with Vocation Vacations, exercising my designer skills by trading spaces with the neighbors over the weekend, adding a new entry about Hello Kitty to Wikipedia.org.
- I am buying fun new tools and toys. Embracing all the opportunities that new technology offers—investing in a home podcast studio, creating professional-quality photos, pimping my ride, tricking out my phone.
- I am releasing my inner rebel. Exploring the edges and keeping you on your toes—teaching kindergarten by day and taking tango lessons by night, competing in Red Bull's Flugtag contest. (Flugtag means "flying day" in German, but more important, it's American for a bunch of creative geniuses strapping themselves to totally outrageous homemade, human-powered flying machines and launching themselves off a thirty-foot ramp into the wild blue yonder, or alternatively straight into the water.)

THE TEN CONSUMER CRAVINGS

The new consumer market is a living, breathing model. There is a new structure of participation that has changed the rules and reconfigured the power dynamic. The five essential criteria outlined above inform how consumers operate in the market. These criteria also point to ten specific consumer cravings that cross industries and age brackets as they drive every decision made by members of Generation X and Y:

1. *Shine the spotlight*: Extreme personalization gives marketing a new face.
2. *Raise my pulse*: Adventure takes its place as the new social currency.

3. *Make loose connections*: the new shape of "families" and social networks.
4. *Give me brand candy*: Everyday objects get sharp, delicious, intuitive design.
5. *Sift through the clutter*: Editors and filters gain new prominence.
6. *Keep it underground*: the rejection of push advertising and the rising influence of peer-to-peer networks.
7. *Build it together*: Connected citizens explore their creative power and influence change.
8. *Bring it to life*: Everyday activities are orchestrated to deliver a dramatic sense of theater.
9. *Go inward*: Spiritual hunger and modern media find common ground.
10. *Give back*: redefining volunteerism and the meaning of contribution.

Each of the following chapters outlines one of these ten market cravings. You'll learn why these cravings have emerged, what they look like, and how to build on them. You'll also get insider lessons from ten individuals and organizations that understand how to play the game and are attracting loyal followings.

People are wary of the hard sell and are quickly finding innovative ways to circumvent any information or stimuli that are unnecessary, inefficient, or irritating. If companies keep pushing, customers will continue to walk in the other direction.

This is not a short-term trend. Every arena will eventually be affected, including politics, nonprofits, education, insurance, travel, and beyond. Industries like technology and entertainment have already felt the shift. Others, such as finance and health care, are still surviving in the old model because they have fewer customers who have adopted the code. These values will soon spread beyond the edges and everyone will need to catch up.

It's time to join the game.

ONE

SHINE THE SPOTLIGHT

Extreme Personalization
Gives Marketing a New Face

Chris Murphy sits down in his bedroom to open the mail. The walls are lined with ribbons, trophies, and newspaper clippings.[1] The headlines say it all: *Murphy has the right stuff. State's top receiver eyes the championship.* The rest of the room is your average teenage haven— an Xbox on the floor, CDs piled next to an iPod, and a stack of comic books in the corner. The pages are frayed and worn, but seventeen-year-old Chris hasn't spent much time reading comic books in the last year. He's been too busy with school, social life, and football. Chris is a senior and the star receiver on his high school team. He's already tasted the thrill of state championships. Next up, college.

Several times a week, a new batch of letters arrives from schools across the nation. They all have the same goal—recruiting Chris. He tears into one crisp envelope after another: *"Dear Chris," "To Mr. Murphy."* They bear formal seals and read like textbooks. At first the attention was flattering. "They all want me?" Chris thought with amazement. Soon it became difficult to separate one school from another.

He opens an envelope from the University of Oregon in Eugene. Poised to throw the paper on the trash pile, Chris stops. It's a partial comic book. "That's cool," he thinks, and starts flipping through the pages. Each frame looks professionally drawn. The only thing that sets it apart from his own stack of comic books is the black and white pages—National Collegiate Athletic Association (NCAA) recruitment bylaws prevent all schools from sending color materials. He's about to set it down and head out for a run when he realizes there's something very different about this comic.

Mouth open in amazement, Chris flips back to the front cover. The whole comic book is about him. The title page reads, *"The Amazing O-Men. Mild-mannered Chris Murphy or Catch-everything C. Mack? A Hero Is Born."* In the top right-hand corner is a personalized "C. Mack" logo intertwined with the Oregon O. Chris is the star of the story, which begins as he joins the Oregon Ducks and starts his collegiate football career, and each frame is drawn with a remarkable likeness to Chris himself. He methodically scans each and every page, then jumps from his bed and dashes out the door. By the end of the week, all his friends, his parents, and even his football coach have read the comic.

For the next few months, Chris eagerly awaits new installments. He receives a new section every couple weeks that takes the story just a little bit further. It's the first envelope he opens when the mail arrives and the only college mailout he reads from top to bottom.

One week, he receives page 13.

"Here's the snap and a quick pass to Chris Murphy."

The next frame shows an ESPN broadcaster looking out over a packed Autzen Stadium, rising to his feet as he describes each play.

The next page is blank. A brief note tells Chris that he'll receive the final piece when he visits the Eugene campus to check out the school in person.

Chris pulls out his duffel bag and begins packing.

College sports are big business. Money, prestige, and school reputations are all at stake, and everyone wants to snag the hottest high-school prospects. In the spring of a student's junior year, colleges begin sending mail to potential student athletes. Most schools work with the "more-is-better" philosophy, flooding their prospects with letters and materials. The University of Oregon has taken a vastly different approach.

Back in 2002, Oregon decided to differentiate itself by combining traditional form letters with graphically rich mailers of different sizes, layouts, and formats. Their aim was to send their prospects more information of higher quality than any other school in the country. Every piece of mail was aligned with the Oregon football "brand"—an in-your-face, cutting-edge look that infuses everything from the green and yellow uniforms to the school's state-of-the-art facilities.

In 2003, the Oregon football staff and a team of twenty sports-marketing interns launched a poster series that featured action shots of uniformed players (the face in shadow) with the recruit's number running through the Oregon "O." The player's name was spelled in bold letters at the top of the poster and the bottom copy read, "The Future of Oregon Football." The idea was to help each prospect build a relationship with Oregon by visualizing himself playing in the Ducks uniform—as if he were already part of the team.

The first posters were sent to a handful of prospects with a personal note from the Oregon coaching staff. People were thrilled. Many recruits mentioned the personalized posters to their coaches, requested extra copies, or even contacted the recruiting staff to inquire about Oregon for the first time. The posters were used to welcome prospects and their families during official school visits. Opposing coaches mentioned the posters to Oregon's staff with considerable envy as they noticed them framed, front and center, in many living rooms during their home-recruiting visits. The posters were clearly doing their job.

It was time to step it up. With the 2004 recruiting season on the horizon, the Oregon staff challenged themselves to create a full campaign that was targeted, personal, and innovative.

Deryk Gilmore, director of player development, and his team of student interns set four key objectives for 2004:

1. Organize a separate mailing campaign for individuals who receive a written offer from Oregon.
2. Individualize all mail in the interest of recruits and their personalities.
3. Create specific identities and logos for recruits that bond them with Oregon football.
4. Strive to be innovative—constantly redefine the cutting edge.

They dubbed the campaign "Coming to Oregon," and launched several initiatives, including the wildly successful personal comic books. Oregon football coaches also sent handwritten notes to each prospect on a weekly basis and outlined their favorite drills and training techniques in graphic postcards mailed to the prospects' high-school coaches.

In the late stages of recruiting, coaches also brought in magazine mock-ups. They entered players' homes with mock-up copies of sports magazines featuring the recruits on the cover wearing Oregon uniforms. Instead of showing magazines depicting former Oregon stars, the marketing team decided to help recruits visualize what a career at Oregon could produce.

Parents were included in the process, too. The team created a diploma series, which reinforced the school's commitment to academics and to helping their sons graduate with high standing.[2]

THE CRAVING: SHINE THE SPOTLIGHT

The Connected Generation is eager for personal recognition. They want to make a difference—or at least a splash. The marketplace is waking up to a national obsession that sees ordinary citizens make their mark, achieve celebrity, and rise to prominence. Whether it's singing on *American Idol,* writing a book or blog, getting their video on *Current TV,* or being celebrated as the next great surfer, this generation longs to be recognized for who they are and what they bring to the party.

People are looking for their big break; they enjoy being big fish in small ponds. They feel ready to be known, and ready to have their dreams and experiences acknowledged and legitimized. Hand over the microphone and start the cameras rolling. Give them the backstage pass and the insider treatment. These folks are itching to stand out, stand up, and be celebrated with their names in lights (or print, or pixels).

In response, companies are waking up to the power of personalization and highly engaging tools that celebrate individuals' talents and potential. Personalized license plates, stamps, and mailing labels were just baby steps. Today, a whole slew of high-end products put you smack in the center of the action. Companies large and small are getting in on the opportunity. Masterfoods has taken M&M's color customization process one step further. The candies can now be printed with two lines of text, up to eight characters on every bite-size piece. Consumers can have their own custom-colored, personally branded treats for $9.49 for an 8 ounce bag (a plain old bag of M&M's of the same size runs about $2.85).[3]

New York independent art and design catalog company Elsewares (www.elsewares.com) offers a custom six-panel comic drawn to order by artist Mark Weber, whose work has run in *The New York Times,* the *Village Voice, Rolling Stone,* and *Playboy.* Hand-drawn, 8x11 art on 11x14 acid-free paper, the custom comic strip is a cool $150. If books are more your thing, husband-and-wife team J. S. Fletcher and Kathy Newbern will write you into one of their romance novels. For about $50, the intended couple can relive their romance in one of eight personalized books that range from "mild" to "wild," incorporating into the text not only you and your sweetie's names, but also your hometowns, occupations, pet names, hair color, perfume, and so on. At Highly Flammable Toys (www.highlyflammabletoys.com) film-school grad Russ Tucker will feature you on a custom 8½x12 inch movie poster ($95, plus shipping). You can add film critic "quotes" and a list of fake credits.

En masse, customers are leaving the audience and taking the stage—ready to stand in the spotlight. Brands that tap into this powerful need with highly creative and customized efforts will get not only some great buzz, but a whole new level of loyalty and brand ownership to match.

Why We Crave the Spotlight

1. **We're hardwired.**

   It's human nature to crave attention. We all want to be recognized and celebrated—whether it's on the football field or in our daily lives. We want to be understood, supported, desired, and even courted. We want to feel special.

2. **We're burned out.**

   We've all spent years being yelled at from the television screen. We don't want to be told anymore to buy the latest detergent or open a savings account. Consumers—especially media-savvy Generations X and Y—are cynical and extremely educated about the entire marketing process. Add in a collective obsession with celebrities, and people everywhere are longing to experience the insider treatment. They want to feel like someone really cares about their dreams and desires.

3. **We've seen what's possible.**

The quest for a high profile is now entrenched in our cultural fabric. Everyone knows a handful of people who have been plucked from the ordinary and enjoyed their fifteen minutes of fame. It's fun to watch and observe real lives, and we feel like our own days might be just as interesting. New venues such as MySpace.com and Current TV, plus podcasts, blogs, reality television, and interactive Web sites, allow us to share our unique personalities and talents with the world. These new tools have made it simple to launch us and our friends into the public eye.

4. **There's a sense of entitlement.**

Members of the Connected Generation see the market intimately tied to their own lives. It's a web of opportunity to explore, not a hierarchical structure to climb or conquer. "I deserve it and I'm ready for it now," is the common attitude. This group is not looking for a slow build, and they don't care about paying their dues.

5. **Every industry has a celebrity culture.**

Celebrated experts are everywhere today—no matter how mini or mundane the industry. From sought-after eyebrow shaper Anastasia (one of Oprah's favorites) to celebrity chefs who teach thousands of home cooks how to make thirty-minute meals, to plastic surgeons and dentists who orchestrate extreme makeovers, to landscapers, carpenters, and mechanics who outfit homes, yards, and cars, people have become famous for doing even the most behind-the-scenes work with flair and personality.

Thanks to the proliferation of new media, including a vast wilderness of television cable channels, there are a greater number of people who receive widespread recognition and global profile. Add reality and unscripted television to the mix and you have a veritable celebrity free-for-all, with has-beens getting second chances and no-namers leaping into the headlines.

6. **People want profile in familiar formats.**

Television, video, magazines—the basics still count. New

media is everywhere, but people want to be where the daily interactions occur. They don't necessarily want to win awards or fellowships; they want *profile*. In the past, only the wealthy got their names out there by funding a library or backing a new hospital wing. Today the options are broader and the criteria for celebrity are random, quirky, and wide open. Consider "Jared the Subway guy," who became famous for losing weight by eating Subway sandwiches.

7. **Youthful celebs wield major power.**

Popular media are celebrating the youth culture more than ever before. The old Mickey Mouse Club has turned into a talent pool for young performers like Justin Timberlake and Christina Aguilera. With so many kids in the spotlight, children begin dreaming about their own celebrity sooner and with greater specificity. They also start preparing earlier. Kids are groomed to play college sports when they're still in grade school, and parents, teachers, and coaches have all signed on to give their prodigies a jump start.

8. **We see where profile can take us.**

Jessica Simpson was a B-list singer living in the shadow of Britney Spears and Christina Aguilera until her MTV reality show, *Newlyweds,* hit the air. What followed was an amazing series of lucrative opportunities, including cosmetic and clothing lines, product endorsements, movie roles, and countless magazine covers. It's not clear how long her star will shine, but she is a stellar example of how greater profile can open the door to financial and social prosperity. As consumers, we watch and learn.

9. **We want promotion without the appearance of self-promotion.**

There's a fine line between self-promotion and having other people celebrate and recognize your contribution. While the Connected Generation craves the spotlight, it's not considered cool to just shamelessly self-promote (to a point). You need other people to celebrate your talents and abilities. If one of the Oregon recruits made his own comic book, it simply wouldn't fly. Currency comes when someone else highlights you.

By all accounts, Oregon's integrated marketing program was a huge success. The materials and innovative strategies were just one piece of the puzzle, but they helped the coaching staff land what many called Oregon's greatest recruiting class ever. In fact, Allen Wallace, national recruiting editor for *Superprep* magazine (www.superprep .com), called the coveted and talented 2004 freshman group the "surprise class of the year" and ranked Oregon's group of recruits number 10 in the nation.[4] The previous year, Oregon had ranked a mere 41 out of 117 competing schools.

Recruits consistently expressed excitement about the materials and attention they received throughout the year. Perhaps the best indicator of success was the number of recruits who assumed their superhero personas while still playing for their high-school team. Local newspaper and online articles highlighting the athletic achievements of "Bone Crusher," "Action Jackson," "The Dominator," and others surfaced in hometowns across the country.

Although the Oregon marketing team was careful to work within all NCAA recruiting regulations, word spread about the incredible materials the school was sending to its prospects.[5] The NCAA no longer allows Oregon to send comic books to their prospects. Although the marketing approach had approval from NCAA governing officials prior to its launch and worked within industry guidelines, competing schools were up in arms over the unfair advantage it appeared to give the team. In a nutshell, Oregon's marketing was scary good and it got them shut down—a minor setback for a crackerjack creative team that has a habit of topping themselves each and every recruiting year.

Oregon's recruiting campaign is an inspiring example of going over the top for a desirable inner circle. It was smart, savvy, and effective. Here are the key lessons to take away from the University of Oregon's considerable success.

LESSONS

Focus special attention on a select group of people.

Each year, the University of Oregon pays extra attention to a coveted group of about seventy top recruits. Within this group, the U of O also pursues a smaller, elite inner circle with extremely innovative and personalized tactics, and in some cases with a dedicated team of marketing interns assigned to a single athlete. As potential recruits begin committing to various schools, the prospect pool narrows and the U of O's efforts become more focused and frequent with their final candidates.

Today, innovation comes from going to unprecedented extremes for a small, select group. It requires a major brain shift, but one that will pay serious dividends. Instead of mass marketing, extreme personalization has the potential to elevate your opportunities and turn your products and services into hot, sought-after commodities. When you go to great lengths for an inside circle, there is a powerful ripple effect that spreads buzz and significantly boosts the "cool factor" of your brand. Your more casual customers will get wind of it and want to become part of that inner circle.

Make each person feel like the center of your universe.

U of O recruits instinctively understood the time involved in creating these graphically rich, highly personalized materials and were flattered to be part of an elite group receiving extreme consideration.

Delight a small group and make them the center of attention. Think about how to make your bull's-eye customers feel flattered and desirable. Most important, explore how your brand can actually bring their dreams to life. Lay their aspirations out in living color and show them how your brand will truly influence their lives. Dream bigger than your customers might allow themselves to dream. Shine the spotlight on them and give them service and attention usually reserved for the rich and famous. Give everyone great service or excellent products, but give your elite circle the most extraordinary treatment possible.

Concentrate on extreme personalization.

Customers today know what they want, and they don't like to be told what they want by marketers. They like to feel understood, so it's critical to know your prospects intimately. Learn everything you can and tailor a full program to satisfy their needs and desires. At the U of O, the recruiting department focused on an elite group who served as a testing ground for highly tailored, personalized programs. As these programs produced great results, they were often streamlined and later rolled out to a larger group (by this time the recruiters had already come up with another stellar idea for their top recruits).

Creativity is the most important currency. It doesn't take a mammoth budget to thrill your inside circle. Explore the opportunities to create a cohesive, personalized program that will give your brand a pioneering, almost rebellious reputation. Remember, reaching more people with a generic message is no longer the goal. The straight math of big numbers doesn't apply.

Case Study—Jones Soda

Jones Soda Company has created buzz, produced 30 percent yearly revenue growth in a flat beverage market, drawn major distribution partners such as Starbucks and Target, and brought in $30 million in annual revenue by featuring one special ingredient in its marketing—their customers.[6]

From labels to flavors, Jones Soda lets its customers lead the way. It all started with the Web site the company launched in 1997. It invited fans to initiate flavors (with more offbeat results, including chocolate fudge and green apple), goofy names (such as Whoop Ass and MF Grape), and bright neon colors. In fact, customers have been a constant source of ideas for this popular underground brand. Even the quirky sayings printed underneath the bottle caps ("76.4% of all statistics are meaningless") come straight from Jones's enthusiastic brand community.

But the biggest win for Jones Soda has been its labeling program. Jones continually changes the photographs on its bottle labels, and the majority of these forty or so photos come from customer submissions. As a result, the company receives thousands of photos daily—most of which are cute but unusable baby snapshots. These toothless models inspired a new company division called myJones, which offers twelve-packs of soda with custom-made labels and bottle caps for $34.95. The program has been available for over five years and has become a cornerstone of the brand, netting approximately twenty orders a day for the customized packs. Weddings and bar mitzvahs fuel the highest volume orders, but photos that reflect inside jokes and celebrate close friendships are also popular.

Leverage popular media.

From comic books to magazine page layouts to graphically rich postcards and mailouts, the U of O spoke to recruits through the mainstream media venues that they already knew and loved. It's a matter of speaking the right language. High-school students don't send much snail mail these days, so why would they respond to boring form letters with nothing but text?

As members of Generation Y, the student prospects are extremely design and media savvy. They judge the competing schools not just by their facilities and reputations, but also by whether they "get it" and would provide a cool, entertaining college experience. To catch recruits' attention, the U of O used every form of media allowed under NCAA rules. To enhance in-home recruiting presentations, the Oregon team created a highly visual plastic map called "Coming to Oregon" (imagine the plastic game board for Twister, with cooler graphics) for Head Coach Mike Bellotti to place on the kitchen table or the living room floor when visiting parents and athletes.

The U of O understood the subliminal power of helping recruits to see themselves in a U of O uniform before making a formal commitment. The U.S. Army has also used this same technique with a successful video game.

Case Study—The U.S. Army

The U.S. Army spends $2.5 million a year on its recruiting "advergame," called America's Army. In 2004, 3.7 million people logged on to track down terrorists or rescue POWs in realistic simulations. The magic of the game is how potential recruits can zero in on specific interests, such as parachuting or working as a medic. It also gives players greater confidence about the challenges and situations they might encounter while on duty. The army says the game has helped it reach recruitment targets in 2004, despite a highly polarized political climate.[7]

Keep delighting them with fresh surprises.

While other programs began to recycle their sales pitches for home visits, Oregon's coaching staff consistently brought new presentation materials to every meeting. They never assumed that the status quo was sufficient and went to great lengths to woo their top prospects. And the marketing team's efforts did not go unnoticed. By keeping the process fresh and interesting, they made the recruits feel worthy—worth the time, money, and creativity it took to secure a firm commitment. It's a lot like dating. Who seems like a better catch—the suitor who arrives late and empty-handed or the one who spells your name in candles on your doorstep?

Personalize and amplify.

Heroes take on an amplified version of their everyday identities. Clark Kent is Superman. Michael Jordan is Air Jordan. Their nicknames and logos identify them as larger-than-life personas. The U of O marketing team wanted to suggest to recruits that by signing with Oregon, they too could become larger than life. By giving each recruit a nickname and an individual logo tailored to that nickname as well as to their playing style, they branded each one a superhero.

In keeping with the school's aggressive, cutting-edge reputation, billboards depicting Oregon players have appeared all over the nation. Even before the school rolled out its full "Coming to Oregon" recruiting campaign, they launched a billboard tradition in 2001 with the Joey Harrington–Heisman campaign, which featured an 80x100-foot-high billboard of Harrington in New York City's Times Square from early June to mid-September. The poster was a photo of Harrington in his number 3 uniform with the tagline, "Joey Heisman, Oregon Football." Harrington's last name was crossed out and replaced with "Heisman" to build East Coast support for Harrington as a Heisman Trophy nominee. The billboards have now become integrated into the student-recruiting campaign. During official visits, each potential player sees a computer-generated image of a fully branded billboard of himself in a location tailored to his interests.

Case Study—Imatoy.com

Imatoy.com is a small Web site with a contagious idea. Owner Tobias Conan Trost creates handcrafted superhero figures for his customers' best friends, bosses, brothers, husbands, wives, or coworkers. Using highly personalized creations, Imatoy builds an alter ego and superpowers for a person based on his/her interests, quirky personality traits, and personal likeness. The character is then fashioned into a 5- or 6-inch, one-of-a-kind piece of pop art that is placed in an acrylic display case and sealed in a blister pack. The figures cannot be removed from the packaging and are for display only. The back of the package has a personalized origin story that explains how each character got his or her powers and describes who they are.[8]

Know your game plan.

Let's revisit Oregon's 2004 marketing objectives:

1. Organize a separate mailing campaign for individuals who have received a written offer from Oregon.
2. Individualize all mail in the interest of our recruits and their personalities.
3. Create specific identities and logos for recruits that bond them with Oregon football.
4. Strive to be innovative—constantly redefine cutting edge.[9]

The marketing team launched its campaign with clear, well-defined goals. There were no hazy ideals such as "attract more recruits" or "target top players." The team took the time to develop a specific game plan, which also worked as a filter for all recruiting activities. Did a new idea fit the objectives? If the answer was yes, the team threw themselves into the activity and made it a success. If the answer was no, the idea was shelved.

Use rules and boundaries to spur creativity.

Deryk Gilmore, director of player development, and his team of interns learned to love rules, which is a good thing, because the NCAA has a complex maze of recruitment bylaws that all colleges must uphold. But instead of feeling hemmed in by the regulations, the Oregon marketing team used rules to spur its creativity. The boundaries inspired them to find new solutions and fresh angles.

For example, NCAA bylaws prevent colleges from sending materials over a certain size. No problem. The marketing team turned one personalized poster into a puzzle. Prospects received the poster in pieces and assembled the large images of themselves decked out in Ducks uniforms. The puzzles prevented the recruiting team from breaking national regulations, but they also made the school look innovative. Rather than trashing the Oregon mailout, prospects and their families would quickly assemble the puzzle in order to see the full poster.[10]

Create materials worth keeping and sharing.

Only the most important, inspiring pieces of our lives end up in scrapbooks and frames. The odd letter might make the cut, but you can bet that every top Oregon recruit still has that comic book, and that by now, it's dog-eared. Even if you hit the big time and become familiar with press and praise (à la Joey Harrington), a personalized comic book, poster, or billboard represents the seed of a major dream. The custom-tailored materials put each player in the center of the action and created a vision for their future in football. They were keepers.

Oregon knew that memorable, permanent promotional materials would take their name further than a drab form letter. When you create cool personalized marketing materials that people want to keep and share with their friends and families, it elevates your brand and creates a powerful buzz.

Case Study—DNA Artwork

Canadian company DNA 11 creates high-end abstract artwork from their customers' DNA strands. The company captures genetic "fingerprints" using a saliva sample and transforms it into an artistic representation of an individual's life code. The DNA is stained with a fluorescent dye and illuminated by UV light, which glows and gives off a fluorescent signal. A special camera captures the image, which is then digitally enhanced, cropped, and color adjusted. Introductory prices range from US$390 to $790, depending on the size of the artwork. "Family" pictures may never look the same again.

Dream big.

Everyone has secret dreams. Whether they're modest or wildly ambitious, there's a special corner in our mind that has quietly envisioned an Academy Award on the mantle or scoring the goal that wins the World Cup. Oregon's recruiting campaign grasped prospects' secret fantasies (playing a starring role on their college team, joining the NFL, becoming a sports superstar) and spun them into graphic realities. They played the ultimate scenario out on the page and dreamed bigger and more outrageously than the students may have allowed themselves to dream.

While it may look like mere fantasy, there's a powerful message behind the comic books, billboards, and posters: This could be you. Lofty ambitions are a key element of the Oregon brand. It's one thing to dream about winning the Fiesta Bowl for your team; it's quite another to see it played out in your own comic book. The personalized materials conveyed unshakable confidence in the recruits and gave them a tangible sense of possibility.

Case Study—ESPN Dream Job

ESPN understands that its loyal audience doesn't just want tickets to the Final Four; they want a chance to step into the shoes of their favorite broadcasters and sit at the *SportsCenter* desk as the newest on-air talent. A talent search competition show similar to Donald Trump's *The Apprentice, Dream Job* films aspiring sportscasters as they compete for a yearlong position as an *ESPN SportsCenter* anchor. Sports fans with dreams of going on-air or calling play-by-play on ESPN get a chance to follow in the footsteps of the original Dream Job winner, Mike Hall, who made his *SportsCenter* debut in July 2005, during the second and third editions of the series. The series performed well for the network, premiering to 1.1 million viewers and maintaining an average of over a million viewers during its six-episode run, despite airing in a highly competitive Sunday evening time slot.[11]

Write your elite group into the story.

Stories affect us on an unconscious level. The U of O could have made slick promotional materials about their team, but they chose instead to tell stories that would resonate with their top prospects. Each comic book was tailored for the individual player, but there were powerful mythologies at work in each and every one: saving the day, realizing your potential, achieving greatness through courage and bravery, coming through for the team in the moment of need. The recruiting materials were more than just cool; they spun potentially boring information into an emotionally compelling story and made the player the star, the hero, the protagonist of the tale. Oregon struck a critical nerve by writing the hero myth that their recruits were already eager to experience.

Case Study—Sony EyeToy

EyeToy (a digital camera for PlayStation2) superimposes video-game graphics onto a player's image and translates movements into on-screen action, giving anyone the ability to become a central character. In the twelve available EyeToy games, the player is at the center of the game and controls the action by moving his or her body in front of the camera.

For example, in a game where the object is to beat back invading hordes of kung-fu fighters who attack from four corners of the screen, players must move their hands (or elbows, head, or hips, etc.) to connect with the fighters on-screen and slap them away. EyeToy is so intuitive that most users will be able to play in a matter of seconds. Watching someone play EyeToy is entertaining because it provides an on-screen mix of live action and animation, similar to the 1988 Robert Zemeckis film *Who Framed Roger Rabbit*. Off-screen, players' movements look determined yet comical.

Don't stop short.

Members of the Oregon marketing team could have high-fived each other for their killer posters and called it a day. Instead, they kept the momentum going and developed the full "Coming to Oregon" program, which included puzzles, handwritten notes, coaching tips, comic books, home visit maps, and more. This cohesive program sealed the school's reputation as an innovator.

Manage timing and emotions.

Oregon's recruiting campaign would begin slowly with each player and rise to a well-planned crescendo—the campus visit. The team expertly built anticipation and linked its campaign with key events. (The final installment of the comic book was available only to those who chose to make a campus visit.) They knew when to push and when to back off. They also knew that the best time to intersect with people is when they're hungry for information and understanding. If a player is ready to check out the school and visualize an academic career on the campus, then it's time to pull out all the stops.

The team also leveraged the positive aspects of peer pressure to sway their most desirable prospects. Instead of organizing solo school visits, Oregon invited recruits in carefully considered groups. Some of the players had already committed to Oregon, and after spending a week bonding and touring with their potential teammates, they would naturally want to convince their new friends to sign up with the Ducks. Even recruits who were still on the fence had a clear sense of who they might be training and playing alongside during their four years at Oregon.

Understand what deeply moves your target.

Oregon took market research to new heights. Coaches gave the interns a list of their top picks and the students gathered interviews, quotes, and chat sessions from recruiting Web sites, along with newspaper articles from around the country and underground buzz on each high-school prospect.

The interns then created detailed bio sheets for each recruit, which outlined everything from nicknames to interests to vital statistics. These sheets also explored the players' decision-making processes. Often, the key to recruiting athletes lay in understanding their criteria for evaluating a school, their key influencers and decision makers, as well as their personalities and interests. Once they had all available information, the Oregon interns worked with the coaching staff to create a profile for each recruit. This enabled them to decide how to most effectively market the school to each prospect.

The team took the campaign another step further by targeting every stakeholder in the decision-making process, including the prospect's parents and high-school coaches. They created strategies to make each person feel valued, pursued, and special. Parents were courted with special mailings and assured that Oregon had the right academic environment and was the ideal place for their kids to excel at both sports and school. The coaches were supplied with information and valuable tools, and given fact sheets that answered any potential questions about the Oregon athletic experience.

The U of O's recruiting team spent hundreds of hours researching an elite pool of desired athletes. They didn't target *all* high-school football players or make assumptions about student athletes in general. Instead, they honed in on their top picks and used every available resource to understand each player's intimate hopes, dreams, and concerns. The program was innovative, but it also relied on underpaid and volunteer labor from student interns.

WORKBOOK

Get Started

1. **Begin by breaking your customers into tiers.**

   You could even come up with names for each level, or divide them into rounds like an NFL draft. Your top tier should consist of the alpha influencers—people who are (or will be) passionate about your brand and feel a strong sense of personal ownership. These highly influential customers are worth more than every other customer in your market. Develop criteria for top-tier membership and figure out who should be in your inner circle.

2. **Think about what rewards and incentives you can offer to your top tier.**

   Don't limit yourself to products or discounts. You could provide full access to inside information or resources, create special events with limited invitations, ask for feedback on early product designs, and much, much more. At some colleges, student athletes work directly with manufacturers to help design team uniforms and some sporting good brands take products to top student athletes across the nation (valuable, long-term customers and brand evangelists) for early feedback and testing.

3. **Step up and do extraordinary things for your inner circle.**

   Go to great lengths for your top tier and create legendary stories. For example, when industry magazines and sports radio programs interviewed the nation's top high-school recruits, the University of Oregon often got airtime for sending them the "coolest stuff." These efforts don't have to be expensive, but they should be highly unusual and surprising. Try to think as widely as possible and focus on generating fresh ideas.

4. **Create ways to give your top-tier members access to each other.**

   A group of BMW motorcycle enthusiasts, for example, have created a club that offers roadside assistance to other BMW drivers. The company didn't create this initiative—the loyal riders did. BMW, however, gave these enthusiastic customers a way to contact each other and share stories, tips, etc.[12]

When your top customers are so excited about the brand that they organize and motivate themselves, it speaks volumes about the company. Your inner circle has drive and enthusiasm that will provide amazing returns on a minimal investment.

5. **Look to mythology to tap into universal themes.**

Look at movies, comic books, novels, and video games and think about how you can re-create mythic stories. There is enormous power and unconscious human emotion buried in these familiar tales. From superheroes to underdogs overcoming natural or personal challenges, there will be at least one universal theme that will resonate with your brand, and more important, with your top-tier customers.

Go for It.

Is there a dogfight in your industry over a certain type of feature or experience? How can you think differently from all your competitors and focus your innovations on an area that no one's fighting for?

What if you spent your entire budget on wooing the top 10 percent of your prospects? What would you do for this group if they had all your time, attention, and resources?

TWO

RAISE MY PULSE

Adventure Takes Its Place
as the New Social Currency

Where are we going to store a thousand chocolate turkeys?
It's a steamy day in early August. Fifteen turkey piñatas the size of bowling balls are lined up on a stainless steel table, ready to be stuffed with candy peas and carrots. At another table, a woman methodically pours chocolate into huge turkey molds. Several other staff members are busy discussing where to keep the finished birds.

I look around. "Is this usually such a popular product?"

The staff shake their heads and laugh. The piñatas are a special order, and all the details have been covered—except the storage situation.

It's just another typical day at JaCiva's Chocolates & Pastries in Portland, Oregon, a family-owned and -operated business that has been creating scrumptious cakes, truffles, and other treats for more than forty years.

On that Tuesday in August, I abandoned my home office to spend the day working as a beginner pastry chef and chocolatier in JaCiva's busy kitchen. My chocolate immersion day came courtesy of Brian Kurth and Vocation Vacations—a Portland-based company that gives people the chance to "test drive" their dream careers. From pastry chef to horse trainer to fashion designer and golf pro, Vocation Vacations has packaged over two hundred vacations across eighty-two vocations that allow people to dive in and experience their ultimate career fantasies, without having to quit their day jobs or finance a new business. It's a risk-free way to see if you really do love the life of a pastry chef, or if the day-to-day work of frosting wedding cakes would send you screaming back to the office.

For eight hours, I was mentored by owner Jack Elmer—his wife, Iva, is the other half of JaCiva's—who explained how treating people right pays off in surprising ways—like the occasional fabulous recipe he learns from other chefs who share only with those they really like. An impromptu roof tour became a lesson in real estate financing and the best way to manage growth. Exploring the frosting room, manned by a talented group of Russian women, was an opportunity to discuss natural group leadership dynamics and cultural values. I stayed glued to Jack's side as he went about his day with grandchildren, honoring talented employees with encouraging words, receiving fresh vegetables from loyal customers, and teaching his insider trick for adding lemon oil to cake batter without upsetting the fragile chemistry.[1]

When it was time to remove the hair net, my back was throbbing from standing all day. I had poured chocolate into heart-shaped boxes, mixed butter cream, and lifted boxes. I arrived ready to learn about baking, but I left with a formula for running a business and running a life.

Pastry and chocolate are not my dream job. My vacation made that clear. But my day was definitely an adventure. It opened my eyes to new possibilities and even clarified some questions I'd been having about my own career. That's the point of Vocation Vacations, which has brilliantly tapped into our growing desire for adventure.

Founder Brian Kurth first envisioned Vocation Vacations when he was stuck in yet another traffic jam on Chicago's Kennedy Expressway. The daily two- to three-hour round-trip commute was beginning to take its toll. As he sat in the car, foot firmly lodged on the brake pedal, Brian imagined all the other ways his life could take shape. His career was going well in the textbook sense, but something was missing. Perhaps he could be a tour guide, or a winemaker or a dog trainer—anything to get off the freeway and into something that resembled a more full and satisfying life.

This was 1999. Two years later, Brian lost his job in the dot-com collapse and spent six months on a road trip across the United States and parts of Canada. In 2002, he moved to Portland, Oregon, and started Vocation Vacations as a self-funded hobby business. In Brian's words, it was a tough sell.

"Everyone thought it was cool but a bit crazy that people would pay to work. I finally had to come back with an analogy: 'Do you drink bottled water?'"

Well, yes.

"Did you drink it five years ago?"

Well, no.

"Would you ever have thought that we'd all buy bottled water for over a dollar?

"It's the same concept of convenience. We're providing people with the opportunity for professional and personal due diligence. The work is done for you. We have the credentialed mentors and the process in place."

Brian launched Vocation Vacations in January 2004 with a handful of packages. Today there are over two hundred vacations, with prices ranging from $349 to $4,999, with 95 percent costing less than $1,200. Requests for specific experiences constantly fill Brian's inbox, prompting him to add new vocations almost monthly. Mentors work with the participants for two days and receive a flat fee for each vocationer that goes through their program. Learning is exciting, but apparently sharing what you know is equally appealing. Many mentors claim that they would work with the vocationers for free because of the sense of satisfaction the interaction provides.

Brian understood that the two-week time-share in Maui is relaxing, but there's a whole group of people who want to return from vacation with more than just tan lines. In fact, the RoperReports NOP survey, which tracks a broad range of vacation trends, found in its 2004 travel outlook that 64 percent of a thousand respondents said that the chance to learn new things was "very important" in planning leisure time, up from 51 percent just a year earlier. Relaxation came in at 69 percent, down slightly from the previous year.

"We're providing people with a tool in their toolbox to change their own lives," explains Brian. "It's a trigger point for change. It's the baby step and the swift kick in the ass that people sometimes need. Others are just curious and have always wondered about the path they didn't take."

According to Brian, the business is split into three main customer groups:

- Career changers who want to explore a new path before they take the plunge. Often these "vocationers," as Brian has dubbed them, want to see if the reality of their dream career lives up to their stuck-in-traffic fantasies.
- Curiosity seekers who have always wondered what it would be like to own a dog day care, become a brewmaster, or go to work as a sportscaster. These customers are often looking for a fun new experience or an out-of-the-ordinary vacation. Few are actually planning a career shift.
- Gift givers who are tired of hearing their friends or spouses wonder "what if . . ." and want to see them try chocolate making (or sports broadcasting or winemaking). These gifts are more than just an ultraconsiderate confidence boost—they're usually a form of loving intervention.

The Vocation Vacations business began with a high number of career changers, but gift givers represent the fastest-growing customer segment. And although women are more frequently the gift givers who present vacations to men, the company's customers are almost evenly split between the two genders.

Vocation Vacations hasn't spent a single cent on marketing or advertising since the company opened its doors. Word-of-mouth has fueled the majority of its business, but the vacations are also popular with career coaches and frequently show up in a variety of online blogs. In March 2004, Vocation Vacations' net profit was a slim $349. The company is well on its way to becoming a multimillion-dollar enterprise by 2006.

Brian's theory is that 9/11 was a massive wake-up call for many people, and has fueled a strong desire for adventure—in life and in work. There's a huge population segment that has realized work needs to be more than a four-letter word. Some people have made drastic changes, whereas others have a subtle understanding that joy and passion should be part of each and every day.

Unfortunately, most people struggle to justify change and adventure in their own minds. They need to understand that it will be okay. "Give yourself permission to take the risk," says Brian. "Just because you have a law degree doesn't mean you have to be a lawyer." Personal beliefs, fears, and a misguided sense of responsibility can build significant hurdles. Brian says he had the idea for Vocation Vacations back in 1999, but it was another few years before he gave himself permission to try.[2]

Vocation Vacations is thriving because it combines career planning and adventure. Maybe you want to be a professional choreographer; maybe you don't. Either way, you get to temporarily drop into a new life and see how it feels. There are new rhythms, expectations, and concerns and new mental muscles involved in a different occupation. When you try something that obliterates your comfort zone, you simply can't come away from the experience without a fresh perspective on yourself, your life, or your place in the world.

THE CRAVING: ADVENTURE CAPITAL

For the past thirty years, customer service differentiated one brand from another, and companies that delivered the best service would rise above the competition. Today's bar is being set even higher, as more brands begin to deliver exciting, interactive, and compelling *experiences*. There is a new premium placed on venturing into the world, collecting new adventures and memories, and pushing personal limits. Customers are seeking highly interactive encounters that teach and challenge and, in the process, give them personal insight and help them define who they are. In fact, activities like international travel, extreme sports, and out-of-the-ordinary hobbies are now considered more rewarding and impressive than an expensive new car or gadget.

The word adventure usually conjures up images of skydiving or trekking in Nepal. But adventure, at its core, is simply a way to engage ourselves beyond everyday experience. It's trying something new (even a different restaurant) and opening up to fresh ideas, perspectives, and ways of living life. For example, MSN.com features an interactive, graphic slide show that introduces the "400 Must-Try Experiences in America."

Unusual, learning-based adventure opportunities are popping up across the nation. Kids are ditching the generic summer sleepaway camp for rock star camp and robotics camp. New York City fashionistas can build their own stilettos on a Saturday afternoon, chefs are redefining date night with make-your-own sushi lessons, and big-box home improvement stores are drawing women by the dozens to their Do-It-Herself workshops.

Today's adventure seekers are eager to disrupt their typical routines, engage their senses and emotions, and have experiences that they can share with friends and families. In a cubicle-focused work environment, interactive, outdoor, hands-on experiences provide a sharp contrast to day-to-day life. People long to go behind the scenes of coveted professions, dive deeper into casual hobbies, and unearth buried facets of themselves (sexiness, bravery, wit, wild behavior) that they don't experience in their nine-to-five routines. Bachelor parties that typically capped off the dwindling singles days by stirring up dust and hitting the bars are being replaced with action-packed weekends of white-water rafting, mad games of paintball, and race-car driving.

People are increasingly looking to adventure-soaked hobbies to define themselves and to meet fellow adventure seekers. Often, they're looking to experiment with a range of activities. This sampler mentality is evident in the new "experience clubs" launched by trendsetters across the nation. Club members designate one day a month to try a new activity or to learn a new skill. One experience club member said her group's agenda has already included stripping, poker, shooting, knitting, trapeze flying, cooking, and self-defense lessons. These clubs allow the seeker to try new activities in a noncommittal fashion but, by throwing some edgier activities into the mix, participants can also work collectively to overcome personal fears and limitations. With a constant flow of new experiences on the slate, chances are that one exotic pursuit might actually become a passion.[3]

So why the sudden hunger for experience? Why is everyone so eager to get out and explore, play, or learn? Here are several key reasons why people increasingly crave adventure.

WHY WE CRAVE ADVENTURE

1. **We're bored.**

     The schedules and routines of day-to-day life can become numbing—especially when you're constantly connected and flooded with information. For many people, the average day is filled with mental stimulus (images, words, dialogue, noise, and messages) but very little physical, firsthand experience. In fact, we're often passive spectators of the world around us, which sparks the desire to jump into the center of the action and get our hands dirty. It makes us crave something that shakes up the routine and puts us in an environment that's different and truly stimulating.

2. **We have great new tools to express our creative genes.**

We have a surging belief in our own abilities and creative powers, and we're looking for people to help us fan the flames. New technology and entertainment have made it possible to become creators, rather than observers. We're drafting our own teams in fantasy football and "coaching" them to the fantasy Super Bowl. We're making crisp digital films and sharing them with friends and family. We're altering existing video games and designing our own new games, music, home improvements, furniture, and artwork. There is a sense that given the right tools, opportunity, and support, we can all step up and create at a new, professional-caliber level. For many people, there is a sense that the shoe might fit and they could radically change the focus of their lives and professions.

3. **Behind-the-scenes access has whet our appetites.**

We have a growing fascination with the behind-the-scenes workings of businesses, media, and other industries. We have access to so much information and are becoming so savvy that we begin to think, "I could do that . . . I think I would be a good Oprah. I think I could edit this movie better. I could produce music . . ." Today, we elevate to celebrity status people who create for others, including chefs, home designers, film directors, plastic surgeons, DJs, and more. Reality television, the Internet, and other mediums have erased much of the mystery behind these professions and put us on a first-name basis with people working at the top of their fields. From celebrity chefs to famous carpenters, the creative professions are gaining profile and becoming more desirable than ever.

4. **Learning has become the ultimate status symbol.**

Television after work? Dinner at the usual place? A boring jog through the neighborhood? Been there, done that. We're all trying harder to wake up, to challenge and entertain ourselves, and many people are craving firsthand learning that engages all five senses. Saturday afternoons now offer an exciting lineup of free or low-cost classes ranging from a workshop on creating digital family albums at the local camera shop, to tile-installation classes hosted at the local home improvement retailer, to vegan-cooking demonstrations at the gourmet grocery. We have access to so many ideas, products, and activities that the bar is higher than ever.

5. **External experiences trigger internal transformation.**

People are looking for a trigger—a marathon, a trip through Eastern Europe, a serious mountain climb—to steer their lives in a new direction (such as getting out of a relationship, changing careers, finishing a screenplay that's been in the works for years). Action breeds confidence and spurs more action. People often use extreme physical experiences to boost their sense of power and possibility. This approach works because it gets you breathing new air and opens your mind to fresh ideas.

Kelly Kirkendoll Shafer was struggling to write her first book when she took a two-day Vocation Vacation in Oregon to experience the life of a professional horse trainer. She returned home to Fort Worth, Texas, fired up and used her newfound confidence to complete the book. She now works as the press contact for Vocation Vacations. Once you do something new—whether it's hiking a glacier or hosting an elaborate dinner party—you can transfer that confidence to another, often more significant, goal in your life.

6. **Experiences are the new social currency.**

People who have personal stories that highlight their own courage, creativity, and talents tend to talk about them at a much higher frequency and with greater passion than somebody who just saw something cool. You may be shown a few snapshots from a friend's trip to Puerto Vallarta, but you are sure to hear every detail of your best pal's week as a wedding planner.

7. **We want to be kept on our toes.**

Being predictable is no longer a compliment (if it ever was). Instead, there's a growing desire to surprise people and explore the edges of our personalities. We want to see ourselves in an amplified and expanded way and present ourselves to others in a new light. Today, we admire the risk taker and creative thinker, and these are traits we celebrate in others and want to cultivate in ourselves.

8. **The Internet has made us aware of the possibilities.**

    Adventurous and offbeat exploits are now mainstream fodder in magazines, television shows, Internet sites, and on the news. If it's unusual, we want to hear about it, and the constant exposure to wild journeys and experiences makes these activities seem all the more doable.

9. **Our peers are doing it.**

    The spirit of adventure is all around, and it's easy to find a group of people willing to tackle a scary, fresh, or challenging experience. Just a few years ago, only a handful of people were vacationing in third world countries, jumping out of airplanes, and pursuing activities off the beaten path. Survey a group in the Connected Generation today and you will find an impressive collective résumé of adventure-seeking activities. Instead of feeling isolated in a thrill-seeking pursuit, there is growing peer pressure to get out there and shake off the cobwebs.

10. **Packaged adventures make it accessible.**

    In the past, if you wanted to have an adventure, the details were pretty much up to you. Think up the idea, find the companions, get the supporting materials, and make it happen. Today more brands and organizations are realizing that people want adventures, and they're building and streamlining the experiences for us. From adventure travel to exciting new classes, it has never been so easy to raise your pulse.

    Transforming work to match personal passions has become the ultimate national adventure, and Vocation Vacations has tapped into a powerful collective craving. Here's what we can all learn from their success.

LESSONS

Make it accessible.

Convenience is one of the most important features of the Vocation Vacations program. The company has covered the details, so people can just dive in and enjoy the experience. Brian Kurth compares the process to jumping out of a plane in tandem. You want to take the risk but still feel safe and supported as you leap. With a tandem jump, you get the full experience with the help of a seasoned professional who will pull the cord if you freak out and don't. Vocation Vacations' mentors provide similar tandem support for their leaping customers.

The Connected Generation is not content to be passive viewers; they're ready to step into the shoes of admired movie stars, musicians, and leaders in high-profile professions. Confident and curious, this group wants to "try on" the lives of those they admire and possibly get discovered in the process. Their only challenge is finding the time to take each new idea for a spin. Companies that build adventure into their brand and make it fun, fast, and seamless will be rewarded by this adventure-seeking generation. Encouragement, convenience, and belief create the winning formula.

Case Study—Scratch DJ Academy

New York City's Scratch DJ Academy trains students in the popular musical art form of the DJ. The school was founded in 2002 by Rob Principe, Reg E. Gaines (author of *Bring in Da Noise, Bring in Da Funk* and a two-time Grammy and Tony award nominee), and the late Jam Master Jay (legendary DJ of Run DMC).

The school combines formal curriculum and hands-on training with over fifty turntables and celebrity DJ instructors, offering an incredible opportunity for amateur and aspiring mix masters to learn everything from blending and scratching to mixing and beat juggling. Offering six- and ten-week courses that range from beginner to advanced, the Scratch DJ Academy has graduated over five thousand students ages five to seventy, who hail from London, Tokyo, Chicago, San Francisco, Cleveland, Atlanta, and beyond.[4]

Create interactive test-drives.

Vocation Vacations knows that sipping wine from plastic cups in a classroom pales next to three days at a full-scale winery. According to Kurth, most vocationers haven't tasted their dreams yet: "The more you can taste it, feel it, experience it, the more you are going to want to make it happen." What wine enthusiast wouldn't jump at the chance to move beyond the community college and get hands-on with the grapes, barrels, and a seasoned winemaker? The key is to get your customers as close to the action and the authentic experience as possible. It can't feel too far removed. Give people the opportunity to hit the ground running in a self-directed yet supportive way. There's an incredible sense of prestige that comes from being on the inside—a prestige that will carry your brand far beyond a one-time purchase or interaction.

The adventure category is not just about dream jobs or extreme sports. It's also about having more entertaining experiences while shopping or interacting with a brand. This is sampling at its best— granting customers the ability to interact with a new product or service before they buy. Interactive test-drives give customers more confidence in the product and the company, and allow them to imagine how it would feel to use the item in their everyday lives. It also makes shopping a heck of a lot more fun. If a company can create a Technicolor vision of the product experience, the customer-product bond will grow much stronger.

Case Study—Maytag

In early 2003, Maytag created an innovative experiential marketing strategy where prospective customers bring their dirty dishes, stained clothes, and family recipes to stores. Maytag found that women were more interested in understanding how a product would fit into their lives than listening to a pitch about the merchandise, so they created the "try-before-you-buy" strategy with the help of independent, dealer-owned stores. Think about it. With the high cost of upper-end appliances, it makes perfect sense to take a potential washer-dryer for a trial spin.

Maytag also understood the social element of shopping, so they designed a new environment that includes wider aisles, brighter decor, and kids' play areas. The new Maytag stores display ready-to-use appliances in vignettes of home kitchens and laundry rooms.[5]

Be the baby step.

Take away the hurdles—make it simple for customers to try your new adventure (whether it includes wine, travel, music, or theater) by providing an easy entry point. Lower the risk, eliminate the research, provide the connections, package the opportunity, and hold their hand through the whole process. Explore the commitment threshold. What's too much? What's too long? Make it simple for people to jump in and try, and remember that the details really do matter. No one wants friction or stress when they're trying to escape.

Case Study—Rutabaga Water Divas

For almost thirty years, the Rutabaga Paddlesport Shop has served residents of Madison, Wisconsin, with clothing, equipment, and other water necessities. Their innovative Rutabaga Water Divas program, which began in 2004, draws out tentative, first-time paddlers—women who've always wanted to try kayaking or canoeing, but who are overwhelmed or unsure about how to get started. The Rutabaga team created a comfortable atmosphere that allows newbie paddlers to learn about kayaking, try the sport with the help of their trained staff, make mistakes, ask questions, and bond with other women.

Whether you're hosting a snowshoe workshop, a bike repair class, or a sailing clinic, "for women" events tend to work best when your customers are trying something for the first time. Helping newbies get up to speed can actually be great for business. By focusing on attracting new women to the sport of paddling and cultivating an excited new community of Water Divas, Rutabaga achieved a robust 10.8 percent growth in 2004 and continued to expand the program in 2005 with community paddle nights and yoga for paddlers, among other fun classes.[6]

Provide different levels of commitment.

Once you've established a commitment threshold, design ways to attract both the casual seeker and the committed adventurer. Provide a low-risk, low-investment opportunity for a casual comfort zone. For example, the Vocation Vacations Web site helps people explore new jobs based on their inspirations. The next step is booking their own vacation, which is still a baby step compared to quitting your job, borrowing money, and opening up a horse-training business.

Let your customers "go out for coffee" with you before they decide to commit and get married. Start with easy entry, and then help them go deeper with increased services, opportunities, support, and information. Courage builds greater courage, so understand that your business model can be there for every step.

Help people give themselves permission.

As Brian Kurth suggested, it can take a major mind shift to realize that just because you have a law degree doesn't mean you have to be a lawyer. Justifying change can be the toughest step for your potential customers.

Build a case for why it's okay to take the leap, try a new job, explore a passion or book the trip. Word of mouth is powerful with Vocation Vacations and other adventure-based experiences, because seeing someone just like them diving in can help justify their own explorations. It makes them think, "If Susan did it, so can I." Giving people permission as part of your language or tagline is also an effective strategy. L'Oreal understood that many women didn't color their hair because of the expense, so they adopted the tagline, "Because I'm worth it."

Hire staff with the right skills and spirit.

Nervous adventurers are often looking for a mentor, so showcase your staff as companions on the journey. Customers want support, future contacts, and a personalized touch, so make the experience feel personal and real. Potential vocationers can read the profiles and credentials of career mentors and coaches on the Vocation Vacation Web site, and see pictures of the horse ranch where they will work or the bed-and-breakfast that they will help to run.

Adventure often generates fear, so the people who guide you through the experience make all the difference. Honor and celebrate the fact that people are putting themselves "out there" and opening up to your staff and mentors. Make them feel safe and comfortable.

Inspire and expand their dreams.

Develop your Web site and other brand materials to put your customers on a path of inspiration. The Vocation Vacations Web site fuels latent passions. If your customers are thinking interior design, they'll discover that you also offer fashion, set, and floral design vacations. Suddenly their design cravings have several new outlets. People who pursue adventure are often open to a whole category of experience, meaning that you may offer something they hadn't previously imagined but which is actually a better fit, or they may choose to try several options on the menu.

In a similar vein, show that you believe in their dreams. Your support can take away the tension and give people the boost they need to go for it. Home Depot's tagline—"You can do it. We can help"—is a fantastic example. In two simple sentences, Home Depot offers its customers encouragement, mentoring, belief, and a sense of ease and simplicity.

Offer opportunities to talk about the experience
and create memories.

Build in discussion among participants, exit interviews, a chance to write about the experience, talk into a video camera, sign their name on the rock, or whatever works for the adventure. Give well-thought-out quality souvenirs, take photos, or provide take-home materials that remind them of the experience. The social currency that comes with sharing is one of the great joys of adventure. Award participants with certificates (thoughtful or crazy or funny, based on their specific personality or experience). After their Vocation Vacation, chocolatiers bring home their own truffle series, river raft guides take home a paddle, and stylists keep videos or pictures of their fashion adventures.

Learn from your customers and respond to their needs.

Make sure you gather feedback (with surveys, exit interviews, staff trained to ask key questions, etc.) so you know how to continuously improve the experience. In their exit interviews, Vocation Vacations discovered that fear often played a critical role in the process. After their trip, most vocationers would say, "I didn't tell you before, but I was really afraid to do my vacation." Brian retooled the prediscussion to address participants' fears, explore their concerns, provide support, and offer the chance to discuss and identify their jitters before the experience. This one simple change has been extremely positive and reassuring for his clients.

Be the source of juicy and surprising ideas.

Victoria's Secret created a million-dollar, diamond-studded bra. Virgin Group billionaire Richard Branson is working to make space travel available to the consumer. While the vast majority of us will never wear a diamond-crusted demi-cup or see the Great Wall of China from the moon, these over-the-top efforts fuel buzz and keep everyone on their toes. In the adventure category, it's critical to keep dreaming bigger and better by offering extraordinary experiences.

For example, Vocation Vacations could offer premium vacations that include international travel, such as learning to be a chef or a fashion designer in Italy. They could also cluster a series of related vacations into a longer experience, such as an Ultimate Design Week in New York City, where the vocationer samples fashion design, television set design, and furniture design in one luxurious shot.

Surprise your customers with more exciting, adventurous, outlandish, and juicy ideas than they've ever imagined, and it will reinforce your brand as a force to watch. Even if most people don't choose premium adventures or services, they will feel special and served simply by knowing that you're ready to exceed their wildest dreams.

Infuse adventure and activity into buttoned-up industries.

Career development tends to be a staid process and involves résumé building, information interviews, and dog-eared copies of *What Color Is Your Parachute?* Vocation Vacations has put a spark in the formerly glazed eyes of hundreds of job seekers (and dreamers) by infusing hands-on action and play into an often-dry industry.

Even if your product doesn't have an inherent element of experience, there are still opportunities to build adventure into the brand. Many innovative companies are now creating live experiences around their products. Offering a "play day" or engaging your brand community in an interactive world gives them something to talk about. Today, brands are expected to deliver fun and excitement along with quality and customer service.

Case Study—Nokia 20Lives

In September 2005, cell phone manufacturer Nokia followed up on its successful Nokia Game—providing skill-based adventures, time trials, and puzzles—with a new adventure called Nokia 20Lives. The Web-based game allowed participants to step into not just one, but twenty fictional "lives" during the twenty-five-day adventure.

Nokia 20Lives was played in twenty-one countries and eleven languages across Europe during fall 2005. The contest used video and animated Internet images, plus SMS (text messaging), e-mail, and voice messaging to help players see the world through the eyes of twenty fictional characters from the world of media, movies, fashion, and music. Participants meet the characters' friends and family, do their jobs, make their decisions, and for one day live as actresses, playboys, salesmen, paparazzi, and power business mavens. Players' choices determined whether the characters triumphed or failed, and they competed for real-world prizes, including helicopter rides, spa weekends, or Formula 1 racing in Monaco—more adventure, thrill-seeking opportunities connected to the lives of the twenty colorful characters.

Case Study—Nike Operation 6453

In 2004, Nike created an adrenaline-filled promotional event to infuse excitement and urban adventure into the official launch of their new Air Force-X MID shoe. Nike's Operation 6453 was an on-foot scavenger hunt that navigated participants through the streets of New York to find sixteen different poster locations. To get involved, would-be participants sent a blank text message to 6453-NIKE and received registration instructions. Players sent text messages to Nike for poster locations, and in turn were sent coordinates. The hunt took place over the course of four days, and when players located posters, they messaged a code on the poster to Nike. The shortest times between receiving and finding the posters received the highest scores. Winners nabbed a limited-edition version of the Nike Air Force-X MID, designed by New York City street artist Stash. Runners-up got a chance to buy the shoes at an exclusive prelaunch event.[7]

Access a dormant aspect of your customers' personalities.

Go to the edge. Don't play it safe. Your customers don't want to be tame, so don't just color in the lines. Redefine the edge. Understand what's fueling their fantasies and tap into their hidden desires. Vocation Vacations actively listens to their brand community and constantly rolls out new vacations. Their latest adventures-in-development include video game producer, art auctioneer, and celebrity personal assistant.

Adventure calls out the elements of our personalities that can starve in day-to-day life. The most successful companies tapping into this craving give people an opportunity to explore dormant aspects of our personalities such as recklessness, creativity, power, or sex appeal. In the fitness industry, for example, the wildly popular strip and pole dancing aerobics classes help women get in touch with their inner sexpot.

Case Study—Thrillseekers Unlimited

Thrillseekers Unlimited was founded in 1992 and leads the nation in action and extreme sports and stunts—coordinating, producing, and performing in hundreds of films, television shows, commercials, music videos, live performances, and advertisements. Their latest offering is extreme "stunt vacations," which have become popular with individual adrenaline junkies and, increasingly, as corporate team-building exercises (an action-filled alternative to the usual golf getaway). Stunt vacations are the all-in-one solution for anyone craving a serious thrill fix with a multiday buffet that includes bungee jumping, rock climbing, paragliding, faux fighting, covert operations, and fire stunts. Founder Rich Hopkins has said that no request is too outrageous, as long as it can be done safely. If Thrillseekers won't do it, you probably shouldn't either.[8]

WORKBOOK

Get Started

1. **Tap into new emotions.**
   What do you want people to feel when they are experiencing your brand? Make a list of the emotions you seek to evoke and imagine all the environments where people tend to experience these feelings. Use these examples as a launch point for your brainstorming:

   a. Relaxation and luxury (Kohler)
   b. Active adventure (Nike)

    c. Passion and sexiness (Victoria's Secret)

    d. Innovation and creativity (Lego)

2. **Create stories in your messaging with adventure as the theme.**

    The choice to take an adventure is made from the heart, not the brain, so go in through story lines, images, and metaphors to capture people's fancy. Royal Caribbean did a great job of this with their "Get Out There" ad campaign. Suddenly the idea of a stodgy cruise and shuffleboard on deck was replaced with an array of outdoor challenges.

    Remember that in the most compelling stories, the characters face some sort of challenge and undergo personal transformation—and there is a happy or poignant ending. To offer people adventure is to help them create such an experience in their own lives. Build emotion and adventure around your brand, create excitement, and give your customers a crescendo.

3. **Reimagine your gifts, rewards, and incentives.**

    Especially with women, companies tend to go for the spa route instead of providing customers with a more adventurous option. Don't underestimate the power of adventure, and imagine all the different ways that you can inject it into your brand.

4. **Partner with others in your category who are creating adventure.**

    Sears has transformed its image from tired retailer to active champion of struggling homeowners through its partnership with the top-rated (and emotionally charged) television show *Extreme Makeover: Home Edition*. Through a highly integrated partnership, Sears' extensive collection of quality appliances (plus its retail stores, installation staff, and charitable division, which pays off mortgages) is showcased on a regular basis. This action-packed show format is helping to revive the formerly stagnant Sears brand and bringing it into focus for a new generation of consumers.

Go for It.

If the barriers were removed and customers had an all-access pass to your brand or industry, what could they experience?

Play a game where you put two nonrelated items in the same bucket and try to make them fit together. Make a list of five things that your customers like to do for adventure or fun (play video games, travel, jump out of airplanes, start businesses). Link each one with your brand and try to create an adventure experience around it.

THREE

MAKE LOOSE CONNECTIONS

The New Shape of "Families" and Social Networks

It's Monday morning. Natasha Duprey sits down at her computer, coffee in hand, to begin another busy day. Duprey is a thirty-six-year-old music supervisor at MX Solutions Inc. in Vancouver, Canada. She chooses and oversees the music for films and television series, including Showtime's *The L Word,* Stephen King's *Dead Zone,* and Bravo's *Godivas.* Duprey began her career in the music industry while studying communications in college. She nabbed the enviable job of producing videos in 1991, worked in artist management, and later ran an independent recording studio and record label. She's been a music supervisor, her self-described "dream job," for four years and feels passionate about her work—and about providing exposure for talented singers and musicians.

Before she's even fully caffeinated, Duprey logs on to MySpace.com, a social networking portal that has quickly become a formidable cultural phenomenon. MySpace was founded in September 2003 by Tom Anderson and Chris DeWolfe and officially launched in January 2004. By early 2006, MySpace had 54 million registered members, with 180,000 more joining every day. This sticky, highly addictive site—the average user stays for more than an hour during each visit—generates 2.5 times the traffic of Google. MySpace is such a hot place for the coveted teen, twentysomething, and early thirties demographic that in 2005 Rupert Murdoch's News Corporation bought Intermix Media, the parent company of MySpace.com, for a reported $580 million.[1]

At MySpace, you can sign up for a free account page and express your creativity by uploading songs, videos, photos, and writing blogs, and customizing your page with graphics or personal messages.

The site also has a designated MySpace Music section, which helps to launch unsigned and emerging recording artists. Major bands, including Nine Inch Nails, R.E.M., Black Eyed Peas, and Weezer, have also previewed singles from their upcoming albums through MySpace—well before they're available on bricks-and-mortar store shelves. Former Smashing Pumpkins front man Billy Corgan even posts his autobiography chapter by chapter on his MySpace page.

Before creating MySpace, Tom Anderson played in a San Francisco band called Swank during the late 1990s and clearly feels a strong connection to the music world. It's one of the reasons why MySpace has gained such an incredible following among musicians and music fans alike. When you're living through those high school, college, and twentysomething years, little else defines your life and social circles more than music. It's the perfect fit for a social-networking community. It's also why MySpace has formed marketing partnerships with the Warped Tour and Rock the Vote.

Friendster was the first social networking portal to gain significant attention, but at some point, everyone left that party and moved over to MySpace. According to Duprey, who began using Friendster to keep in touch with friends in faraway places, Friendster was slow to load, seemed unable to deal with major traffic, and didn't respond to changes and user requests. "When MySpace came up, it was an easier, more accessible site, so everybody moved over there." Now when she visits MySpace, Duprey spends three-quarters of her time researching and following new bands and the other quarter staying connected with her friends and family.

As a music supervisor, Duprey seeks out new, emerging bands and musical artists to feature on the shows she oversees. She receives a massive pile of CDs every month from record companies and publishers and reads industry magazines, but says MySpace is the ideal place to discover bands that are flying under the media radar. "For me, it's great to start a relationship and listen to their music before they become famous or become the hip new band." Whereas indie artists control the rights to their own music, established acts often have a bureaucratic chain of label staff, publishers, and managers to contact before a deal can be inked. When Duprey finds a band that she likes on MySpace, she's often the first person who has ever licensed their music and can get in on the ground floor of their burgeoning careers.

In fact, over 50 percent of the artists whose music Duprey has licensed for film and television were groups or solo acts that she initially contacted through the Internet or through MySpace.

MUSIC AND COMMUNITIES

Online communities have become potent social influencers. They're much more than a place to troll for dates (although that's certainly a popular reason to log on) or to bid on a vintage porcelain monkey. Internet communities have changed the rules of the marketplace and revolutionized entire industries. The music world, for one, will never be the same again.

Technology first sparked the recent musical revolution, fueled by the availability of MP3 players and file sharing through Napster. These two developments laid the groundwork for a huge shift in how music is now discovered and shared. In the past, the only way to hear about hot new bands was to turn on the radio, visit a record store, or eventually watch MTV. "Now, it's a lot easier to create a record," explains Duprey. "You don't need to spend $50,000 a day going into a recording studio. You can do it all on your computer at home." Full albums can be quickly recorded, mixed, produced, and released without red tape or fanfare. That means there's a flood of new music available to listeners, and there's a lot less money invested in marketing this independently produced music. Emerging bands don't have to spend ten years touring the country in a broken-down van, waiting for a record label to swoop in and save them from obscurity. They can do it themselves, their way, without a lot of cash, connections, or equipment.

Artists not only have the means to go it alone, but many have absolutely no desire to sign with record companies. They want to market the music themselves and retain control over how and where it's distributed. This is a massive paradigm shift, given that distribution used to be the toughest stumbling block. Sure, you could sell tapes from the stage after a local show, but who had the resources to distribute them across the country or the continent? With online downloading (legal and illegal), everyone has immediate access to digital music files.

Being self-sufficient can also generate greater credibility in today's decentralized marketplace. "There's a certain customer base out there that's interested in independent music," says Duprey. "They're not interested in Mariah Carey or Nickelback or whoever's being pumped by the record companies. They want to find out about new and independent stuff, so they've formed these online communities." It's a simple yet revolutionary new reality: You can now be an unknown, underfunded band and still sell records.

Duprey also believes it's difficult to mismarket yourself through online communities in the same way that you can in the marketplace. "It's almost like the marketing is progressing constantly on these Web sites, as opposed to saying, 'Well, we've printed a thousand posters and we have to live with them until they're gone.'" Bands can constantly update their MySpace sites with new photos, graphics, and details. It's also an effective way for artists to gauge fan reactions to their music. If a particular song rarely gets played or another single generates an incredible response, that's valuable (and free) market research. On the flip side, there's a new obligation to keep your materials fresh. An old, out-of-date page with no discernible activity is a red flag that you're out of the loop.

Duprey says MySpace helps her uncover promising artists, but it also enables her to network more efficiently and to stay on top of a fast-moving industry. The bands labeled as "friends" on her personal MySpace page are artists that she has either licensed in the past or whose music she especially likes. These online friends send electronic updates about their tour schedules, photo shoots, recordings, and other news, or post personal messages on her bulletin board. "I can keep in touch with the trajectory of their careers without having to sit down every day and say, 'Okay, here's a list of all the bands that I want to check up on,'" says Duprey. "I spend all day in front of my computer, and if somebody wants to start an online relationship with me, I'd much rather do that than sit down and have coffee for forty-five minutes. You just don't have that kind of time in a day." Her work depends on a keen ability to pick the right artist for the right scene in the right project, and online portals such as MySpace add a valuable dimension to her search. Built-in rankings and visitor traffic are early indicators of who and what is hot, and exactly how people respond to specific musicians. It's a rich and authentic research tool.[2]

Communities Take Control

Online communities have changed the rules of commerce. Amazon.com was one of the earliest examples of the link between communities and purchasing power. Users rate titles on the site, suggest other favorite books, and provide raw, unedited opinions about what they love and hate. Now sites such as epinions.com, buy.com, eBay.com, and many, many others provide firsthand news and reviews about every product imaginable, and consumers have come to expect this feature. Blogs, niche interest sites, and webzines also have potent communities that will quickly spread the word about whether something is worth your valuable time and money. Marketing can attract initial interest, but when a product is truly subpar (anyone remember J.Lo and Ben Affleck in *Gigli?*), the community will swiftly spread the word. On the other hand, communities might rally behind a small venture that doesn't seem to have a prayer in the marketplace. If members deem it smart, cool, funny, hip, or worthwhile, anything is possible. Such loose groups of like-minded people can even rediscover existing products and elevate them to bestseller status in record time.

Consider how fading brands like PUMA have gained new life by finding favor with a small group of trendsetters who are key influencers with their peers. PUMA was revived by the hip-hop community, which embraced the company's retro styling and made it a popular choice for a fashion-forward new generation.

As MySpace clearly demonstrates, communities are also changing the way business is conducted. They've revolutionized how we make deals, discover people, award status, and distribute products and services. They've dismantled the old hierarchical system and set up their own networks. Brands are now held accountable for everything they do and say, and will be swiftly punished for a lack of accountability. Try anything strange or underdeliver on your promises and your brand community will bring you to task—sometimes by dumping you like last year's Uggs. An incident involving the Kryptonite lock company is one of the most stunning examples of the power of online communities.

In mid-September 2004, a twenty-eight-year-old New York City graphic designer named Benjamin Running was one of several people who posted online videos explaining how to pick Kryptonite Evolution 2000 U-Locks with a ten-cent Bic ballpoint pen. Kryptonite had always proudly portrayed the fifty-year-old lock design as impenetrable and even invited notorious Greenwich Village bike thieves to try their hand; they stripped the bike of everything but the frame, which was secured to a metal post with the U-Lock. The stunt showed that Kryptonite locks were the best protection against bike theft—until the Bic pen incident, that is. In a matter of days, word spread beyond the online cycling community to mainstream media, including the Associated Press and the *New York Times*. Suddenly, everyone knew the story. At first Kryptonite denied the problem and remained firm that the locks would deter theft. The company later changed its tune and announced that it would exchange vulnerable locks for free. By September 2005, Kryptonite had exchanged over 75,000 consumer locks worldwide and continued to send postage-paid labels to customers who wanted to swap their U-Lock for an Evolution Disc Lock.[3]

When communities gather, rules change. Music was the first industry to get an extreme makeover. A few young guys created Napster, sparked controversy (and lawsuits), and for better or for worse unshackled music from its corporate masters. If history is the guide, what will be next? Thanks to blogs, affordable print technology, and international exposure at the click of a mouse, the publishing industry may well be ripe for an overhaul. Film, television, and gaming could also be waiting in the wings. But one thing is clear: Online communities, whatever their form, are a powerful market force that should never be underestimated. Regardless of whether your organization or industry has online communities (and it probably does—even if you don't know about them) or your company manages a virtual community, everyone needs to listen and respond. Such communities have created a new power structure that will continue to shift and evolve. Now let's explore why these communities have such a deep-seated appeal.

THE CRAVING:
CIRCLES AND LOOSE CONNECTIONS

Today, people are increasingly seeking close friendships and forming tightly knit yet nontraditional communities. A *U.S. News & World Report* article, "Tribal Culture: Single But Not Alone, These Urbanites Are Redefining the 'Adultescent' Years," reports on the families of friends being formed by men and women of Gen X and Gen Y in the now greatly extended single years before a typically delayed marriage.[4] These familylike circles of peers, these tribes, which have been depicted with humor and affection in television shows like *Friends, Sex and the City,* and *Will & Grace,* are now evolving into a new form.

Many people are currently seeking less structured social and professional networks by moving away from traditional associations and club-style memberships in favor of loose connections that more accurately reflect their interests, lifestyles, and general lack of time. According to Robert Wuthnow, author of *Loose Connections,* the new shapes of social interaction are less formal, demand shorter periods of commitment, and are more focused on specific goals in response to the demands of modern life.[5] In response to this new mind-set, traditional social groupings such as the Elks, Rotary Club, and women's associations are experiencing a decline in membership. Instead, Gen X and Y are creating loose connections around brands, activities, and specific passions and interests.

Recent technologies have influenced a basic dynamic in American society—the relationship between the individual and the group. In the next few years, brands can expect to see increasingly empowered individuals actively coming together in new forms of connection, and this chapter illustrates how to leverage this phenomenon. In 2000, Starbucks bewildered many in the business community by working with Microsoft and investing millions of dollars to install wireless networks in their stores. Forward-thinking Starbucks planned to tap into the burgeoning desire to merge home, work, and play with the assistance of rapidly developing technologies. They predicted a future where customers would enter Starbucks to pick up a cup of coffee as well as work, catch up on e-mail, and hang out. Starbucks, in other words, realized that when a person enters their store for coffee, they weren't just looking for a skim vanilla latte; they were seeking a "third place," a clubhouse of sorts that's distinct from their home (first place) and their work or school environment (second place).

With traditional association membership on the decline, people are not just buying brands, they are interacting with them more deeply and informally "joining" them. Companies need to wake up to this important shift and understand the complex dynamics that surround a brand-focused community.

Online Networks

The familiar groupings may have shifted, but community has not gone away. It is too important to people. Instead, it has evolved to fit today's lifestyle and interests. People simply have less time to spare, are relocating more often, and if they have time available, don't want to commit themselves to organizations that have large, obscure objectives with significant time requirements. A group that works to build a new school soccer field or to protest industrial construction in a historic neighborhood is more likely to draw membership than older institutions that had lifetime memberships and sought to remedy everything from hunger to litter.

As the railways, highways, airways, telephone, mass media, and Internet erode the concept of the traditional community, they also create new ones. Unanchored and conceptual communities of others that share a state of mind rather than physical proximity have joined the geographical neighborhood. A filmmaker in Seattle has realized that he shares more community interests with other filmmakers in Los Angeles, or New York, or even Australia, than with his neighbor down the street who is a passionate organic gardener.

As the traditional icons of community (such as conversations with neighbors over the fence) have slipped away, they've been replaced by communities of ideas and mutual interests. The electronic age has enabled this evolution in ways that few imagined even two decades ago. The Internet has catapulted friendship, dating, and straightforward networking beyond anything that was possible when the world was trapped by traditional, geographically based contact. When organizations understand how Gen X and Gen Y are creating connections, they learn how to gather communities around their brands, learn from these tightly filtered groups, and advertise with a laser-focused, nontraditional approach.

The Connected Generation filters much of its communication, entertainment, and life interactions through technologies such as e-mail, ICQ (a popular instant messaging system, pronounced "I Seek You"), cell phones, texting, and online communities. This layer of technology adds entertainment, control, new possibilities, and a different kind of social schedule to their relationships. It is tightening up their inner circle relationships and giving them loose, interest-focused connections.

WHY WE CRAVE CIRCLES
AND LOOSE CONNECTIONS

1. **New forms of media create new social possibilities.**

   Social networking is becoming a widespread cultural phenomenon. It's evolving beyond a social experience into a powerful (even addictive) form of entertainment. While older generations might read the newspaper with their breakfast or watch a morning news show while sipping their coffee, younger generations will start their day by checking into sites such as MySpace or Friendster. It's how they feel connected and grounded for the day. Bottom line: Meeting new people—especially those who deeply share your passions, interests, or values—is fun and satisfying.

2. **Real life can be stranger than fiction.**

   From MTV's *Real World* series to *Survivor* and the subsequent explosion of reality television programming, there's a hunger for unscripted access to other peoples' lives and unique experiences. With online communities, people watch the human drama (or human comedy, depending on how you see it) unfold on the Net, rather than on the television screen. It's a step closer to the action, and it puts you in the cast, with unlimited access to the "show," 24/7.

3. **There are new ways for existing circles to communicate.**

   Today, it's not uncommon to find your closest social network spread across the country and even across the world. Your best friend relocates to San Francisco while another friend teaches English in Korea. E-mail first made it simple to keep these connections close, but online communities provide an even looser, more free-form way to chat, share, and stay involved in each other's lives, regardless of physical geography.

At sites such as MySpace, friends can post blogs about their day-to-day lives and instant message each other when they spot a friend online. You can indulge in a bit of harmless cyber-stalking (look up an ex-boyfriend to find out who he's currently dating, for instance) or chat with like-minded fans of an emerging punk band. Being highly connected is a new form of social currency, and for Gen Y it's fun to layer technology between friendships and daily communications. This tech-savvy group doesn't feel that the virtual barriers of a community site create distance, and it's often their preferred way to bond. Just as they're more likely to text someone to ask them out on a date, virtual communications are a comfortable way to stay close and interconnected.

4. **We want private space.**

Online communities can foster a secret world of relationships and connections—a private space that you might not discuss in your day-to-day interactions. You might tell your coworker about going for drinks at a downtown lounge, but you may be less likely to explain the thirty minutes you spent chatting online about a new video game. It feels special, exclusive, and fun to keep it private. In addition, your coworker may not have ever played a video game. The online community encourages relationships of common interest, validation, opportunity, entertainment, resources, and passions.

On the other hand, there's a strong illusion that these are truly private spaces. Many Gen Y community members don't even consider that their parents, professors, or bosses could go trolling through the site—reading their blogs, checking out their photos, and scanning each posting. A January 8, 2006, article in the *New York Times* titled "In Your Facebook" by Nancy Hass discussed privacy issues and explored the clever ways that both police and students have responded to this complex new social dynamic.

According to Kyle Stoneman, a senior at George Washington University, it was the campus police who launched a Facebook war. "We were just being, well, college students, and they used it against us," he told the *New York Times*.

In the story, Stoneman said he believes that campus security learned about a party he was planning with friends last year by monitoring Facebook.com. The officers waited until the party was underway, then shut it down when they found underage students consuming alcohol, said Stoneman.

The group decided to retaliate by using Facebook to set up a prank party. They chatted up a beer blast and spread the word online. When the campus cops arrived, they saw forty students and a table of cake and cookies, all decorated with the word "beer." Stoneman said the looks on the officers' faces were priceless. In true Facebook style, he snapped a few party photos, including a shot of one unimpressed officer, and posted them on the popular networking site.

5. **We need major flexibility.**

Online communities are never all or nothing. Members can move in and out of the space throughout their days, weeks, or months and adjust their involvement depending on their needs and desires. We all crave community, but our busy lifestyles can increasingly limit our ability to nurture and create it. At sites such as 43Things and Match.com, the show's always on. It's up to you how often you tune in and participate.

6. **We want to be able to "shop for people."**

Virtual communities can add a fun new layer to social experience by allowing people to have conversations around their deepest passions. You can chat with someone who already knows the intricacies of film editing instead of having surface-level conversations with your "regular" group of friends. This familiarity allows the discussion to go deeper and enhances the possibility of learning and discovery. You can create a network focused around your interests. The Connected Generation is full of leaders and innovators. They love to learn, but they also want to teach. They find satisfaction in being the one who knows what they're doing or spreading the word about something cool.

Virtual communities can also enable people who are living isolated lives to reach out and find like-minded friends. If you live in rural Alabama, it can be intoxicating to connect with someone in New York City who shares your passion for modern art—a relationship that might be difficult to come by in your corner of the globe. You can keep up with your chosen world and stay connected with the people, events, and news that are an integral part of that network.

Online worlds can even connect people who share common geography. Sites such as Facebook create an insider community for college students who attend the same school. College students use the site to stay in communication with friends, post information about parties and school events, gather support when running for school offices, and troll for dates. Everyone travels the same campus and shares a collective experience—whether or not they ever meet face-to-face or attend the same microbiology class.

7. **We're offered new sources of attention, affirmation, and popularity.**

Just as e-mail and BlackBerries have us constantly checking in with our networks, these forums provide multiple ways for people to interact, praise, comment, and connect with us. On MySpace and Facebook, users can even "measure" their popularity and sociability by how many friends are in their networks, how many times they've been "poked," and how many comments they have on their message boards, as well as through more subtle clues such as party photos, inside jokes, and streaming videos. For high-school and college students—and let's be honest, the rest of us—this can be a powerful motivator.

8. **We leap at the chance to break out and get discovered.**

Some communities offer a public platform to gain personal recognition for your talents. MySpace is providing a forum for bands to share music with their fans and get some all-important exposure to a potentially global fan base. It's another chance to get that big break. The same logic applies to writers, actors, filmmakers, artists, Web designers, video game developers, and social activists.

9. **The Internet allows for convenient centers of influence.**

A Gen Y student council hopeful wouldn't dream of handing

out chocolate to gain votes—she'd be much more likely to launch and run her campaign on Facebook. That's where everyone hangs out and would read the posts or promotional materials. Virtual communities can also provide a convenient way to mobilize people for specific causes or political purposes, or to start a real-time networking group.

10. **We can tap into multiple scenes.**

Maybe you're a surfing fanatic who loves cooking and graphic design. Virtual communities present the unique ability to satisfy all these interests among different groups. You don't have to watch your surfing buddies' eyes glaze over while you discuss the virtues of aged balsamic vinegar. There are people out there who can engage with all your separate and overlapping passions—even if they're not part of the same circles.

11. **We want control and immediate results.**

Traditional social groups, including Rotary, Elks, chambers of commerce, and other associations, are struggling to maintain membership. To Gen X and Y, these formal networks seem time-consuming, not very productive, and limited in structure—these are their parents' clubs. Making an impact might mean serving in a way that just doesn't fit their lifestyles. The old guard often requires young members to slowly earn their wings and follow rigid policies. They can lack immediacy, fun, and a true sense of impact. So this generation is switching channels and making its own rules—creating networks where they don't have to climb ladders or get stuck in messy group politics. They have an inherent desire for speed and an ingrained sense of entitlement, which means that they won't wait around to earn their stripes. They've got their own plans and ideas, and they're ready to implement them right away.

12. **There are no barriers.**

The Connected Generation has a much higher level of trust for strangers and feels little fear about meeting people online. No one would bat an eyelash to hear that a friend or coworker uses an Internet dating site. It's not strange, desperate, or frightening. In fact, many people feel that the layers of technology give them more control. They can think through each connection and politely reject a potential date without having to do it face-to-face.

It's easy to block or stop communication altogether with a pesky person.

LESSONS FROM MYSPACE

Stay connected and committed.

MySpace has continually upgraded its features and launched improvements as the community evolves. In 2003, the site added group profiles, the ability to block friend requests and approve comments before posting, classified ads, "online now" status, and picture rankings, among other key changes. In 2004, music gained presence when artists were allowed to create profiles and post streaming MP3s. MySpace also added conversation forums, games, more features for group communication and organization, the ability to give "kudos" to praiseworthy members, and event invitations. The year 2005 brought school-based home pages, "sticky threads" (an online discussion entry that always shows at the top of the threads listed in a forum), a calendar system, and customizable name URLs.

It's critical to listen, notice, stay connected, and respond to your online community's members. MySpace is highly flexible, continually changing and adapting to the community. Similarly, once your site is up and running, you've got to stay close to the community and develop ways to gather members' feedback. Even better—watch carefully, anticipate your customers' needs, and provide useful tools before anyone even requests them.

Link like-minded people with similar goals and interests.

MySpace would not be half as successful if you couldn't search for people by interests. In a virtual space, it would be impossible to quickly find common ground. There have to be convenient mechanisms in place to pinpoint other U2 fanatics or competitive gymnasts. Most people already have social networks in their daily lives, so there has to be a compelling reason to take the experience online. Passions and common interests are the threads that tie communities together—

whether members live on opposite sides of the world or take the same English lit class.

Link fellow fanatics.

As a lead singer in a local band, MySpace founder Tom Anderson understood the needs of undiscovered bands and built MySpace to link artists and fans. People are passionate about music, and this energy has driven MySpace's success. This generation is often equally passionate about their pets. Date My Pet created a community (it's not exclusively focused on dating) based on people's love for their furry friends.

Case Study—Date My Pet

Independently owned Web site Datemypet.com is less a dating service than a social network for pet owners. It's great for meeting people who share a love of animals—or for simply finding your pet a playmate. Launched in 2004, the site allows members to upload photos of themselves and their pet and search for like-minded animals and humans (for now, membership is free). Even if you're just looking for someone to chat with over dog walks or cat-grooming sessions, it's a great way to ensure that any new humans in your life get the green light from your four-legged friends. Datemypet.com is a prime opportunity for a dog food manufacturer like Science Diet to build a community around its customer base of pet lovers.

Provide a virtual space for an existing community.

MySpace effectively reached out to independent and aspiring musicians and attracted a community of music lovers from across the globe. Facebook took the same concept and flipped it. Attending the same college is the common thread that links members in this popular online community.

Case Study—Facebook.com

Developed in February 2004 by Mark Zuckerberg, Chris Hughes, and Dustin Moskovitz at Harvard University, Facebook is a social-networking site modeled after traditional school facebooks, which collect names, photos, personal interests, and other information about students into a bound paper booklet. The three creators originally designed the site (registered as the facebook.com) just for Harvard students, but the phenomenon quickly spread to other schools. By 2005, Facebook had the largest number of registered users among all post-secondary networking sites and has launched a version for high schoolers. In January 2006, the site ranked ninth in overall Internet hits, behind fellow online network MySpace.com. The college directory logs over 250 million page views in any given twenty-four-hour time period perhaps because it appeals to the average student's life and daily rhythms.

Anyone who has a valid .edu e-mail address—including school students, staff, faculty, and some alumni—can access the site, but the vast majority of users are current students. Members create an online profile and upload a personal photo. Once they're registered, they can search for specific fellow users and request to be added to friend pools. They can also use search features to find members by interest or location, and to create or join specific groups. Although Facebook is school specific, you can create "friends" status and find like-minded groups among people from other schools, which is helpful for promoting regional events or simply making wider connections.

Facebook has been successful because it takes a strong mutual interest—attending the same school, college, or university—and uses it as a way to link and network members. Everyone who joins the site already has a solid bond through their educational institution, and Facebook builds on that connection. Users can view only profiles of other users at the same school, but mutual friends who are attending different institutions can view each other's profiles.

One of the most popular features on Facebook is called "poking," which is a digital way to say hello to friends and new contacts or to start a conversation. When you poke another Facebook user, the system sends text that reads "you have been poked" and gives them the option to return the "poke." It tells someone that you're thinking about him and provides a quick, informal way to stay in touch.

All the features of Facebook are free, except for public announcements, which members purchase like classified ads to sell an extra couch, find players for a volleyball league, or get used textbooks for a specific class. The site also survives on revenue from corporate advertisers who are eager to reach college and high-school students.

Don't strangle the network.

Let the community lead the way. MySpace trumped Friendster because of its additional features and greater freedom. Just like a cocktail party, online communities are live and unpredictable. The dynamics are subtle. Holding the reins too tightly by overmonitoring interactions, limiting the ways people can communicate, or dictating how people will use the site will only silence the conversation, and if the party gets dull, the room will empty out.

Extend functionality around existing behavior.

MySpace didn't debut with all its features in place. It started with the basics and let the community develop its own ways to interact. The music section evolved as people began sharing news about bands, recruiting fans, and ranking music. No one pushed it into place. Trust the process and honor the changing needs of the community. Make it easier for them to do what they want to do. That could mean changing course or bringing on new tools as demand grows.

Sometimes the community is created for one purpose but builds profile and momentum when it's leveraged for another reason, such as when Democratic National Committee Chairman Howard Dean used MoveOn.org and Meetup.com in his political campaign. According to *Trend Letter,* the very nature of the political process is being changed by the "power of the Web to mobilize and elicit responses from constituents."[7] Through MoveOn.org, Meetup.com, and various blogs, thousands of like-minded people became active participants in the political process rather than passive bystanders during Dean's push for the 2004 Democratic Party presidential nomination.

Add relevant and expanded features.

Bandwidth is a huge cost for MySpace. Members can upload full-length songs and videos and post large-file photos for free. Other sites might limit those files to save some cash, but providing room for emerging artists and musicians to showcase their music is a key part of the community's success. (These high server costs were a potential gamble that paid off when the site's large audience commanded powerful ad revenue and a stunning $580 million price tag at the time of sale.) MySpace has also created its own versions of the most successful online services, including Evite-style invitations, Craigslist-type classified ads, AOL's instant messaging, Match.com's dating profiles, and live meeting facilitation like Meetup.com. MySpace has established itself as a one-stop-shopping site with its integrated, relevant features.

Respect people's needs.

Be careful with pop-up ads or too much advertising. Make it too commercial and it just doesn't feel cool or underground anymore. MySpace gives users full control of their profiles and activities, and doesn't have laborious rules. It's a freewheeling, almost-anything-goes environment that mimics natural social interactions.

It's all about multimedia.

Technology drives online communities. People log on to share music, blogs, podcasts, and video. It's essential to keep up with the new stuff and to adapt as the community brings in fresh technologies. No one's going to stop reading posts, but they'll go elsewhere if they can't show their vacation photos or pull out the guitar to play a song.

Never underestimate the lure of attention.

Provide new ways for people to attract and give attention, such as MySpace's "kudos" or Facebook's "poking" functions. They're simple tools that keep people coming back. Create additional opportunities for profile, leadership, popularity rankings, and the ability to influence or make an impact. It's interactive and it gives clout to individual members.

Support highly personal, one-to-one communications.

The ability (or even the perceived ability) to connect directly with another community member is an attractive feature of MySpace. Regardless of whether you're e-mailing Chris Martin, lead singer of Coldplay–a band with a huge MySpace following–or your best friend, there's a direct sense of peer-to-peer connection. It breaks down the barriers and gives the community a feeling of democracy. It also shows fans that famous people are human. A hot band will have the same kind of rambling, cluttered page as everyone else on the site. There's a grassroots spirit that puts people on the same personal level.

Case Study—43 Things

At online social network 43things.com, people publicly compile their goals and the site automatically connects them with others who share the same goals. In fall 2005, over 99,000 people in nearly 3,000 cities were making plans to perform stand-up comedy, get out of debt, kiss in the rain, get a tattoo, smile at a stranger, eat fewer sweets, grow their hair long, or volunteer in Latin America. Currently 423 people want to make a movie, and 1,788 plan to go on a road trip with no predetermined destination.

The site works because it connects random people in pursuit of a common ambition. On 43 Things, you state a goal such as "write a novel," which immediately links you to all the other people who have chosen the exact same goal. You also attach tags to your aspiration such as "writing," "novel," and "fiction." Tags are

not selected from a precodified hierarchy set by the site designers, but arise from grassroots activity. Now you're suddenly connected to everyone with similar goals, such as "write a good
novel" and "write a book and have it published" and "finish my
novel."[8]

Add tools for self-expression and creativity.

When you're not meeting people face-to-face, it eliminates all the subtle clues that come from what they wear, how they speak and act, and
what they say. Online communities provide a place for people to
express themselves without censorship. It's a free space to do and say
what they want. For community members, their MySpace space is just
like a locker, bedroom, or apartment—the images and songs they post
represent their personalities. Customization is key. MySpace gives
members a range of tools for decorating and creativity. From artwork
to cell phone photos to songs and poems, anything goes.

Case Study—Flickr

Flickr didn't invent online photo sharing, but it was the first site
to identify itself as much more than a hosting service for personal photo albums. Flickr has won a devoted following by offering the Web's most robust and intuitive set of tools and features,
not only for self-display, but also for visual conversation. Flickr
permits what cofounder Caterina Fake calls a "rich, sharing
experience."[9]

Each member has his or her own photo page where people
can leave comments on each image through a process called tagging. You can upload photos by e-mail or from a camera phone
and post photos to any blog. Flickr allows users to form private
groups for events such as reunions and public groups based on
interests such as hiking or fashion. Users can also chat and share
photos in FlickrLive and sort their photos into albums with
Flickr Organizr.

It is important to note that new technologies are also generating a whole new vocabulary. As new words are introduced, the definitions can be fuzzy and several companies might use the buzzword to define slightly (or completely) different functions. Terms such as "tagging" may take on multiple meanings that change slightly within the context of different brands and Web sites. As these new technologies become more mainstream, their definitions will also become more concrete and less confusing.

Provide insider peeks and perks.

Album previews, television launches (such as NBC's *The Office*), and all manner of exclusive access have kept people coming back to MySpace. Everyone wants to see what's next. Gen X and Y love the undiscovered. They don't want to be handed everything in an official package—they want to log on, find something great, and spread the word. Communities that provide early admission to the latest and greatest will stay sticky.

Don't needlessly edit or censor the community's opinions.

When News Corp. bought MySpace, many users worried about the Big Brother effect—the Orwellian idea that the multinational corporation would breach privacy by monitoring pages and censoring free expression. These fears were openly shared on the site and to the new owners' credit, they did nothing to squelch the conversation. In general, MySpace has kept censorship to a minimum. (Items such as nude photos, hate speech, and messages about illegal activities are included on their short list of prohibited content.)

Virtual communities need a few core rules and basic boundaries; then they've got to reveal their bumps and bruises. In the old paradigm, Rupert Murdoch's News Corp. would quickly take down any negative criticism. But these communities will abandon ship if anyone tries to squash the spirit of anarchy. Who wants to participate in a careful, highly scripted exchange? It's got to stay free, not too corporate, and open to real dialogue.

Be transparent.

Nothing will kill a community faster than hiding motives and practices, or fudging the truth about corporate policies. Users' privacy must be paramount. MySpace members come back to the site because they feel that they truly own their spaces—it's a wide-open place to play, chat, share, discover, and forge connections. Owners must maintain their credibility and be clear about their motives. The community can sniff out false claims or corporate spin from miles away.

WORKBOOK

Get Started

1. **Develop an architecture of participation.**

   Make it easy and fun for your customers to participate in your brand by creating content, exchanging ideas, and sharing solutions with each other and your staff. Map out your current architecture of participation, making note of on- and offline locations where your brand community goes to communicate directly with people from your company, industry, and fellow customers.

2. **Invest in your community.**

   Invest at least as much in the member community as your customers do, in terms of the emotional and financial commitment. Who is working directly with your community members? What have they learned about the needs and wants of the community? If you don't have a liaison in place, consider how you will address this major opportunity.

3. **Nurture and empower your community.**

   Rethink your position from being a commander-controller to being a community nurturer. Enable enthused customers to gather around your brand and form their own peer-led communities. What software will help your customers to connect with each other? Can you identify where your brand community resides online? Do they gather on your site or elsewhere? What are they discussing? What are they hoping your brand will provide for them? Do they want information, access to the insiders, architecture for participation, solutions to challenges, a listening ear for improvements, or the opportunity to help you test new innovations?

Go for It.

Select an established but ineffective and outdated form of community that your company is holding on to (usually out of pure tradition or laziness). Using the steps in the previous section, reconceive this ineffective event or model (and its budget and staff power) into something truly inspiring and effective.

Identify a hot point where members of your brand community are trying to intersect with each other and with your company. Create an architecture that would allow free-flowing connections and communication around this issue. Troll through the customer response communication for clues and talk to your people who work on the front end.

FOUR

GIVE ME BRAND CANDY

Everyday Objects Get Sharp, Delicious, Intuitive Design

This is the story of an industry pioneer that lost its way and used "design thinking" to get its groove back.

Since it inception in 1928, Motorola had been dominated by engineers. This led to some exciting innovations, including the first mobile phone over two decades ago. But in the early 2000s, Motorola was floundering a bit. While the company still held a respectable share of the worldwide market, it had produced a string of unpopular phones and developed a reputation for somewhat unattractive, industrial-looking designs.

Nokia had maintained its number one market position. Samsung was leading the design charge, and was known for creating aesthetically pleasing phones that put it firmly in the number two spot.

The industry was caught up in feature mania, and manufacturers were focused on adding more and more gadgets to their mobile phone headsets in order to gain a competitive edge. Historically, Motorola had relied heavily on innovative features to generate breakout products, but this time they launched a design-driven initiative—to create the world's thinnest, sleekest phone.

In 2004, Motorola shed its stodgy image and introduced an aesthetic marvel—the ultrathin Razr V3 cell phone. Simpler, smaller, and sleeker than its rivals, the Razr weighed just 3.35 ounces and measured a half-inch thick. The Razr was impossibly compact and simple to operate, featuring an artfully hidden antenna and impressive photographic capabilities. The phone marked an elegant detour from the drive toward bulky, unattractive features. At $450 per handset, the

Razr was an instant hit, selling more than 1 million units in the first six months and 12.5 million units before reaching its first birthday.

Motorola had its mojo back and was suddenly a cool brand for design-conscious buyers. The Razr gave Motorola the image makeover that it desperately needed and positioned the brand as forward thinking and stylish.

Analysts were suddenly applauding the communications industry titan for its groundbreaking design. "With the RAZR V3, Motorola has created the most eye-catching handset on the market," said Yankee Group analyst Matt Hatton. "For most consumers, form-factor is the crucial hook when choosing a mobile phone, and the V3 has form-factor in spades. Couple this with the functionality you'd expect on a top-end phone and Motorola seems to have a winner on its hands."[1]

The Yankee Group analyst told the Associated Press that the Razr represented a departure from Motorola's stodgy, engineering-driven Midwestern roots. "These guys have to evolve from an engineering-focused company to a hip, slick, dynamic, rapidly moving consumer electronics company. Thus far, they've been able to do that."

The idea of a thin, small phone wasn't exactly original. In fact, communications companies had been gradually shrinking their models for years. What made the Razr impressive was that no company had ever been able to create a phone quite as small or quite as physically attractive. In fact, it was generally believed that it was technologically impossible to make a mobile phone that thin, especially if it included advanced features such as a camera.

While small phones were on people's radar, most of Motorola's competitors were distracted with technological one-upmanship, such as creating smart phones that offered BlackBerry-like options, streaming video clips, and adding MP3 players into the handset.

The field was crowded and focused on a different flavor, so Motorola went into stealth mode and put together an IT department team to build a phone prototype that was less than a half-inch thick. The goal was clear—size and simplicity. The ultimate prototype caught the attention of Chief Marketing Officer Geoffrey Frost, who had become frustrated with Motorola's stodgy image and was hungry for products that could reposition the brand in consumers' minds. Frost fully backed the project, commissioning the team to use any means necessary to make this ultrathin model a usable reality.

Roger Jellicoe, a director of operations who managed the Razr development project, also believed the concept had tremendous promise. "I badly wanted to do this phone," he said. "I saw the potential and realized it could change the industry." The further the team delved into the project, the more convinced they became that they had a hit on their hands. "From the beginning," said Jellicoe, "once you picked up the Razr and used it, you never wanted another phone."[2]

Motorola's internal innovation process was the biggest challenge facing the Razr team. Developers bypassed the standard procedure of running new product ideas past regional managers across the world. The company wanted to lead the market, not just give customers and managers what they thought they wanted, so the team put aside its normal practices. This was something different.

The team also sidestepped the cumbersome rounds of customer research that might have slowed development or provided conflicting information that could compromise the product. Motorola confirmed the demand in simpler ways, such as noticing how enthusiastic Motorola employees and their families all were clamoring for the Razr.

Finally, the team chose not to work closely with mobile phone operators such as Vodafone and Cingular. Stealth allowed Motorola to get a leg up in the marketplace.

"One of the big successes of Razr was that it took the world by surprise," said Jellicoe. "There are very few Motorola products that do that."[3]

When Motorola introduced the Razr in August 2004, both customers and industry watchers took notice. The Razr was such a hit that it achieved the company's total lifetime projections for the product in just the first three months.

Design is the main character in this success story. Innovative design is the new vehicle for steering troubled brands out of mediocrity and taking leaders to new heights. Motorola laid the foundation for breakout, design-driven products like the Razr a few years ago, when the company first began to embrace fashion and aesthetic innovation.

In 2001, Mike Zafirovski, then chief of the cell phone division, expanded Motorola's design team and hired famed Jim Wicks away from Sony, where he'd headed the Sony Innovation and Design Center in San Francisco. At the same time, Motorola opened a design center in downtown Chicago called Moto City, to attract young talent who were not exactly eager to work at its cell phone headquarters in the distant suburb of Libertyville, Illinois.

Today Wicks leads a worldwide staff of over two hundred design employees who reflect a mixture of right- and left-brain thinking, including sociologists, psychologists, musicologists, engineers, graphics designers, and software and color specialists. Technology is a way to serve consumers' tastes and priorities, so Motorola poured more money into consumer research, including global studies of lifestyle trends and aspirations.

Design has become a core competency for being in business—any kind of business. Motorola's Razr phone offers important lessons about the value of design for today's brand leaders and all future innovators.

THE CRAVING: GIVE ME BRAND CANDY

Design creates emotional attachments. The look and feel of objects, places, and things are becoming increasingly important. Humans are sensory creatures, and we naturally respond to things that look beautiful, smell good, have wonderful textures, delight the ears, and work intuitively. Design has emerged as a sign of the good life.

Design is shifting paradigms and spurring innovators to rethink established products and industries. Starbucks led the charge by turning plain coffee into made-to-order designer beverages to be savored in cozy reflective spaces. Apple has given computers and MP3 players a sleek and sometimes colorful exterior, and fully invented the look and feel of its (electronics) stores. Cirque du Soleil has ditched live animals and hay-scattered tents for a dramatic reinterpretation of the circus, which blends street performance, opera, rock music, and astounding human acts.

Business and cultural commentators are increasingly documenting the phenomenon of "universal design"—a shift from creating new pieces to reinventing everyday objects to make them more functional and pleasing. This upscaling trend has given rise to new forms, colors, and shapes, which have become markers that help customers determine the quality of products. And major retailers, including category leader Target, have partnered with recognized designers such as Cynthia Rowley, Thomas O'Brien, and Isaac Mizrahi, who bring a potent sense of cool and simplicity to the brand.

By rethinking the way people use mops, the Procter & Gamble Design Continuum has completely changed the cleaning paradigm. The result? The clever family of Swiffer mop products are on their way to becoming P&G's newest $1 billion brand.[4]

The abundance of styles and choices has brought design out of our peripheral vision and into the spotlight. In 1970, there were three design magazines; today there are over fifty. Even product names are getting a playful high-concept twist. Ben & Jerry's pioneered the clever-names trend back in the 1980s with flavors like Chubby Hubby and Cherry Garcia. Today, with products like OPI's nail polish titled "I'm not really a waitress," design has come to encompass the entire brand experience. Even Crayola has taken their crayon colors to a whimsical new level with names such as purple heart, razzmatazz, tropical rain forest, and fuzzy wuzzy brown.

Design is a powerful form of self-expression, helping us match who we are on the inside with how we present ourselves on the outside. Interior design has become a national pastime, and shows such as *Trading Spaces, Extreme Makeover: Home Edition,* and *Queer Eye for the Straight Guy* have achieved enormous mainstream popularity. We are less intimidated by design rules, feel free to experiment, and are having more fun with our choices and creations.

The definition of a branded product has expanded to include the entire experience and not just the isolated product. For example, when people say that they love their iPod, they are not just referring to the slick little MP3 music player, but also the iTunes Music Store, iTunes system, and the iPod software. In short, the iPod experience encompasses the entire system.

Improbably, the consumer market for adhesive bandages has also exploded in the past decade, driven by design and technological advances in hospitals. Consumers now browse store shelves jam-packed with new wound-care designs: liquid and spray-on bandages, ionized-silver bandages, waterproof bandages, easy-to-remove bandages, or anti-itch, antibleeding, or antibacterial bandages. Not to mention the bandages shaped to fit fingers or knuckles, medicated to minimize scars, or cushioned to heal blisters. There are eye-catching bandages for kids, decorated with licensed cartoon characters or tattoo designs, and clear ones that appeal to adults because they're nearly invisible.

Design (along with its strategic twin, innovation) has become a vital tool to stand out and stay strong in an increasingly competitive market. Design methods are helping managers to better understand their customers. Design-driven research is helping company leaders to visualize future opportunities to outwit the competition. Design-driven strategies are helping companies stay on the innovative edge and helping businesses connect with customers on a deeper level by anticipating their real desires and needs. That vital connection can be the difference between leading a category with a passionate brand community that drives growth or scrambling for market share with flat, dated offerings.

"At Sony," says Norio Ohga, the company's recently retired chairman, "we assume that all products of our competitors have basically the same technology, performance, and features. Design is the only thing that differentiates one product from another in the marketplace."[5] Design, in other words, offers great rewards for organizations that use it to lead every aspect of their business development, from product creation to advertising and marketing.

Many brands are aiming to boost their creative edge by adding or promoting talented designers into their leadership ranks. A growing number of companies are adding chief creative officers, or CCOs, to their executive teams. Experts predict that the new destination for young, talented leaders will be "D-school" instead of B-school. Stanford University has established a new institute of design that teaches design principles and strategy to business, engineering, and design students. Founded by Stanford engineering professor David Kelly (who just happens to be the founder of design powerhouse IDEO), this D-school is poised to give Stanford a significant edge over its business school rivals as design innovation becomes more intimately linked with bottom line revenues in every industry imaginable.

Brands today face fierce global competition. Design innovation is one of the strongest ways to generate organic growth, new revenues, and wider profit margins.

WHY WE CRAVE BRAND CANDY

1. **Design makes life easier.**

   Life can get overwhelming and design is a primary way to simplify products, spaces, and experiences. Design helps to create real-world product solutions, such as allowing three busy cooks to work side by side in a cramped kitchen. Design also makes technology more immediately usable and intuitive. It's easy to forget that everything around us has been designed, and that these aesthetic decisions affect nearly every part of our lives, from navigating an airport to booking a flight, baking a pie, or text messaging an important piece of information. When systems and products work, it's taken for granted. But, according to Bill Moggridge, IDEO cofounder: "A lot of trial and error goes into making things look effortless."[6]

2. **Design is a key differentiator in a sea of choice.**

   With shelves packed with look-alike products, distinctive design creates the "wow" factor that visually pops a brand out of the mainstream and into the spotlight. Time is at a premium for just about everyone, so well-designed and easy-to-use products quickly build loyal fans who spread the word to their friends and networks.

   In her book *The Substance of Style,* author Virginia Postrel argues that we increasingly make purchasing decisions based on how products make us feel. "In a crowded marketplace, aesthetics is often the only way to make a product stand out."[7]

3. **We want to feel we are in good hands.**

   Design has become an important factor in our decision-making process, often disproportionately tipping the balance toward products and experiences with superior design. In short, good design lends credibility. In fact, a study conducted by the Stanford Persuasive Technology Lab, along with Consumer Web Watch, found that the "look and feel" of a Web site are more important than the content. Nearly half of all consumers (46.1 percent) in the study assessed the credibility of Web sites based in part on their visual design appeal, including layout, typography, font sizes, and color schemes.[8]

4. **Good design makes the products' use transparent.**

   Intuitive design helps to communicate how objects will be used, making their purpose more immediately apparent. Design can reveal the built-in technological abilities of a product and help the consumer to see it, touch it, and figure out how to utilize it to full capacity. Good design takes away the friction and solves common problems. It also eliminates the "work-around" (the common adjustments people make when products are not streamlined or efficient to use).

5. **Design evokes emotions and delivers pleasure.**

   The typical phrase is "form follows function." Nancy Lafferty-Wellott of Habits & Habitats design firm teaches her clients a different phrase, "form follows flow." She defines "flow" as the feeling of enjoyment people get when they're working with an intuitive, well-designed product. It's a natural sense of pleasure and ease. People literally relax and breathe evenly when a product works intuitively, instead of tightening and clenching in anticipation of solving a product's puzzle.[9]

   Alex Lee, president of the New York–based OXO International environmental design firm, explains the "flow" experience: "Ultimately, what sells the product is the emotional side of design. We aim to create products that intrigue people, invite a question: 'There's something different about this thing. What does it do?' The critical moment is when they smile and say, 'A-ha!' If done right, the process makes people feel clever. They think, 'How come nobody ever thought of this before?' They get it, and somehow, they belong to this exclusive club of people who get it. That club could have ten million members, but it doesn't matter."[10]

6. **Design is widespread, inexpensive, and easier to achieve.**

   Remember the old days when only people with fat wallets could afford stylish kitchen appliances or bathroom fixtures that looked like they arrived straight from Italy? Today, our homes, offices, and closets are filled with affordable and beautiful objects at every price point. Good design has become highly accessible, and even mundane items like toilet brushes or water bottles have visual appeal. From pet products to cell phones, design has crept into every category and every niche and has become a heightened priority in our daily lives.

7. **Design shapes our environment and elevates our behavior.**

Imagine drinking wine from a plain white Dixie cup. Picture the way you would handle the cup, how quickly you would drink the beverage, and the position of your hand. For most people it would be a quick guzzle, a cup smash, and a chance at two points in the nearest trash can. Now picture holding a gorgeous 1917 Austrian-designed wineglass made of leaded crystal. When you go from the paper Dixie to this masterpiece, it modifies your behavior. You become more conscious of your movements, take your time to savor the drink, and might even straighten your posture, deepen your voice, and say something a bit more thoughtful during dinner. That's an extraordinary transformation for $70. Good design elevates your behavior and changes how you operate in a given environment.

8. **Design adds beauty to everyday products and spaces.**

In the past, designers focused on making one new product. Today, they create a much broader story—a complete and highly detailed experience that feels memorable from start to finish. The holistic design experience creates whole environments for people to sink into and provide richness that has a significant impact on the bottom line. Even doctors' offices have taken a stylish turn that parallels the popularity of cosmetic surgery and less invasive aesthetic treatments like teeth whitening and dermabrasion. Warm palettes, clean lines, and comfortable, living room–style seating have replaced dated colors and hard chairs.

It's not enough to have a good product anymore. You have to evaluate how your products make people feel by examining the sum total of all the parts and players in the experience.

9. **Design helps us evaluate quality and desirability.**

People make judgments based on design. It's shorthand for our lives and beliefs, and it provides cues for full experiences. Imagine that you're planning a vacation, and the travel agent hands over two brochures for two similarly priced resorts. The first brochure is a lifestyle magazine with glossy, high-quality paper, gorgeous photos, and an amazing map of the property done to scale. The second brochure is poorly translated, using words like "gastronomy" for the gourmet restaurant, and includes photos from the early 1990s, complete with guests who have huge bangs and hideous neon bathing suits. Despite equally enthusiastic endorsements from both friends and previous guests, where would you choose to stay? For many, the brochure alone would tip the sale. After all, if the brochure hasn't been updated, the bath towels and the free snorkel equipment might not have been, either.

10. **Design choices shape our personal identity.**

Whether we like it or not, we define ourselves through aesthetic choices and symbols. Whether we choose the fanciest or the most practical clothes, cars, shoes, jewelry, bags, ties, furniture, dishware—these are all ways of communicating who we are and what we're about. People make snap judgments based on design that extend to our values, preferences, and priorities.

11. **We are more confident and empowered.**

It used to feel as if designers belonged to a secret club and possessed mysterious powers. Today, we all seem to think of ourselves as designers in one way or another. We're celebrating our own abilities and expressing our personalities. Many experts have noted the rise of the creative class, and there's a high value placed on individual creativity.

Now you don't have to go to design school to sell your own fashions; you can just start ripping things up, sewing them together, and posting the creations on eBay. Technological advances have given us professional-level tools. While these tools may not give us the skills of trained designers, they do provide the motivation to at least try to express ourselves and create. Everyone is throwing their hat into the design ring, as there's greater acceptance of diverse creative projects and an appreciation of truly brilliant design.

12. **Design makes brands stand out above the competition.**

Many companies have designed their way out of failures and into market leadership by creating products that serve and delight their customers in fresh, new ways. Design gave Microsoft a leadership position in computer operating systems; it rescued Apple Computers from a downward spiral and made it a buzz-worthy frontrunner; and it launched Starbucks as a global powerhouse.

There is compelling evidence showing that businesses that leverage good design perform better financially. A Design Council study demonstrates that design-led businesses on London's FTSE (Financial Times Stock Exchange) 100 outperformed the index by 25 percent, while 90 percent of businesses that are growing rapidly say that design is an integral or significant part of their operations (only 26 percent of static companies say the same).[11]

As well as increasing market share, design can help to reduce costs by making manufacturing processes more efficient and cutting materials spending. It can also limit the time it takes to get new products and services onto the market.

LESSONS FROM MOTOROLA

Make design a core business strategy.

There was a long season at Motorola when engineers led product innovation and designers functioned in a secondary role of essentially providing a wrapping for the technological circuitry. Today the focus has shifted. The heart of Motorola's breakout new product developments is a company-wide commitment to design as a core business strategy. Customer-focused design leads the way, and engineering and technology take a strong supporting role in the overall vision. Motorola designers are an integral part of every product development team and are present in key decision meetings for the brand.

John Zapolski, an expert in human-centered products, systems, and strategy design, explains that businesses get the best from design only when they view it as a core competency. "Companies that are successfully exploiting the full potential of design do so because it's present in all of the decisions the company makes . . . These companies aren't choosing to apply design to their respective business strategies, but have chosen design as the fundamental strategy itself . . . Design isn't something that the design department does. It's a way of operating the company. It's an ongoing set of choices about how the company is going to exist, to compete, to grow."[12]

Aesthetic initiatives can drive performance innovation.

Design-driven innovation can generate breakout solutions that improve performance beyond the original focus area. Motivated design groups push boundaries and often create unexpected innovations along the way.

One perplexing challenge in designing the Razr phone involved the placement of the antenna that sends and receives radio signals. In order to keep the phone as small as possible, the antenna had to be designed into the phone's casing, but no one in the mobile phone industry had a solution for that challenge. Jellicoe sent five engineers off for a week, each charged with dreaming up two different designs that would solve the problem.

After the results were in, the team sifted through the proposed solutions and picked three that had the highest potential for success. Next was an intense two-week period when the company developed rough prototypes to test the three options. The resulting antenna design was a hit. Not only did it fit the product's specifications, it performed extremely well in the field. The new antenna was so superior to its predecessors that it's now being adapted as the new standard.

"That antenna is showing better performance in the field than any other antenna we have in GSM," says Jellicoe. GSM stands for "global systems for mobile," the technology standard used in most of Europe and Asia and by Cingular and T-Mobile in the United States. "Obviously, all of [Motorola's] GSM programs from this point on are adopting this same style of antenna. This is clearly a big win."[13]

Case Study—iPod Nano

The fusion of small and stylish has been a winning formula for Apple, pushing the design-oriented company to stay on the innovative edge and create solutions that improve current products and inspire new favorites.

The iPod Nano debuted in 2005 and took small and slim to

new heights. While the outside of the Nano resembles a shrunken iPod mini, the inside has been painstakingly reengineered to accommodate the ultrathin design. Older iPods (except for the iPod Shuffle) have miniature hard drives, but the Nano is built around a chunk of solid-state flash memory. The color screen is sharper, which increases readability despite its diminutive size. The click wheel on the front, battery, and chips all had to be reinvented to fit the Nano's slim 6.9 mm profile. The result is a player that is thinner than a pencil and lighter than eight quarters. It's one-fifth the size of the original iPod that Apple introduced four years earlier and has 4 GB of memory, enough to hold a thousand songs, and it also displays album art and photographs.

"We use every fraction of a millimeter of space to get things in there," says Apple senior vice president Phil Schiller. "It's like a puzzle to fit all that stuff together. It has the tightest tolerances of anything we've ever made in the history of this company."[14]

Discarded ideas can be refit together to create one powerful solution.

In creating Motorola's Razr, the team tapped into a rich source of free ideas—discarded concepts from other Motorola projects. Jellicoe discovered through informal discussions about the design needs of the Razr that several engineers had already developed important breakthroughs. Several clever and promising concepts had been cast aside because they didn't work well with existing projects on the table. Repurposing some of these ideas, Jellicoe created a sketch that incorporated elements from different projects.

"None of those ideas was the complete solution, and so the trade-offs or risks were judged unacceptable when each was considered separately," he says. "When the novel ideas were put together, however, the risks seemed manageable. This illustrates both the hazards of group thinking and the fact that innovation can sometimes move forward only when ideas are evaluated in combination rather than in isolation."[15]

By repackaging existing technology, Motorola created a cutting-edge, ultrathin phone that moved from concept to market in just one year, instead of two or three times as long.

Design for a mobile life.

As you walk the halls of Motorola's large Florida campus, it becomes quickly apparent that most of the men have their mandatory cell phone clipped to their belts while most of the women carry them in their hands. The idea of clipping a cell phone to a stylish pair of wool trousers topped off with a cashmere sweater makes many female employees shudder. It's bulky and unfashionable. The women at Motorola are not alone—there are millions of women who would love a less geeky way to keep their cell phones close at hand.

Moni Wolf, director of design for Motorola's iDen group, is working to solve the belt-clip puzzle. One of her innovations includes a phone with a small outer display lens that can pop out for remote use (such as clipping onto a wristband or being worn as a pendant). This means that women can keep their phones in handbags or briefcases but still have ready access to a thumb-sized device that will vibrate, flash, and show the caller's ID. Phones without the pop-out lens might use a Bluetooth-enabled accessory to indicate when the handset is ringing. (Bluetooth is an electronics-industry standard for wireless connectivity between devices.) Other future phones will offer a wallet hinge for better wearability and discreet, built-in handles that can be attractively attached to the outside of a purse or hung on a lanyard and worn as a necklace. As often happens, such innovations will probably appeal to both women and men.[16]

Case Study—Yoplait and Campbell's Soup

Many of us now eat meals and snacks on-the-go in cars and at desks. Food manufacturers are responding by reinventing established food products in carefully designed, convenience-focused packaging. When General Mills debuted Yoplait Go-Gurt in tubes nationally in late 1999, it was a breakthrough for outside-of-the-cup thinking. The first-ever yogurt in a tube was the perfect snack for on-the-go kids and adults, and single-handedly increased the total U.S. yogurt market volume by 2 percent.[17] Campbell's Soup is similarly scoring big-time with Soup at Hand: sippable, heat-and-go soups. The convenient new microwavable packaging has made Soup at Hand one of the most successful new product introductions in the company's history.

Assemble a "hot group" in a creative environment.

Motorola made a conscious decision to put the best, brightest, craziest, and most passionate people they could find on the Razr development team. Breaking away from standard procedure, this "hot group" left their cubicles in the sprawling research and development facility in suburban Libertyville, Illinois, to team up with designers and marketers fifty miles southeast in Moto City—the orange-and-gray downtown Chicago innovation lab. The open, democratic layout, central location, and collaborative atmosphere encouraged closer teamwork and broke down barriers, contributing to the enormous success of the Razr project.

Today's design labs have abandoned assembly-line thinking and, instead, gather diverse teams from different disciplines. These reimagined spaces support strong design thinking and are quickly becoming standard for organizations across a number of different industries.

Fisher-Price is just one of those companies whose innovative new space, called the Cave, inspired winning results for the toy division.

Case Study—Fisher-Price

Beanbag chairs, comfy couches, and adjustable lighting make the cubicle jungle feel like a distant memory. At the Cave, a design innovation center for Mattel's Fisher-Price toy unit, teams of engineers, marketers, and design professionals meet with child psychologists and other specialists to share ideas. The groups observe families at play in the field and then return to brainstorm, or "sketchstorm," as they call it. Next, the teams build new toy prototypes from foam, cardboard, glue, and acrylic paint.

Staffers such as Tina Zinter-Chahin, senior vice president for research and development, call the process "spelunking" because it's based on the idea of taking a deep dive into product development. It also means mixing and mingling employees from a range of different disciplines. "People at first were skeptical," says Zinter-Chahin, who says that toy designers weren't thrilled about spending time with marketers. "They said: 'Come on, I'm going to go away for five days and take a marketing person?' We found that while [marketers] aren't great with foam and glue guns, they're great at hashing out an idea and positioning the product."

The Cave is already producing tangible results for Fisher-Price. After observing babies and their moms playing at home, the spelunkers realized that parents typically spend a lot of time teaching kids about everyday household items such as light switches, drawers, and kitchen utensils. Fisher-Price had a large toy lineup, but it was short on real-world, practical stuff. The company developed the Laugh and Learn Learning Home, a $64 model home made of plastic, where kids can crawl through a front door and explore the alphabet, numbers, music, speech, and different sounds. The new toy debuted in 2004 to enthusiastic parents and has now expanded to a full Laugh and Learn branded line of toys.[18]

Expand the role of color in communication.

While colored phones such as the hot pink Razr have created a fashion stir, designers at Motorola are also exploring color as a communication tool. Consider a traffic light, says Wolf, head of design for Motorola's iDen group. "Red, yellow, green. Three simple colors, yet on their own, they regulate traffic across the globe with surprising success. There is no text, no talking, no human motioning. Just three colors that speak volumes in an instant."

The idea of a "color vocabulary," for example, may even reshape how we use cell phones. Imagine if you could recognize your inner circle of family and friends by the blue light that surrounded the keyboard when they called. Or, if a red emergency light signaled that it was wise to answer a certain call even during a meeting. Perhaps lovers will eventually send pink "love lights," as the modern equivalent of texting XOXO (hugs and kisses). Or if four green lights meant that all your kids had arrived home from school, and three purple "I'm thinking about you" messages arrived from friends. Instead of listening to sixteen voice messages, the colors could do all the talking.

At Almus Generic Pharmaceuticals, strategic use of color has given this company a coveted edge in the ultracompetitive generic drug industry.

Case Study—Almus Generic Pharmaceuticals

For years, prescription drug boxes have traditionally been white. Crowded pharmacy dispensaries are often a sea of white, which makes it difficult to distinguish between different medicines, strengths, and quantities. United Kingdom–based Almus Pharmaceuticals has changed all that with new packaging designed to reduce the possibility of dispensing errors.

Almus's strategic partner, Creative Leap, realized that the company needed a bold yet simple color system that would enable pharmacists to quickly distinguish between various drugs. They designed a color-coding system that would visually instruct the pharmacists before they even read the text on each box. A stark two-color system uses block color on the whole box, with a single stripe in a different color to denote the strength. Using a twelve-color palette for the whole Almus range, each drug type was assigned one symbolic color and a different stripe tone.

Almus launched the new packaging in 2003 to universal acclaim from pharmacists, who praised the new system for its simplicity, quick restocking potential, and, most important, its enhanced safety. With just thirty-five total products, the company enjoyed an 18 percent growth in sales volume in the first year alone. By 2004, Almus had ninety-five products on the market and aimed for two hundred by 2005.

The straightforward, intuitive color system demonstrates that existing design practices should never be taken at face value. There are always fresh ways to reimagine the status quo.[19]

Develop solutions by reading between the lines.

Sometimes customers don't actually know what they need or want. Great design anticipates new solutions and opportunities that may not even be on the table. At Motorola, for example, customers constantly request bigger displays and keypads to make the handsets easier to use. But after a while, the phone gets as bulky as a potato, and no one is happy. Designers like Wolf have begun to probe deeper, and translate the desire for a "bigger keypad" into "easier-to-use keys," and have introduced strategically placed textures, simple layouts, and QWERTY touch-typing functionality into the keypads.

Companies like 3M follow this same read-between-the-lines methodology to develop breakout new products.

Case Study—3M

When customers said that they wanted bigger batteries to power their new, larger computer screens, 3M decided that they were actually asking for better visibility and developed new ways to create brighter displays.

The St. Paul, Minnesota, industrial conglomerate—with an R&D staff of 6,500 people in thirty-one labs worldwide and a $1.1 billion budget—innovates by decoding the deeper meanings in customer feedback. Instead of mechanically responding to each request, the company carefully interprets what customers actually need.

"One of the tools is how we train our people to ask the probing questions," explains Jay Ihlenfeld, 3M's senior vice president for research and development. "So, when a customer says, 'We need a battery with a longer life or one that can put out more energy,' 3M knows to ask the next question: 'Why do you need that?' It's our job to drill down to understand what is the underlying solution."

The drilling down is clearly paying off. Today, 3M's hottest product is an ultrathin plastic film that's now put on virtually every flat-screen display on the market. The film enhances image clarity and brightness, and channels more light to the viewer, so the screens require less light and hence less battery power. That means that portable devices can get by with smaller rechargeable batteries.

Whenever you use a laptop or personal digital assistant or turn on a flat-panel television, chances are you're looking at a 3M product. It's a great example of how design-based thinking can solve sticky challenges in surprising ways.[20]

Watch the user (translation: Go home with your customers).

Design innovator IDEO has an expression: "Focus on the verbs, not the nouns." Translation: If you focus too much on the product (especially in the beginning), it will lead your process astray.[21] For Motorola, the most important breakthroughs have come from watching cell phone users in their daily lives.

For example, the design teams observed that many people don't have the patience to read the manual, so they use only features that are readily apparent by fiddling with the handset. Younger members of the Connected Generation (raised on computers and video games) tend to excel in learning how to use electronic devices. There's a large segment of the population, however, that gets overwhelmed by all the available features. All they want is a phone that looks good and makes calls.

Motorola is responding to this need by making phones that are more intuitive to learn. The design teams are exploring options such as preprogramming phones with three different levels of usage ranging from minimum features to advanced tools.

OXO's Good Grips line, one of the most celebrated product designs in today's market, was inspired by the founder watching a very special customer—his wife.

Case Study—OXO International
Good Grips Kitchen Tools

When Sam Farber started OXO International in 1989 and set about developing a new range of easy-to-use kitchen tools called Good Grips, his primary interest was meeting the needs of just one customer—his wife, Betsey, an architect who suffered from arthritis in her hands. Betsey was frustrated with poorly designed kitchen equipment that made it impossible for her to carry out basic chores such as peeling potatoes. Farber asked himself: "Why do ordinary kitchen tools hurt your hands, with painful scissor loops, rusty metal peelers, and hard skinny handles? Why can't there be comfortable tools that are easy to use?"

Fed up with user-hostile kitchen gadgets, Farber approached Smart Design, a New York–based industrial design firm he had commissioned during his time at Copco (the leading manufacturer of ergonomic and stylish teakettles and other kitchen tools). The brief: to develop a range of kitchen tools that were comfortable in the hand, dishwasher safe, high quality, good looking, and affordable.

OXO wanted to develop tools that would cater to a wide range of user dexterity while still remaining stylish and desirable. Video research provided significant insights that led the team to deeper innovations. Sharpness, for example, emerged as an important way to make the tools easier to use. The design team also divided tool types according to wrist and hand motions—twist/turn (used to scoop, stir, and peel), push/pull (graters and knives), and squeeze (scissors, garlic presses, and can openers). Smart Design quickly made a series of models from foam and other materials to test the initial concepts.

Since its launch in 1990, the design quality of OXO's Good Grips has been commercially and critically successful, winning almost every major design prize, including one from the Arthritis Foundation. Good Grips tools can even be found in the Design Collection of New York's Museum of Modern Art.[22]

Forge smart partnerships and co-branding opportunities.

Motorola is embracing partnerships as a design strategy to create user-driven products and solutions that overcome the technological obstacles customers face when they want to stay seamlessly connected while on the go.

Launched at the 2005 Consumer Electronics Show, Motorola

partnered with Burton Snowboards to create a line of Bluetooth-enabled jackets, helmets, and beanies that will give snowboarders the ability to switch between their iPod playlists and incoming calls in midair. These three new innovations provide riders with wireless, high-performance connectivity and playability on the slopes.

The alliance represents a powerful collaboration of global industry trailblazers: Motorola is recognized for introducing the first commercial wireless products and Burton is known for producing some of the world's finest snowboarding equipment and apparel.

Motorola and Burton's relationship also includes a three-year global sports marketing alliance, which includes a strong Motorola presence at Burton's world-renowned Open Snowboarding Championship Series and event tour.[23]

Brands in every industry are partnering to develop smart new products and services. Instead of forming long-term alliances, these companies often work together on a project or brand over a short period of time. For example, PUMA has styled a Mini Cooper vehicle (christened the "PUMA Mini Cooper S") by applying PUMA's air-mesh footwear technology to the car's seats, which injects more comfort and breathable shock absorption. After the official launch in Frankfurt in 2003, the PUMA Mini went on tour, visiting flagship stores in London, New York, Santa Monica, Santa Barbara, San Francisco, and Milan. Mini driving shoes were also made available, based on PUMA's motorsport shoe.

WORKBOOK

Get Started

1. **Engage in your own product design experience.**

   Have your leadership and decision makers experience your products and the brand experience. Andrea Ragnetti, the newly appointed chief marketing officer for Philips Semiconductors, which makes a range of audiovisual products, recently gave each member of the board of directors a collection of Philips products. He had one request: Try them out over the weekend. The results were shocking. On Monday morning, many of Philips's leaders had to confess that they could not work some of their own products.

2. **Get your team out of the office and into the homes of your users.**

    Watching users in real-world situations offers behavioral insights and sparks ideas that would never come to life if the designers simply sat in their cubicles thinking about the situation or relying on generalized market research.

3. **Use design to attract top talent.**

    Attractive aesthetics and innovative design-based companies can serve as a powerful recruiting tool to attract top-notch creative personnel.

Go for It.

To what degree does your brand currently appeal to all five senses? Take each of the five senses, one at a time, and explore how you will appeal to each one. Evaluate how these new avenues of connection with consumers can set you apart in the marketplace or solve your existing brand challenges.

Find a product with a design that you absolutely love. Explore all the reasons why this product speaks to you and delights you. Take the exploration as far as it will go.

Consider brand partnerships to extend your design message. What is a good match for your brand? What other products out there appeal to your target audience (even if they are in an entirely different industry)? With which brands would you like to be on par in design?

FIVE

SIFT THROUGH THE CLUTTER

Editors and Filters Gain New Prominence

Stuart Hunter had a simple goal: He wanted to buy a bicycle. Hunter—who spent fifteen years developing retail store concepts and working with brands including Adidas, Target, Best Buy, and Circuit City—was ready to kick-start a new, healthier lifestyle. Years of working long hours and neglecting his health had added sixty pounds to his frame. Hunter had cycled earlier in his life and thought it would be a good way to achieve his new goals. All he needed was a bike.

But this basic purchase proved to be the ultimate thorn in his side. Hunter found that shopping in bike stores was a miserable experience. Young gear geeks completely ignored him while he shopped, whereas others saw his expensive car and immediately steered him toward the most expensive bike on the floor.

He concluded that bike stores were impenetrable for anyone who was uninitiated into the world of cycling (which is almost everyone). He did some further research and found that despite a 25 percent surge in Americans' spending in health and wellness categories, the cycling industry was stagnant at best. Hunter linked the poor sales directly to dismal shopping encounters. He saw a huge opportunity to create positive shopping experiences in the cycling industry and dove in headfirst.

Hunter's first roll: bike store opened on March 26, 2005, with a radical new concept: Offer fewer bikes and create a familiar, comfortable, helpful experience for customers. While the typical bike retailer will display over one hundred models on its showroom floor (one store owner even bragged to Hunter that he carried three hundred models), roll: stocks four bike categories divided by lifestyle—road, mountain, trail, and family. In total, roll: carries eighteen product styles and each bike has a clear difference, such as best in class or best in value. Hunter has sifted through the best product each bicycle brand has to offer and carries the top picks. Most of the stores are about 4,000 square feet, including the back-end office and storage, which leaves 3,000 square feet for the retail floor.

The roll: inventory is highly edited, which is a technique Hunter first honed in his work with Circuit City. As part of a project to develop a concept store targeted toward women, he helped the electronics retailer to overhaul the digital camera department, taking it from twenty-four SKUs to only six. The result? They reported higher sales volumes with the six carefully edited SKUs than they had achieved with twenty-four. This is when Hunter first saw the power of editing in action.

Hunter also tapped into his own bad buying experience to develop the roll: Perfect Fit System. This innovative process blends the inherent geometry of bikes with accurate physical measurements to produce a great new way to choose the right size and model. Staff members use a noninvasive, "hands-off" laser scanning system to measure five key points on a customer's body. A computer uses the data to generate algorithms and select the ideal bicycle size and style. In the process, the system also fits customers for shoes, helmets, seats, and other related purchases, giving them tremendous confidence in their final choices and providing roll: with a higher-than-average conversion rate from prospects into customers. In fact, roll: will not sell a bike without taking the customer through the fitting process. An experienced bike racer may visit her favorite bike store and work closely with the staff to achieve a highly customized fit, but the average bicycle consumer does not know what he or she needs and rarely receives a level of service that would equip the consumer as a newbie in the field. Hunter's fit and sales process provides much-needed guidance and customized information to a large group of people who often get lost in the sales process offered by most bike stores.

The Perfect Fit System is a central part of the roll: experience because it eliminates the fear of bike shopping and creates a sense of theater—not just for the customers being measured, but for everyone browsing in the store. It also helps customers to feel more invested in the brand. If you purchase a bike at roll: but don't know whether you want to immediately buy shoes and gloves, it's simple to return with your personal measurement printout to purchase the additional items later.

roll: stores are drawing enthusiastic reactions and a loyal fan base of new bicycle converts. Hunter says his favorite roll: customer is someone who hasn't been active for a while, decides he or she wants to start cycling, and visits roll: before checking out other bike stores. After browsing the store and being fitted for a bike and accessories, this customer will often leave to do some comparison shopping. Not surprising—bikes are big-ticket items. Invariably, this same customer returns to Hunter's roll: store that very same afternoon ready to purchase after wandering around aimlessly in many of his competitors' stores without proper guidance.

While other bike stores expect that the customer is—and wants to be—as knowledgeable as the staff, roll: assumes that you just want the right bike for your life at the right price. The stores, the service, and even the fit system are all highly edited, which leave customers free to think about what they really want and need in a bicycle. When a brand does the heavy lifting and sifts through the clutter, customers are left to explore, play, and enjoy the most interesting part of the experience—and in the case of roll:, that's cycling itself.

Hunter's secrets for success:

- Respect the customer.
- Have a clear understanding of the customer's experiences and motivation behind the purchase and the use of the products.
- Provide a carefully edited inventory that highlights the distinct and compelling differences between bike models.[1]

THE CRAVING: FILTER OUT THE CLUTTER

In a world that's increasingly inundated with choice, editing is a critical market phenomenon and an important process in our daily lives. Consumers rely on editors to sift through the raw data and identify the top picks. As a result, many savvy brands are learning to build editing mechanisms into their brands, products, and Web sites. In today's global world, it feels good to be "in the know," and to avoid costly and frustrating purchases.

People naturally edit every day, all day long. Consider the way you grocery shop. There are hundreds of thousands of choices in the supermarket, but somehow most people seem to choose the same twenty-five items almost every time they visit. We have to edit or it would take two days every week just to get the groceries. When I go into an Asian food market, I'm overwhelmed by the options. I have no idea what to buy, what to make, or how to use the unfamiliar vegetables. I tend to leave with some rice candy and anything that feels familiar. I have the desire to buy more items from the market, but not the expertise. I need an editor.

When someone else—a brand, an expert, or a trusted insider—does the sifting and sorting, it frees you to engage more fully with the experience. Someone else has trolled through the clutter, so you don't have to search. It's an incredible breath of fresh air in a crowded market. Editing also inspires a sense that you'll find the best fit for your taste and lifestyle. It's not a matter of reducing choice. Smart, savvy, user-friendly editing filters through the chaos and makes it easy to see what's important. Editing gives you more choice, rather than less, because you can forget about the extraneous details and focus on what you truly need and want.

People Like Me

An ideal editor could also be called your "twinsumer"—a term coined by the New York marketing firm Trendwatching to describe someone who shares your interests and deserves your trust.

According to Trendwatching's Web site, a twinsumer is someone (who you may or may not personally know) who is your taste twin—someone whose interests, values, lifestyle, and consumer habits mirror your own. A twinsumer's edited advice is relevant because it fits your life. As Trendwatching writes:

> After all, what good is a jubilant hotel recommendation on Trip advisor.com (a travel review site with more than 1.8 million consumer reviews) to a 27 year old bachelor from Vancouver looking for some sun and fun near Singapore, if the reviewer happens to be a father of four from Stockholm, whose positive rating of the Shangri La Rasa

Sentosa Resort was heavily influenced by the abundance of kid-friendly amenities or the presence of dozens of other families?[2]

Your twinsumer might share your values, interests, and tastes in important areas, such as family, lifestyle, politics, finances, or location. It's an imaginary someone who would have a discerning palate, and who would make choices as well, or better, than you would for yourself. Your twinsumer would see the world through a lens very similar to yours. When your best friend says that she loved a certain film, do you take her advice or discount it? It depends whether she shares your taste in movies. This is an example of the natural editing process that we all undertake, usually without a second thought.

A twinsumer wouldn't just be a shopping buddy, either. In the last ten years we've seen an explosion in news, opinion, and current events programming. To be a smart news consumer, you need to take in a variety of sources. A political twinsumer would look at all the information and pull out the news and perspectives that matter to you. For some people, that might be a Jon Stewart. For others, a Rush Limbaugh.

While most of us won't ever find a perfect twinsumer—someone we could count on to pick our food, clothes, entertainment, and political parties (and what would be the fun in that?)—the concept underscores what's most important about editing. Regardless of the industry or arena, we have to trust the editor and feel that his or her life is like ours. We need to believe that whoever is telling us where to go out to dinner has combed through the options and picked what's best for our lives.

THE HUMAN EDITORS

High-profile Editors

More than ever, celebrities, musicians, self-help gurus, and nationally renowned experts are naming their top choices and favorite products. Customers identify with these recognizable names and trust their knowledge, so their recommendations feel like advice from an admired friend.

Consider the success of the *Queer Eye for the Straight Guy* lifestyle

gurus, "What Not to Wear" fashion stylists, and Makeup 411.com
(where customers can learn which makeup products their favorite
celebrities wear). Each of these well-known brands uses filtering as the
foundation of their work.

Aspiring and Everyday Influentials

The rise of bloggers has paralleled the rise of the editing phenomenon. In today's marketplace, where even the smallest purchase category has multiple choices, everything needs editing. The editors who
step in and meet our needs are enjoying unprecedented rewards,
ranging from positive posts on their blogs to higher status and even
publishing and television opportunities. These everyday influentials
are rapidly becoming minibrands in and of themselves, sharing ideas
with the public and establishing expertise on a particular subject.
Up to 100,000 visitors a month peruse blogger Josh Rubin's carefully
edited collection of cool stuff on www.coolhunting.com, and independent food critic Steven Shaw, the "Fat Guy," has enticed a passionate following of urban diners with his Web site www.egullet.org.

Shopping Magazines and Guides

"Magalogues," a new blend of shopping catalogue and magazine,
such as *Lucky* for women and *Cargo* for men, focus exclusively on
what to buy and experience. Magazine giant Condé Nast recently
launched another magalogue, called *Domino,* dedicated to the boom-
ing home decor and renovation industry, and a Canadian magalogue
called *Wish* brands itself as a "shopping list for life."

Daily Candy has a free daily e-mail newsletter and Web site,
including editions for many large cities, including New York, Los
Angeles, Atlanta, and San Francisco among others, plus an insider's
guide to what's hot, new, and undiscovered—from fashion and style
to gadgets and travel. It's like getting an e-mail from your clever,
unpredictable, and totally in-the-know best friend who always has the
scoop on must-have jeans, secret beauty treatments, cool tech toys,
and hot new restaurants.

The Respected Industry Expert

Respected industry experts are people with strong credentials and a breadth of experience in their area who provide an uncanny level of access and insight. They have tried the product or service and know how it compares against many others in the category.

Founded by Edward M. Swartz, W.A.T.C.H. (World Against Toys Causing Harm, Inc.) issues an annual "10 Worst Toys" list to help parents, friends, and relatives avoid giving children toys that could lead to serious injury or even death. W.A.T.C.H's annual toy conference generates extensive media coverage and has established the organization's position as a top industry watchdog.

The Source for Breaking News and Secrets

A true Web pioneer, Matt Drudge has earned a huge following for covering—and uncovering—news, events, tips, and rumors before they surface in mainstream media outlets. In 1996, Drudge broke the news that Jack Kemp would run with Republican Bob Dole in the U.S. presidential election. Drudge later revealed that *Newsweek* magazine had obtained (but not yet published) information about a brewing relationship between President Bill Clinton and a White House intern—Monica Lewinsky. When Drudge broke the scandal, *Newsweek* published the story. Drudge also beat other news outlets to announce comedian Jerry Seinfeld's million-dollar television contract, Connie Chung's departure from CBS News, and the 1997 death of Diana, princess of Wales.

The Drudge Report Web site (www.drudgereport.com) now generates more than 100 million page views a month. His methods may be controversial, and some journalists say his news leans toward glorified gossip, but the Drudge Report has become a media force to be reckoned with—a clear example of how ordinary people can gain fame as information filters.

Local Editors

From Craigslist sites to local arts and entertainment listings and Lonely Planet travel guides, these are local insiders who know their home stomping grounds inside and out. When traveling to a new city or country, they can list great restaurants, suggest tourist sites to both explore and avoid, and in-the-know tricks and tools to make the entire experience safer and more enjoyable.

THE VIRTUAL FILTERS

Collaborative Filters

"Collaborative filtering," which Wikipedia defines as the "method of making automatic predictions about the interests of a user by collecting taste information from many users," first emerged at Amazon.com. The online book giant's recommendation software points customers who bought Malcom Gladwell's *The Tipping Point* to new reads such as *Freakonomics* by Steven Levitt and Stephen Dubner. Boasting over 6 million product reviews, Amazon claims that the click-through and conversion rates of recommendations based on collaborative filtering vastly exceed those of untargeted content such as banner advertisements and top-seller lists. Amazon may have pioneered this practice, but others have honed it beyond the sometimes clunky, broad links it makes between books.

Others who have embraced collaborative filtering include TiVo, which in 2005 had 100 million user ratings on approximately 30,000 television shows and movies. While often helpful, collaborative filtering can also land its share of misses. In 2002, *Wall Street Journal* reporter Jeffery Zaslow wrote a hilarious article titled "If Your TiVo Thinks You Are Gay, Here's How to Set It Straight." Here's an excerpt:

> Basil Iwanyk, 32, first suspected that his TiVo thought he was gay, because it inexplicably kept recording programs with gay themes. A film studio executive in Los Angeles and the self-described "straight-

est guy on earth," he tried to tame TiVo's gay fixation by recording war movies and other "guy stuff."

"The problem was, I overcompensated," he says. "It started giving me documentaries on Joseph Goebbels and Adolf Eichmann. It stopped thinking I was gay and decided I was a crazy guy reminiscing about the Third Reich."[3]

He mentioned his TiVo tussle to a friend, who told an executive at CBS' *The King of Queens,* who then wrote an episode with a My-TiVo-Thinks-I'm-Gay subplot.

RSS—Really Simple Syndication

Keeping up-to-date with the information you want can be overwhelming. Instead of trolling through endless Web pages, imagine having the latest news and features delivered directly to you. A clever service called "really simple syndication" (RSS) frees you from clicking from site to site and allows you to identify the content you like, which is sent right to your in-box. It takes the hassle out of staying up-to-date by providing the latest information that you're interested in.

Not all Web sites currently provide RSS, but it's rapidly gaining popularity. First, you need a news reader (also called a "feed reader"), which is a program or aggregator that can check RSS-enabled Web pages on behalf of a user and display any updated articles. There are many versions, some of which require a browser and others that are downloadable applications. All allow you to display and subscribe to the RSS feeds that you want. Once you've chosen a news reader, all you have to do is decide what content you want. By choosing key words, you can read from numerous sources simply by glancing through the highly edited selection of articles, blogs, and wikis in your RSS news browser. RSS is widely used by the blogging community to share headlines or full text entries and attached multimedia files. RSS usage is expanding as more people take advantage of this time-saving service. Other applications include marketing, bug-reports, or any other activity involving periodic updates or publications. It is now common to find RSS feeds on major Web sites, as well as many smaller ones.

WHY WE CRAVE FILTERS AND EDITORS

1. **We want a range of choices tailored to our needs and sensibilities.**

   The market is flooded with choices. Time has brought more models, more options, and more possibilities in every single category—from food to fashion to finance. We're all overwhelmed by the options, but that doesn't mean we want to give them up. Instead, we're looking for *the best choices for me.*

2. **We don't have the time or know-how to tackle the due diligence.**

   In the past, people would usually research only big-ticket items themselves, but routinely surveying the market before opening our wallets has become a regular part of the shopping process. It's the new standard. You can go online to check out laptops or the nutrition information on that new energy drink with the same few mouse clicks. It's convenient to research just about anything, but it can definitely become overwhelming. When editors do the work and we reap the benefits of their expertise, we're more likely to go with that brand or product.

3. **We want the confidence to make purchases, and we want to avoid expensive, time-consuming mistakes.**

   Making fewer mistakes in our product and service purchases means fewer returns and less of that nagging buyer's remorse. Selecting from an edited list of top picks makes life simpler. Editors give us a breather because they've already weeded through the possibilities, eliminating the stuff that doesn't work or that offers poor value. They've done the time-consuming research so we can feel more confident in our choices. An editor can also affirm or help us develop a gut instinct by narrowing the scope and eliminating the lemons or even the mediocre choices. We're left with the good stuff and are free to follow our own intuition from that point on.

4. **Niche discoveries make us feel in the know.**

   A good editor will also introduce new products and services. The act of pointing like-minded consumers in the direction of "obscure" or "niche" goods and services is an addictive part of the editing phenomenon. Editors give us a guided treasure hunt, where half the fun is the unexpected "find" that delights and surprises.

Editors also level the playing field for niche and indie brands. The Internet gave us unlimited access to products, information, and people, and now we have the sense that there's access to anything—if we just knew it was out there. Niche discoveries feel more valuable because they're rare and unexpected.

5. **Carefully cultivated choices mean more fun.**

A well-edited space or experience lets you relax and exhale— even if you didn't realize that you were holding your breath. Go into a Pottery Barn store, for example, and you can immediately see how all the items work together. There's a sense that you don't need to shop around for a better chair or sofa (if you like the one on display) because Pottery Barn already made sure that it fits with a mid-century modern end table or a vintage-style lamp. If you trust a brand's quality and taste, you feel free to play. Smart editing removes customers' hassle and lets us go deeper into the experience.

6. **Technology makes the editing process easier.**

From blog software to collaborative filtering and RSS feeds, we're now equipped with easy-to-use tools that make editing simpler than ever. Many technological advances let people edit to make their lives easier, while many filters are seeping into our daily routines. Many afternoons, my friend Rachel surveys the contents of her fridge and types a few ingredients into the Epicurious Web site database, which contains over 50,000 recipes. The smart search engine matches her ingredients with a list of possible recipes and she's ready to make dinner—no shopping trip necessary.

7. **There is so much crap out there.**

To put it bluntly, amid all the online gems and retail finds, there's a lot of crap that effective filters save us the hassle of sorting through. In today's information explosion, editors can help us avoid the bad and focus on the good. Many categories (such as music, movies, books, news, Web pages) have become so large that a single person cannot possibly sort through everything to select the relevant picks. This is where editors become crucial.

8. **Again: We want a sense of community.**

Editing defines a position, a point of view, and even communicates a sense of style. This invites loyalty and passion as like-minded communities are drawn to a given filtered experience. Communities often develop around trusted filters because they're hungry for connection with fellow fans. For example, diet guru Dr. Atkins swayed an entire nation to forgo carbs, and Atkins devotees formed hundreds of online solution and support groups.

9. **Personal growth is often built into filtered experiences.**

Ongoing relationships with filters require that the entire community take a journey together. Personal development and discovery keep it fresh and ensure that editors and their fans evolve over time. A diabetic chef continues to develop innovations for his loyal blog readers, including clever substitutions for sugar and new cookware that works perfectly for sugarless baked goods. As editors grow and mature in their craft, their point of view and edited choices grow with them—as do their followers.

LESSONS FROM ROLL: BIKE STORES

Take a position.

Before you start trimming your offerings or eliminating a category, service, or approach, it's critical to know who you are and who you're seeking to serve. Hunter created roll: as a "bike store for the rest of us." This tagline clearly pinpoints the target customer. If a buyer wants to cycle competitively or to prepare for the Ironman triathalon, he might need to consult a serious gearhead at a traditional bike store. If he just wants to breathe some fresh air on his bike—whether it's during the daily commute or on a weekend ride in the mountains—roll: is probably a good fit.

Many companies fear that by taking a position, they'll lose customers. It seems counterintuitive to eliminate a whole segment of buyers. In fact, people respect an organization that has a clear purpose. Be distinct and committed to your value position.

Case Study—Starbucks Hear Music

In 1999, the ubiquitous coffee giant joined forces with a catalog music company from Cambridge, Massachusetts. Now rebranded as Hear Music, this Starbucks division chooses music for the coffeehouses, creates the Hear Music compilations, and interviews artists about their favorite albums for the Artist's Choice series.

Hear Music also has a clear position: "At Hear Music, we are dedicated to helping people discover all the great music beyond the Top 40. We find great albums, old and new, and bring them together in ways that make them interesting to explore."

Their approach has produced some wonderful—and successful—results. In 2004, the Hear Music brand coproduced, marketed, and distributed an original album by Ray Charles called *Genius Loves Company,* a collection of duets he performed with Norah Jones, James Taylor, and others. Released just after the musician's death, the album went triple platinum (selling over 3 million copies) and garnered eight Grammys.

Hear Music also offers some exclusives via their "Hear Music Debut" CD series, created specifically to introduce new and developing artists. New York rock band Antigone Rising, which was selected as the inaugural band featured in the debut series, has sold more than 70,000 copies—a phenomenal start for an unknown group with little radio support and a limited touring schedule. Selections from the Antigone Rising CD are supported by heavy rotation in Starbucks cafés.[4]

More than just a café sound track, Hear Music has a unique editorial voice in its programming for Starbucks locations, CD compilations, and now, in partnerships with other music labels, its production, marketing, and distribution of a wide range of music.

Provide context.

The roll: concept would have fallen flat if Hunter simply cut 290 of the 300 possible models and opened a dingy little store with ten lonely bikes on the floor. There has to be context and purpose to the trim-ming and filtering. A small inventory sitting in a vacuum is just not the answer. roll: works because it's attached to four lifestyles—road, fam-ily, mountain, and trail. All the bike models, accessories, and extras are chosen because they will help customers experience these four styles with ease, fun, and value. From the store's carefully designed layout to the strategically scripted sales process, every aspect of the brand provides inspirational context for people seeking the joy of the ride.

Edit both primary products and supporting accessories.

If you've ever bought a bike, you know that the actual bicycle is just the first step. Once your gleaming two-wheeler is parked in the garage, all the real questions start to emerge: Where can I safely ride my bike? How can I keep my hands from chafing on the handlebars? Where do I put my wallet?

Hunter knew that bicycles were just the beginning. In order to bet-ter serve customers and tap into the lifestyle aspirations that surround cycling, the roll: team created accessory bundles. The essentials package, for example, includes a helmet, water bottle, a small seat bag, a trail map, and a multitool. There are different packages for dif-ferent lifestyles at an all-inclusive, discounted price. "Customers love them because we've taken all the mystery out," explains Hunter.

The accessory bundles are just one example of the dynamic cate-gories created in every roll: store. The same principles also apply to their displays. Most bike stores hang their stock in the same cluttered way, day in and day out. roll: creates changing displays that tap into the true emotion of what customers are actually purchasing. A sum-mertime vignette, for example, might include images of a family cycling to and from a picnic. When customers enter the store, they immediately understand that bikes could help their busy family to spend more active time together.

Help people discover your brand as their "twinsumer."

Customers interacting with your brand are looking for shared values, taste, and perspectives, just as they would with another person.

They want to feel "that's me" or "that's who I want to be." Help people trust your brand and your editing ability by building a personal profile.

roll:'s "bike store for the rest of us" is just the beginning. Before launching the roll: concept, Hunter and his team spent hours discussing who and what the brand was all about. They even have a few quirky sentences that sum it up:

> We believe . . . that not everyone looks good in spandex.
> We believe . . . that you don't have to cycle 2000 miles through France.
> We believe . . . that you should be able to get off your bike and go into the café without feeling like an idiot.

These statements shape a sense of personality that endears customers to the brand—just as they would if the editor was a best friend or neighbor. The profile builds trust and helps customers understand why and how specific choices are made. In essence, the brand becomes a twinsumer—an editor whose taste and values you inherently trust.

Brands need to give customers cues to help them feel like twinsumers, and these cues are most effective if they're shared on a number of different levels, from staff attitudes to signage, from inventory to advertising and beyond.

Case Study—del.icio.us

The Web site del.icio.us allows consumers to post their favorite bookmarks, categorize them with tags, share them with others, and subscribe to other people's list of links. Through a simple software tweak known as tagging, this bookmark-sharing system has found a new way to organize information and connect people. You simply submit your links to a Web site, add descriptive text and keywords, and then del.icio.us combines your post with others from the Web. The system creates clumps from posts with the same keywords, and loose classifications emerge when many people link to the same URL. The sites people are viewing and saving online become the basis for deeper learning and connections. As a specialist on Generations X and Y, I could share all my favorite blogs, Web sites, articles, and books, thereby saving a fellow marketer dozens of research hours and providing a shortcut to my sources for ongoing intelligence.

Smart Mobs author Howard Rheingold has called del.icio.us part of the "collective intelligence of the Web," giving you the ability to find useful things and allowing others to feed from your knowledge. Others have acknowledged that tagging isn't exactly foolproof. The system uses keywords, so terms with subtle and multiple meanings can lead you down a variety of rabbit holes.[5]

Case Study—Chipotle Mexican Grill

Consumers are also finding each other in the non-virtual world. Consider Chipotle Mexican Grill and their passionate fans who seek "burrito soul mates." Chipotle Mexican Grill serves just two things: tacos and burritos. The Denver-based quick service restaurant chain creates twenty-ounce burritos stuffed with fresh high-quality ingredients that each customer designs on the spot. Starting with cilantro-lime rice on a tortilla, you then choose ingredients from among beans, meats, grilled veggies, guacamole, cheese, sour cream, and three types of salsas—all for under $10. But don't think this focused menu means your options are limited. There are officially 262,140 possible combinations (327,675 combinations at locations that have salad). In the case of Chipotle, an edited but flexible menu means more customer control and, in the end, more possibilities.

CEO and Founder Steve Ells graduated from the Culinary Institute of America and worked for two years as a chef at a five-star restaurant in San Francisco before he came up with the idea for Chipotle (named for the chipotle pepper, a jalapeño pepper that is smoked and dried). The first location opened in 1993 near the University of Denver.

As Ells explains, "When I created Chipotle in 1993, I had a very simple idea: Offer a simple menu of great food prepared fresh each day, using many of the same cooking techniques as gourmet restaurants. Then serve the food quickly, in a cool atmosphere. It was food that I wanted, and thought others would like too. We've never strayed from that original idea. The critics raved and customers began lining up at my tiny burrito joint. Since then, we've opened a few more [400-plus locations and growing]."[6]

Chipotle has an incredible fan following, including the Web sites ChipotleFan.com (created by a student at George Washington University) and ChipotleLovers.com. At ChipotleFan.com, you can check out nutrition stats, read more about the restaurant, and find your "burrito soul mate"—the person who orders the exact same meal as you when they go to a Chipotle restaurant. According to the site, there are 11,858 people searching for their burrito soul mates, 8,833 have been linked, and 74.49 percent have found "burrito love." I might discover that Susan in Los Angeles shares my love of whole wheat chicken guacamole burritos with mild salsa and extra sour cream. We love the same burrito and are therefore burrito soul mates. The odd person who takes his burrito completely dry or adds all three salsas for extra heat might be one of the 11,858 people still looking for their burrito match.

Let customers self-navigate and steer the experience.

No one likes to be pounced on before both feet are in the door. At roll:, the first few minutes in the store are completely self-navigated. For example, the retail stores use what Hunter calls a familiar apparel store layout because it's intuitive to people. There are mannequins, uncluttered displays, and the same principles that you'd find at work in, say, Banana Republic—where you already know how to browse the store. This is more revolutionary than it might sound. In most bike shops, the only clothing you see is a rack or two of spandex. It's tough to tell what's designed for men or for women, and if you don't necessarily want to wear spandex on a first-date bike ride, forget it.

The roll: team put a lot of time and effort into changing the customer experience, and the store layout is one of the first signals that you're in for something different. Customers feel relaxed and at home as they wander around the store. It relieves anxiety and gives them time to evaluate the options. That way, the "first question they ask can be an intelligent one," says Hunter. The highly edited inventory then helps people make meaningful value comparisons.

Trust—live and die by it.

Editors live and die by their honesty. If brands take advantage of customers' trust, they may never regain it and will pay dearly in bad word of mouth. For example, if it cost more to buy a roll: accessory bundle than to pick out each item separately, all credibility would be lost. Customers would no longer trust the store's editing and would always be suspicious of everything, from the bike selection to the prices to the fit system. There would be no solid ground.

If people think an editor is getting paid or incented to make specific choices (such as carrying one substandard helmet brand simply because the manufacturer offered a great deal), a brand immediately becomes unappealing. The Connected Generation, more than any other, can sniff out insincerity from miles away. Your edited choices must be congruent with your standards, values, and brand personality, or it will destroy your legitimacy.

Make the buying experience fresh and interactive.

The roll: Perfect Fit System does much more than ensure that each customer gets the right bike for his or her body proportions. It engages everyone in the store because it's unusual, interactive, and captures the senses. It's also completely new. As one customer is fitted using the noninvasive laser scanner, others will naturally gather to watch. They ask questions and get involved in the process. The laser scanner creates buzz and gets people talking so they become participants, rather than passive observers. Successful brands create a full sensory experience. Customers want to see, feel, touch, taste, and interact with your products and services.

Provide great design and consistency.

Every aspect of the roll: brand reinforces its unique perspective and personality, including the store layout, signage, advertising, online presence, and even the colors and images it chooses. Design and brand consistency demonstrate editorial credibility and show effective filtering in action. Editing can't be a matter of picking one element and ignoring the rest, such as editing the bike styles but offering no guidance with accessories and clothing. Every brand space, from retail stores to Web sites and catalogs, needs to be consistent—blending the key position (such as roll:'s "the bike store for the rest of us") into a potent customer experience cocktail.

For the Connected Generation, design is critical. It's a form of shorthand for this savvy group and a tool that immediately captivates or alienates them. Imagine, for example, if a car manufacturer introduced a blog about women and driving, but used a photo of a girl lounging on the hood wearing a skimpy bikini. The image would obliterate everything positive about the blog and the brand, and would show that the manufacturer just didn't get it. Design provides visual cues and helps customers answer questions such as, "Would people like me come here, listen to this band, buy these clothes, or use this cell phone?"

Provide familiarity.

We all know how to grocery shop. Pick up your cart or basket and begin to circle the store. You expect that produce, dairy, meat, and bakery items will be on the outside perimeter. If you want cereal or a can of kidney beans, you need to venture into the middle aisles. The same kind of logic applies to Web sites, medical clinics, and movie theaters. We have an expectation for these spaces that transfers into unfamiliar categories and experiences. When that expectation is thrown off in a confusing or unpleasant way, it's very frustrating.

The roll: team designed their stores to feel comfortable and familiar. There are clear categories with well-marked merchandise, clothing mannequins, and legible signage. The stores are clean, brightly lit, and never stuffed with too much merchandise. You'll never get hit with bikes crashing down from the ceiling or have to wander into a service room just to get some help.

Let your brand personality guide the filtering.

It's important to develop a clear brand personality before taking the role of a filter or editor for your customers. If the brand was a person, imagine the conversations you'd have, the wine you'd drink together, how he or she would speak and dress, and what the two of you would have for dinner. roll: developed their position as the bike store for the rest of us. Popular retail store Anthropologie embraces whimsy and inspired choice, which translates into an attractive brand personality. Those who wander the stores' engaging format might envision the brand as an eclectic friend who always has the greatest new skirts mixed with vintage or one-of-a-kind jackets, accented with her own artisan jewelry. Full of spontaneity and inspiring in her choices, you never know if she's going to take you out for Moroccan food or whip up her grandmother's famous Belgian waffles with fresh lingonberry sauce for dinner.

Case Study—Anthropologie

Founded in 1992 by a small group including Richard Hayne, who also created Urban Outfitters (a hip chain of clothing, accessories, and home wares for Gen X and Gen Y), entering an Anthropologie store feels like you're wandering into the coolest garage sale on earth—in a chic, bohemian Parisian apartment. Each store quadrant has a distinctive theme, such as the wash-room (complete with luxurious soaps and lotions) and the boudoir (with pillows, wrought-iron bed frames, sheets, and nightwear).

The store goes against traditional retailing wisdom by mixing disparate merchandise in an unconventional, controlled-clutter kind of way. Most important, the books, clothing, jewelry, and home items make customers feel like they've discovered a rare artifact, providing a signature piece to further highlight their eclectic sense of personal style. Anthropologie hires two artists for each of its store locations to create unique, store-specific art. This savvy move makes the brand seem like an inventive, independent retailer instead of a mass-market chain.

Anthropologie clearly knows its position: "Our buyers and designers are on a tireless quest for those simple objects that bring beauty to our daily rituals, deepen our experiences, and to put it simply—make life inspiring." To find this ever-changing mix of products and fresh inspiration, Anthropologie buyers and designers travel the globe to far-flung locations, including Copenhagen, Parma, Budapest, Tokyo, and Marrakech.

The approach simply works. Anthropologie customers spend in excess of $90 per transaction, leading to average sales of approximately $800 per square foot of retail space annually.[7]

Explore your editing opportunities.

Here are some of the different ways that roll: edits its customers' experience:

Visual editing.

Customers know roll: is different from the other bike stores from the moment they enter the store. Instead of dodging tires and metal frames, the apparel and lifestyle merchandise is positioned in the center of the floor. Most bicycles look basically the same, so the lifestyle merchandise taps into customers' deeper reason for purchase—the pure joy of the ride. The bikes themselves are on the outside perimeter. Mixed in between are the sales and fit elements, including the noninvasive laser-scanning system. There are also accessory racks, or as Hunter says, items for heads, feet, hands, and seat, where accessories are packaged both individually and into kits based on different needs.

Staff and customer-service editing.

roll: divides its staff into teams based on their knowledge and interests, including bike, apparel, and service experts. All staff work collaboratively and are not paid by commission to avoid competition.

The service process is tightly scripted, which is novel to the industry. Staff members are also chosen for their passion and energy—and their commitment to the mission of helping ordinary people enjoy cycling. When roll: hires new staff, Hunter says they're looking for "accomplices."

Filter your brand using a less traditional lens.

roll: filters their bikes according to lifestyle, but the home improvement industry has also been exploring new ways to edit their offerings.

Case Study—
The Debbie Travis Paint Collection

In spring 2005, home decor icon Debbie Travis paired with Canadian Tire (Canada's original home improvement and auto store) to launch a new paint collection that eliminates the guesswork in choosing a wall color. Customers pick from four moods—nostalgic, calm, dramatic, cheerful—then choose a paint color that will evoke that feeling. There are approximately eighty colors in each group, plus twelve whites imbued with the palest hues of cream, blue, pink, lilac, and green. The collection also includes practice pots with a built-in brush so customers can pretest the colors at home on a four-foot-square wall area.

WORKBOOK

Getting Started

1. **Ask the right questions.**
   Stuart Hunter starts the editing process by asking, "Who are we doing this for and what do they want to get out of it?"
2. **Create filters in both "practical" and "passion" categories.**
   Progressive Insurance's Web site has made it easy to filter through the benefits of all available insurance offers. It's a wel-

come solution for a boring yet necessary purchase. At the other end of the spectrum, fans will spend hours and days consulting editors in categories they're passionate about, including books, fashion, music, gaming, travel, sports, collectibles, and politics.

3. **Create an influential insider.**

Consider creating an internal brand personality who shares his or her favorite related purchases. For example, a travel company could profile its CEO and have her discuss her favorite vacation destinations, top packing tips, luggage-buying criteria, the best ways to rebook a canceled flight, and insider tips to avoid travel disasters.

4. **Filter out the unnecessary.**

Sometimes what not to buy is more valuable information than what to purchase. The trusted author of *The Girlfriends' Guide to Pregnancy* has released a shoppers' guide to steer new moms through the dizzying array of products available for their little one. New moms appreciate the scoop on what's essential to buy new and what's okay to pick up used or to skip altogether.[8]

Go for It.

If you had to decrease your inventory by 75 percent, what criteria would you use to edit the mix and what products or services would be left in your lineup?

You have been commissioned to create straightforward content for your Web site that helps people make edited buying decisions. You have thirty days to create some form of editing or filtering that will make the purchase process simpler and faster. What aspects of the purchase process will you tackle and what formats will your editing take?

SIX

KEEP IT UNDERGROUND

The Rejection of Push Advertising and the Rising Influence of Peer-to-peer Networks

Brett Riepma, age thirty-one, is waiting at a red light when a fellow Toyota Scion driver gives him a nod and a wave. Brett smiles. *It feels like you're part of an underground club.* When he pulls into the parking lot of Target, several people come over to ask how he likes the car and to check out his customized interior. A few more ask to sit in the driver's seat. Currently, Brett is the only person in his circle of friends who owns a Scion. It's kind of fun to be ahead of the pack.

For Brett, owning a Scion has been a great experience from the moment he ventured onto the car lot. In fact, it was the first time he actually enjoyed buying a car. "I hate going to car dealerships," he says. "I always feel like I'm going to get ripped off by the salesperson." This time things were different. Brett was told that he could haggle on any Toyota car in the lot except for the Scions, which have a pure pricing model. What you see on the Web site is what everyone pays at the dealership.

So far it sounded good to Brett. The salesperson was easygoing and casually answered his questions, opening showroom models for Brett to sit in, examine, and test drive. Next, he was directed to a laptop computer where he was left in peace to customize his car using the online vehicle configuration tool. It was fun and easy. Brett hit "print" and his Scion order was ready. Two days later, his fully customized Scion xB was sitting in his driveway.

Brett continued customizing the car after it was delivered. This weekend, he will install tinted vent visors. He originally purchased the car with $4,000 worth of add-on accessories. "The base model is so affordable at $14,500 and already comes loaded with features like air-conditioning, a great CD stereo, and power windows, doors, and locks," Brett explains. "It was fun to add a bunch of accessories without feeling like I was spending too much. It is pretty rare to be able to fully customize a car for around $20,000."

Brett added a bass box, exterior pinstriping, new wheels, a spoiler, and a myriad of other personalized touches. His favorite accessory is the lighting kit, which uses the newest LED technology to illuminate light bars in the foot wells and the cup holder. It produces a subtle light and gives his interior a soft blue glow after dark. In fact, his cup holder offers ten different colors with the flip of a switch, illuminating water bottles into artwork. Later he added stylish seat covers and more deeply tinted windows.

His most talked-about accessory, however, is one that Brett personally designed. While enjoying his morning bowl of cereal, Brett noticed a small toy car pictured on the box with the words, "Actual Size" printed next to it. He contacted a friend who owned a graphics firm and had a large black-on-white, see-through vinyl sticker created for the windshield with the message "Actual Size." Wherever he goes, the sticker gets more than its share of attention and comments.

For Brett, his Scion xB is a canvas for his personality. It's also an expression of his personal style, urban sensibility, and playful approach to life.[1]

Nearly two years after a strategic underground launch to urban trendsetters, Scion's outreach is having the desired ripple effect—influencing buyers outside the original young, urban male core target. Scion is firmly established in the "cool ride" category for many young people, and Toyota has set the pace in the auto industry by innovating a program that hits the right notes and organically spreads its popularity to a broader customer base. It's a grassroots, underground marketing model that's in high contrast to the "go big, go loud" approach often used to lure young buyers.

Toyota Scion is the first automotive nameplate created specifically for a young car buyer. Baby Boomers put Toyota on the map over thirty years ago, and winning over their children is now considered the key to future success. The 80 million Baby Boomers who currently dominate vehicle sales will be followed by their Gen Y offspring—and these 65 million young Americans spend $172 billion a year. This burgeoning generation is projected to purchase one in four vehicles (totaling 5 million new vehicles annually) by 2010.[2] Because of the size and spending power of this emerging market, Toyota has made a long-term commitment to serving the needs of Gen Y. The company had one false start with a program called Genesis but quickly got serious about learning how to best reach the Connected Generation. Genesis failed on several fronts. The cars lacked distinction beyond an affordable price point, but more important, Toyota failed to understand this sophisticated young demographic and to tailor a sales and marketing approach that reflected their complex and integrated relationships with brands.

Toyota did not attempt to target the entire Gen Y consumer spectrum with the Scion nameplate. Instead, they focused their attention on reaching urban trendsetters, an important consumer group that actively seeks out the newest styles and innovative brands. Their target market consists of college-educated urban males under twenty-five with above-average incomes, who function as "thought leaders" among their peers.

Toyota began by launching three completely different vehicle concepts at three price levels—a Euro-sedan (xA), an urban utility vehicle (xB), and a sporty model (tC) in 2003. The xA and xB were previously sold in Japan and reconsidered with Gen Y styling cues based on feedback and research from the U.S. market. The tC was the first car created using all the Scion market intelligence. In 2005, Scion unveiled the t2b, a new concept car that reinforced the company's focus on pushing the envelope in styling and entertainment.

Simplicity is important to Scion's target buyers, so the customer has to make only a few key choices when purchasing a Scion: model, transmission, color, and accessories. Scion vehicles are considered "monospec," which means that everything is included for the base price ($13,680 for models with a five-speed manual transmission; $14,480 for automatic-equipped models). Buyers automatically get air-conditioning; power windows, door locks, and outside mirrors; rear wiper-defroster; antilock brakes with traction, stability control, and brake assist; halogen headlamps; remote keyless entry; privacy window tinting; full "ground effects"–style body valances; and a monster sound system.

All 2005 Scions were equipped with a new 160-watt, six-speaker AM/FM/CD Pioneer sound system that's XM satellite radio–ready and MP3-media compatible. The Scion Pioneer audio system also comes with a user-customizable welcome screen similar to those found on cell phones, and Sound Retouch digital equalization for clearer MP3-CD sound.

Scion has also developed approximately forty accessories for each vehicle. They offer a wide array of appearance, convenience, and under-the-hood items, such as a cold air intake or a strut tower brace, which essentially brings a build-to-order process to the average consumer.

Toyota completely reworked the sales process to meet the demands of a new culture of car buyers. Scion's vehicle distribution strategy is structured as a dealership within a dealership, where 400 square feet of showroom floor space is dedicated entirely to the Scion brand. Many dealerships even have dedicated entrances, so Scion customers don't have to walk through the main Toyota store.

The product area includes highlights of the vehicles' features on 50-inch plasma screens, several accessory display cases, freestanding paint and fabric selector stands, and in many showrooms a Scion vehicle customized with accessories. Self-service Internet kiosks and printer stands allow users to log on to the Scion Web site, virtually customize their chosen vehicle (including installation of any of the approximately forty accessories), and then save or print the details for future reference. This streamlines the purchase process and facilitates a more personalized shopping experience. Certified Scion sales staff are trained to foster an environment that supports buyers who want answers when they have questions, but who also crave the freedom to explore at their own pace, demonstrating a "pull" versus a "push" sales philosophy.

A nontraditional, underground marketing approach is the final strategic piece, which Toyota developed by partnering with a consulting and urban-marketing specialist called the Rebel Organization. According to Jeri Yoshizu, sales and promotions manager for Scion, "Rebel is as close to the customer as you can get. Their knowledge of urban culture was invaluable to everyone on our team."[3]

The Gen Y–focused car line and strategic partnership has generated impressive results. Scion eclipsed its sales projections for all three models in 2004, falling just shy of 100,000 units. To put that in proper perspective, Scion sold 20 percent more vehicles than Audi of

America during that same year, and at least 85 percent of Scion buyers are new to the Toyota family. Most of them previously owned a Honda—especially the Civics—or a domestic brand. About 25 percent of buyers were purchasing their first car ever.

Scion is the industry's youngest nameplate, and with an average buyer age of thirty-five, which is well below the industry average of forty-six, Scion draws more Gen Y buyers than any other car brand, according to J. D. Power and Associates. A full 19.1 percent of total Scion sales are to customers age twenty-five and under.[4]

The marketing campaign is emerging as another big success, says Todd Lassa, the Detroit editor of *Motor Trend* magazine. "I originally wrote a column two years ago criticizing Toyota for trying to market a youth-oriented automobile, but I admit I was wrong." His initial editorial had focused on the advisability of targeting an audience that resents being targeted, and discussed whether a big company like Toyota could successfully produce something that these young consumers would deem cool.[5]

THE CRAVING: KEEP IT UNDERGROUND

As long as there has been human culture, there have been subcultures—centered around politics, lifestyles, leisure activities—that exist outside mainstream society. These independent or countercultural forces have traditionally held more sway for youth, but today people of all ages are increasingly affected by subcultures of every form.

The Connected Generation has grown up feeling saturated by advertising and marketing. They are suspicious of ordinary push campaigns and gravitate toward integrated, contextual offerings that emerge from trusted friends and members of their networks. If you've read Malcolm Gladwell's *The Tipping Point,* you understand the "Law of the Few": A select group of people discover something new—from shoes to bands to politics to neighborhoods—and translate it in a way that it becomes acceptable to a much wider audience.[6] This is the way of the underground.

Sales and advertising have historically relied on an invasive model. Customers put up with incessant ads because it seemed like a fair trade-off for free television and radio programming. Today, technology empowers consumers to skip ads and customize their programming, which flips the traditional model on its head. Thanks to services like TiVo and media such as podcasts, consumers can bypass ads entirely. Advertisers can no longer invade homes through television without consent, and the "go big, go loud" approach is now ineffective because people are put off by it.

Too much advertising can also dampen word-of-mouth buzz. People don't share new things with their networks if the information is already out there. Why would you spread the word about a new teeth-whitening product, for example, if the television ads play every fifteen minutes on major networks? Unless you had an exceptional personal experience with the product, there would be no reason to say anything. We are quickly moving from a push model to one where highly networked customers learn about products and services from each other and choose to pull in the information that they find interesting or useful.

It's increasingly critical to create compelling experiences and relevant communication channels that are respectful of, and carefully tailored to, customers' true needs and values. Even the market is becoming more fragmented, as people travel in social groups based largely on personal interests. Reaching people en masse is becoming difficult to do, so companies need to learn how to communicate with these private subcultures and get invited to take part in the underground communities. Today, the opportunity is to add value to these communities and build authentic, long-term relationships with small groups that take the message out to larger networks. It's a delicate balance. Many subcultures believe that going mainstream means "selling out," so organizations need to show careful consideration for their group beliefs and sensibilities.

Sincere, respectful, pull-based marketing will lead consumers to reward their favorite brands for showing true relevance. They not only accept the brand as part of the community, but then share it with a wider circle. The marketing message so closely matches the audience's needs that they don't feel intruded upon. And research shows that nonintrusive approaches are the best way to satisfy the Connected Generation. According to Forrester Research, there is increased consumer resistance to intrusive marketing:

68 percent of consumers agree there are too many ads today.

63 percent of U.S. households wish they got less direct mail.

66 percent of e-mails received are unwanted.

Secondly, consumers are actively taking control away from marketers:

75 percent of consumers have or intend to sign up for do-not-call lists.

74 percent have or intend to install pop-up and spam blockers.[7]

Savvy brands understand that underground marketing is more than just a good sales technique—it's a way to mitigate the growing frustration with aggressive, invasive advertising tools.

At its core, underground marketing works to foster a sense of shared experience and belonging. Underground brands are self-consciously different from their rivals, and are bound by a set of clearly defined and rigorously enforced values. They fulfill a range of needs for their customers or members, and the fastest-growing brands project an attractive aura or group identity. Underground brands also inspire proselytizers—customers who will naturally chat up the brands to their friends without pay or rewards.

As we discuss throughout this book, underground brands often evolve in unexpected or unplanned ways. Customers adopt the brand as their own and manipulate it however they see fit (Scion owners self-organizing car events, or iPod fanatics creating new accessories and software for their beloved Pods). For brand builders, the key is to give your active, empowered customers a great product and the tools to use and develop it however they like.

Harley-Davidson is a classic cult brand. This 101-year-old company earned $7.1 billion in 2005, a 4 percent increase from the previous year. There are sleek new models such as the V-Rod line and features designed to reach women, but the 866,000-member Harley Owners Group is the most telling piece of the puzzle. This company-sponsored club organizes rides, training courses, charity fund-raisers, and social events. Club members wear their Harley logos with pride because they symbolize rugged individualism with a whiff of danger. The community is diverse: Some of these people live the Harley lifestyle twenty-four hours a day, but others have three kids under the age of ten and drive a minivan to the corporate office. These club members hit the road on their bikes to express a dormant part of their primarily respectable, grown-up personas.[8]

This desire to unleash some submerged part of ourselves is also fulfilled by indie music and film, which are artistic creations that exist outside the commercial mainstream, without the support of a major record label, film studio, or another large-budget source. *The Blair Witch Project* (1999) reportedly cost $35,000 to make, grossed $240 million, and probably kept thousands of people away from wooded campsites that summer.[9] More recently, *My Big Fat Greek Wedding* (2002) transcended cult status (thanks, in part, to the Greek community) to become a box-office smash.

All these projects were fueled by word-of-mouth marketing, which is becoming an increasingly influential method, according to a survey from *CMO* magazine. The survey asked marketers, "Which of the following emerging marketing techniques are you currently using or planning to use within the next six months?" Over 69 percent responded with "customer influence via word of mouth," which was second only to "e-mail marketing."[10]

The Word of Mouth Marketing Association (WOMMA) formally organized in November 2004. WOMMA is expanding at a dizzying rate, enrolling 200 corporations and organizations in less than a year. Many of these major brands and agencies are turning to WOMMA as they integrate word of mouth into their core marketing strategies.[11]

A 2005 national study from NOP World also confirmed that face-to-face interaction is the strongest medium for spreading word-of-mouth buzz. When asked how they make recommendations, 80 percent of consumers say they tell people in person, followed by 68 percent who say they make recommendations over the telephone. Nine in ten consumers say word-of-mouth recommendations are the most important source of information in making a purchase decision.[12]

But Yankelovich Research President J. Walker Smith says that public attitudes about marketing techniques are still overwhelmingly negative. In 2005, for example, 56 percent of consumers say that they shun products that make them feel flooded with marketing and advertising messages. And in what seems like a particularly odd paradox, while the majority of consumers surveyed expressed attitudes of resistance, 55 percent also agree that they "enjoy advertising."

"Consumers are anxious to be engaged by marketers in a more satisfying and compelling way," says Smith. "Marketing resistance is not a desire to stop shopping altogether. Consumers just want a better way to interact with marketers. Smarter, technologically empowered, time-starved consumers want marketing that shows more respect for their time and attention. Consumers don't feel that the current practice of marketing fulfills this requirement."[13]

WHY WE WANT TO KEEP IT UNDERGROUND

1. **We are sick and tired of advertising.**

   Mass advertising is dying. Experienced consumers couldn't care less about commercials, ads, banners, and other common marketing tools, except perhaps as objects of scrutiny in an American studies course. Instead, people are drawn to spaces and brands that feel like advertising-free zones. No one wants to feel like they are being hustled, yelled at, manipulated, or begged, so brands need to find authentic and interesting ways to ignite conversations with the Connected Generation.

   "Peer-to-peer word of mouth is really key to these consumers," says Josh Levine, president of the Rebel Organization. "They are more interested in companies that they've heard about than those that get pushed on them from TV."[14]

2. **We crave authentic interactions and spaces.**

   This generation values transparency. Brands that initiate authentic interactions with customers will always have an upper hand. We're all ready to inhabit genuine spaces that don't feel commercial—where the best products and services float to the top, and companies enhance the experience, rather than exploit it.

   People like to know that they're receiving what was promised, and that a brand can be trusted to deliver without spin, hidden rules, or costs. The most effective brands simply capture what's real about the product or service and present it in a straight-up manner. Honesty sells. Instead of being gimmicky, invest in the community in a way that truly adds value.

3. **There is power in the act of discovery.**

    People do not want to be told what's cool. They want to feel like they've stumbled upon your brand and your message all by themselves. The most successful brands seamlessly integrate with social and cultural movements and provide exciting new experiences for the brand community to enjoy on its own terms—and to share with others. It's a matter of trust and honesty. Each generation wants to find its own way in life and discover its own likes and dislikes. There's social currency in being one of the first to discover something new and sharing it with your network.

4. **We're embracing roles as independent brand owners.**

    When customers are truly thrilled about their experience with your product or service, they can become outspoken "evangelists" for your company. This group of satisfied believers will be a potent marketing force to grow your customer base.

    Ben McConnell and Jackie Huba, coauthors of *Creating Customer Evangelists,* are experts at taking a company's best customers and building them into influential, loyal, and enthusiastic evangelists. The duo has created a loyalty ladder that demonstrates customer progression on their way to evangelist or "brand owner" status.

    The bottom of the ladder represents satisfaction, which simply means that the product wasn't returned. On the second rung is the repeat purchaser, someone who would buy the product more than once. On the third rung are people who would recommend your product to others. The top of the ladder holds the true brand members, which is also called "ownership," because this group feels as if "this is my brand and my product." These brand members actively talk to friends and strangers about the product and buy it as a gift for others. We're entering an era where such brand owners are highly connected and more influential than ever before through their personal, underground networks.[15]

5. **We put a new premium on getting respect.**

    The Connected Generation responds to honesty and respect. They want to be treated as peers and not as "targets." This group likes communication that recognizes their intelligence and acknowledges their equality. Don't speak down to them or use tired "sales speak." It's important to have a true understanding of their culture and to reach them in their natural environments. It's the old golden rule, updated for today's marketing mores: Show respect to get respect. Let the setting dictate the type of interaction you design and add value to the community instead of disrupting their unique interactions and unspoken codes. Consumers are in control, so marketers must find a way to be welcomed in by the consumer. This process always begins with understanding the community and embracing what they value.

6. **The model for creating awareness has rotated 180 degrees.**
    Big, loud, and often. This used to be the proven formula for reaching consumers. Today, it's better to quietly seed a group of influencers and have them naturally spread the word, creating excitement that spills outward. In order to satisfy your brand community, much of your promotional and advertising investments must fly under the radar screen of mainstream consumers. Marketing choices need to include the important elements of surprise, intrigue, and personalization. As the brand gains acceptance, it will percolate out into other networks, infused with the unique flavor and ownership cues from the community. It will naturally develop its own history, stories, and a richer personality over time.

7. **Customers are in control . . . and we're not stupid.**
    Consumers are more sophisticated than ever before, and increasingly they control the media that advertisers use to reach them. They notice details and are not easily fooled by gimmicks.
    It's important to speak the right language and use the right people to spread your message, because your projects will be effective only if you stay true to the underground culture. If you miss the mark, watch out. Ten years ago, Nike alienated the skateboarding community by using unknown athletes and print ads featuring skate tricks that true enthusiasts knew could not be landed. Nike has only recently made inroads back into this subculture with more authentic brand messaging. McDonald's also got blasted from the underground for depicting rappers wearing preppy shoes and performing cheesy raps about Big

Macs. The hip-hop community was not impressed. The question is no longer "What can we sell to the consumer?" but "What can we learn from the consumer about his or her needs, and how can we help to satisfy those needs?"

8. **We have a desire to be special, exclusive, and part of an inner circle.**

Highly individualized consumers are looking for brand choices that express their personality and signal their unique tastes. The clothes and shoes we wear, the cars we drive, the phones we use, even the food we eat, all communicate who we are and what we value. There's such a vast market that we're using brand choices to help us feel both set apart and included. Subcultures embrace specific companies or brands and by doing so provide cues to other community members. For example, fans of *Sex and the City* often shared main character Carrie Bradshaw's obsession with shoes and handbags and helped revive cosmopolitans as the cocktail of choice.

9. **We appreciate companies that fan our flame and support our community.**

Brands that thrive underground know how to create experiences that integrate seamlessly with the community they want to reach. These smart organizations also provide ways to highlight community talent and give back by funding important events and opportunities that would otherwise be difficult to stage. They are community contributors in the best sense of the word.

There's something very powerful on both a conscious and subconscious level about having a person or brand fan the flames of your passion. The person or brand becomes a partner in your growth, and instead of trying to sell you something, helps you achieve your potential, acknowledge your dreams, and makes them feel more possible.

When customers bond with brands through an experience, they also become more open to future messages and contacts. Over 80 percent of people surveyed in the 2003 Worldwide Experiential Marketing Survey said that participating in an experiential marketing process would make them more receptive to advertising, and 53 percent of all consumers (and 61 percent of Gen Yers) said that experiential marketing opportunities are very influential on their brand perceptions. Experiential market-ing drives fast results, and many consumers say it helps them make quicker product choices.[16]

LESSONS FROM SCION

Transform your entire brand experience from "push" to "pull."
Scion knew that the brand relationship would fall apart if the dealer-ship experience ignored urban values. To address this need, Scion created a pricing structure that built trust and a sales process that was both self-directed and fun.

The Scion "Pure Price" solution meets the buyer's desire for con-sistency *and* transparency. It means the advertised dealership price will be the actual transaction price—a principle that applies to acces-sories, financing, and insurance.

The Scion business model has also created a win-win situation for both buyer and dealer. Customers can rest assured that they're not being asked to pay inflated car lot prices, and Scion dealers enjoy an additional profit margin from all the vehicle accessories. Port pooling of dealer stock and accessory installation at the port makes for easier, faster delivery of custom-ordered vehicles and relieves dealers of the need to maintain huge inventory levels. Port pooling allows foreign automakers to streamline the accessory customization process by cre-ating regional ports in key cities, where trained personnel modify the cars after they arrive from overseas, significantly reducing waiting times for customers. The buying process is also faster, because many customers have already priced and customized their cars on the Scion Web site before they even set foot in the dealership.

All Scion dealers have undergone extensive training programs to learn more about their unique target audience and how to provide a sales process more tailored to their needs. In addition to the usual two-day, off-site product-training sessions, each dealership participated in six days of customized, in-store education. The Scion Covenant, key standards that focus on improving the customer experience through sales and marketing, plus specific image and facility require-ments, was introduced at every dealership.

Finally, Scion sells with zero incentives. Most small car brands currently add a $2,000 cash incentive. Other companies are trying to buy Gen Y, but Scion customers simply want to own these distinctive, high-value vehicles.

Case Study—Kiehl's Cosmetics

Any woman familiar with the department store cosmetics counter knows the routine by heart. The salesperson tells you about miraculous new products, extolling their smoothing, lifting, brightening, and downright age-reversing capabilities. You can do a little on-the-spot testing, but there are only so many take-home samples available before the salesperson raises her eyebrows and you feel the pressure to whip out your platinum card.

Contrast that with Kiehl's, where the 154-year-old brand's white-coat-clad sales reps urge you to take home free samples and give the products a shot before you buy. Kiehl's gives away more than 12 million sample packets and tubes each year. This sampling program is the cornerstone of Kiehl's customer-service philosophy, taking the pressure off both reps and customers.

The company has made a strict commitment to swim against the cosmetics industry and reject false claims or promises that are scientifically impossible to keep. Kiehl's does no advertising and prefers to reach customers with quality, generous sampling, and word-of-mouth referrals.

In addition, Kiehl's invests in serious training for its highly knowledgeable staff. The company uses nearly 10 percent of its compensation budget to send new hires on an up-to-four-week residency in New York, Miami, or San Francisco. Sales techniques are a lesson in what *not* to do: Don't promise too much. Don't send customers away *without* free samples. And don't use words like "fabulous."

This low-pressure, sample-focused approach has been a powerful tool to build loyalty and fight off the competition. Kiehl's has enjoyed double-digit earnings for the past several years and earned $70 million in 2004.[17]

Partner to build credibility and develop internal intelligence.

Toyota's lack of experience with Gen Y buyers and their failed Genesis series meant that the company needed to build new relationships and credibility with the urban youth community. With Scion, the company held the internal competencies to offer distinctive vehicles and a unique sales process, but it needed a strategic partner that understood how to engage young drivers. Toyota chose to collaborate with the Rebel Organization, primarily on the strength of their experience, established credibility, and large network of relationships within the urban community nationwide. By partnering with Rebel, the Scion team increased their internal intelligence about the brand community, developed better market instincts, and utilized Rebel's talented staff and networks to roll out a pitch-perfect program.

Focus your efforts on delighting your core brand community.

Trend leaders are early adopters who like variety and never hesitate to try new things. For automakers, these are the people who believe that their vehicles are more than just a form of transportation—they become an expression of individuality.

Scion set its sights squarely on these Gen Y trend leaders. All products, events, promotions, and creative and staffing decisions are filtered through a narrow community lens. What would these influencers respond to? As a result, decisions are not diluted by half-hearted efforts to reach a broader audience. By serving the core market with appropriate promotions and products, Toyota ensured that this group naturally shares its passion for the Scion brand.

This means no cheesy banners, staffed tables, or embarrassing "shout-outs" at Scion-sponsored events. You would never see a primarily Caucasian group decked out in khaki shorts and matching polo shirts working a Scion event in an urban community. Inspired by a shared love of the hip-hop lifestyle and music, the Scion staff reflects a fashion forward, yet highly individual style that confirms their street credibility. The company staffs all promotions with people who naturally match the target audience.

BMW shares a similar philosophy in reaching its core audience. The company works to attract a particular psychographic, and it doesn't matter what the rest of the world thinks: As long as their prospects think it's cool, all is well.

Case Study—BMW Automobiles

"Whisper to shout." This was the internal marketing strategy designed to create buzz around BMW's 2001 short-film series. First step? Hollywood's creative community.

If the writers, directors, and producers of top feature films gave the movies a thumbs-up—not as car ads, but as short films, and even as art—it would give the BMW brand the respectability necessary to draw a larger audience base.

The first two films in *The Hire* series debuted online in 2001. The third film, Wong Kar-Wai's *The Follow,* made its debut at the Cannes Film Festival in May 2001 to international acclaim. Since its groundbreaking debut, *The Hire* has logged more than 100 million film views online at the BMW Web site.

BMW tapped into the talents of high-profile producers like David Fincher and Ridley and Tony Scott. The short-film directors were an equally prestigious group, including John Frankenheimer, Ang Lee, Wong Kar-Wai, Guy Ritchie, Alejandro González Iñárritu, John Woo, and Joe Carnahan.

The Hire received an estimated $20 million worth of PR in outlets, including the *New York Times* and *Time* magazine. In 2002, the Cannes International Advertising Festival awarded *The Hire* with the Cyber Lion Grand Prix prize.

Additional recognition included the "Best Excuse for Broadband" award at *WIRED* magazine's third annual Rave Awards in 2001, and the 2002 Los Angeles International Short Film Festival's Best Action Short award, for director John Woo's *Hostage.* In 2003, *The Hire* series was inducted into the permanent collection of the Museum of Modern Art (MoMA).

Next, BMW created and distributed a DVD of the films with partners like *Vanity Fair* magazine. The full DVD collection (with all eight films) was unveiled at the Palais des Festivals during the 2003 Cannes Film Festival, and BMW further reached out to its essential brand community by partnering with TiVo and creating its own cable television channel based on *The Hire*. What began as a big idea grew into a cutting-edge entertainment event that was unprecedented in the automotive industry.[18]

Don't just say something—do something.

Scion's monthly events have attracted more than 100 million impressions and built a database of more than 75,000 people interested in Scion vehicles. The brand's market research shows that target market members learned about Scion from seeing the vehicles at relevant venues. The nameplate's core philosophy of participation and inclusion means that events are designed strategically for maximum interaction between the participants and the brand. For example, about 400 people at each aftermarket auto show (featuring products to customize your car after purchase) race go-carts for a chance to compete in the final race in Las Vegas. The winner gets a yearlong racing school scholarship and use of a race car valued at $500,000.

Scion spotlights the activity—the Scion brand message is always secondary. The entire marketing strategy positions Scion as a leader and insider that does cool stuff, showcases talent, and invests in the community rather than taking advantage of it.

Case Study—Red Bull Energy Drink

The Red Bull energy drink has developed highly participatory marketing efforts, including its very own Red Bull *Flugtag* ("flying day" in German), a competition in which entrants launch themselves from a thirty-foot ramp in homemade "flying machines" into a body of water—Amazon River surfing expeditions, kite sailing in Hawaii, and social events such as hip-hop dance contests and music jam sessions.

Red Bull sponsors some five hundred athletes around the world. These are people who will participate in extreme sports, such as flying stunt planes through a dangerous racecourse with city bridges and landmarks as markers. All these adrenaline-fueled activities have one objective: to expand Red Bull's presence as it battles the upstarts and major players who have stepped into the energy drink category—a category that Red Bull first created.

The results have been spectacular. In some countries, Red Bull commands an 80 percent market share. In the United States, where Red Bull enjoys a 47 percent portion of the energy drink market, sales are growing annually at a 40 percent clip. In 2004, Red Bull sold 700 million cans in the United States and aimed to reach one billion in 2005.[19]

Make the product a canvas for creative expression.

Scion is a statement vehicle. Heavily accessorized and customized, the vehicle becomes a focal point for personal and artistic expression.

The Scion "Installation" art gallery tour commissioned over fifty artists to paint live on Scion vehicles. A specially designed vinyl wrap was first applied to the vehicles, providing a canvas for these young urban artists to express their creativity. The finished pieces were removed from the cars, mounted, and sent on a thirteen-city gallery tour, with a final exhibit held at Track 16 in Santa Monica, California, with all the artists in attendance to sign autographs and see the full collection. The exhibit attracted more than fifteen hundred art and music lovers, some of whom bid on the pieces, with proceeds going to youth-oriented nonprofit groups.

At the MAGIC Marketplace in Las Vegas—a fashion-focused trade show—Scion commissioned designer Jon Phenom to wrap a Scion xB in denim. Musicians and artists were then asked to work on this open canvas throughout the four-day trade show. After the trade show, Phenom created ten one-of-a-kind messenger bags from the finished denim canvas, which were auctioned on eBay. Proceeds went to the Nikao Youth Project, a nonprofit movement dedicated to inspiring and empowering underprivileged urban youth through fashion, art, and retail experience.

Case Study—Vespa Scooters

Vespa also envisions their scooters as blank canvases by engaging top designers to create special editions and by appealing to young design students for innovations.

From its conception in 1946, the Vespa by Piaggio has always been more than just a scooter—it's a classic style icon. The Vespa reflects a specific personality and lifestyle, including adventure, style, and simplicity, and evokes a sense of tasteful romance as depicted in the films *Roman Holiday* and *La Dolce Vita.*

Vespa has always relied heavily on PR to promote the popular scooter as the ultimate urban accessory. Over the last few years, Vespa has worked with some of the world's most celebrated fashion designers and houses—including Dolce & Gabbana, Julien MacDonald (for Givenchy), Vivienne Westwood, Donna Karan, and Jimmy Choo—to design one-off, customized scooters.

In 2005, Vespa partnered with the renowned Parsons School of Design to reconsider this Italian-style icon in the context of twenty-first-century American culture. Parsons students in the fashion design, product design, and design and technology programs developed a new lifestyle collection, ranging from clothing to wearable technologies, accessories, and new scooter features. The fashions were unveiled at the spring 2005 Parsons Benefit and Fashion Show and launched on the brand Web site at www.vespausa.com/parsons.[20]

By linking Vespa with celebrities and fashion, and targeting the style press rather than focusing on automotive pages or specialty magazines, Vespa has reinforced its reputation as a stylish, aspirational brand for a new generation.

Connect the brand with top community talent.

Scion's brand message is "Independent artistic impression," and virtually all campaigns include music-focused marketing.

These efforts include:

- Enlisting some of the country's best DJs (Jazzy Jeff, Peanut Butter Wolf, Melo-Dof, and the World Famous Beat Junkies) to create Scion CD samplers.
- Producing over eleven volumes of the Scion CD series and distributing more than 4 million copies at lifestyle events, auto shows, and Scion dealerships.
- Booking local, well-respected DJs to play music and draw people to Scion booths at auto and trade shows.
- Licensing hip-hop, rock, and electronic music from both commercially successful and unsigned artists for Scion promotions (including contests, Web sites, DVDs, CD-Roms, and shortwave radio broadcasts).
- Launching a Scion record label to record and produce music from relevant bands, whose work is then released for DJs, tastemakers, and radio stations.

By exposing some of the industry's top talent to their underground brand community, Scion has garnered national attention from radio, retailers, and music-focused Web sites and publications, including *GQ* magazine, *Billboard,* and *Entertainment Weekly.*

Engage customers in surprising ways.

Displaying vehicles and handing out brochures at auto shows or special events is about as relevant to the Connected Generation as cassette tapes and the dial-up Internet. Instead, Scion continually seeks surprising ways to engage their customers and help them experience the vehicles in a fun, contextual environment. For example, instead of backing a big spring break party, Scion might sponsor a breakfast at Denny's the next day. The party might be a highly competitive arena, but the morning-after breakfast offers few distractions and provides a great environment to display or test-drive cars.

Case Study—
Indie Film *Napoleon Dynamite*

Napoleon Dynamite is an American independent film written and directed by Jared Hess. Based on the short film Hess directed at Brigham Young University with Jon Heder, the movie was an instant hit with audiences at the Sundance Film Festival and won best feature film at the U.S. Comedy Arts Festival. Fox Searchlight, which backed the 2003 independent hit *Bend It Like Beckham,* bought *Napoleon Dynamite* at Sundance, and together with MTV Films and Paramount Pictures, mounted a guerrilla marketing campaign to spread the word.

During its mid-run at theaters across the country, Fox added a five-minute epilogue to entice fans to return for a second viewing—shooting the scenes just four weeks before the release instead of cobbling together previous footage. Fox also promoted the Napoleon Dynamite Fan Club, which in fall 2005 had 150,000 members.

At one point there were 25,000 people competing in a contest to become club president (the president got insider scoops and bonuses, including Pedro's actual bike from the movie). The film's Web site also provided an audience participation script (remember *The Rocky Horror Picture Show?*) and the quirky promotional campaign included more than forty iron-on transfer designs that could be printed from the Web site and made into T-shirts.

Viewers loved the film, but Fox knew that the idiosyncratic humor didn't translate well in previews, so the company held free screenings to build publicity. They handed out "Vote for Pedro" T-shirts and frequent-moviegoer cards that offered gifts to people who saw the film three times.

Since its release, *Napoleon Dynamite* has gained cult status among the Connected Generation. In 2005, it won three MTV movie awards for breakthrough male performance, best musical performance, and best movie. *Napoleon* debuted in 2004, earning $116,666 in its opening weekend, and brought in over

$44.5 million by February 2005. Not bad for a film that cost just $400,000 to make.[21]

Invest in your Web site and make it fun and interactive.

Scion's Web site gets a million hits each month, and its rich, intuitive navigation design makes it a fun place to hang out. Two-thirds of Scion buyers configure their cars online with specific colors and options before they visit the dealership. Many know months in advance the exact car that they plan to purchase, and choose every detail with excited anticipation. Once they've bought their vehicle, many Scion owners gather at community sites such as Scionlife.com, which averages about 170,000 page views a day.[22]

"Some people are on the site every day and sometimes all day," says Scion Life Webmaster Darren Seeman. "It's not just about Scion. It's about the lifestyle." The brand has a cult following with over eight popular Web sites dedicated to all things Scion, including scionlife.com, scionzone.com, and scionowner.com.[23]

Create relevant strategies to reach key subsegments.

For Scion, it's far more important to have meaningful interactions with a handful of people than casual interactions with a larger, less-targeted group. Toyota has taken both practical and passionate approaches to serve the dedicated car aficionados in their urban communities.

Purchasing aftermarket turbochargers, superchargers, and lowering kits top the to-do lists for many Scion owners once they have the keys to their new vehicles. Scion anticipated this demand, and developed a process with SEMA (the Specialty Equipment Manufacturers' Association) to transfer technology from Toyota's development side to aftermarket manufacturers who wanted to develop products specifically for Scion vehicles. This innovative strategy launched the same year that the cars hit the road and marks the first time that a Japanese carmaker has participated in this program.

Scion further wooed this project-oriented buyer by commissioning a series of customized vehicles from notable urban artists and "tuners." These souped-up works of art were featured on the cars episode of

MTV Cribs, and Rebel secured a placement deal with Discovery Channel's *Monster Garage,* in which two Scion vehicles were transformed into rock-'em-sock-'em robots.

Product specialists are also recruited and trained to represent the brand at international auto shows and tuner shows such as Hot Import Nights and Import Revolution. Hot Import Nights, the latest generation of car shows, combines highly customized, "macked-out" cars with the latest in sound systems, accessories, music, video games, beautiful women, and popular media to create a compelling night out with fellow car fanatics. These specialists come from the urban youth markets, so they look and act like brand community members and speak the language of Scion's target audience.

Present product information in the context of lifestyle content.

The biannual *Scion* magazine presents attractive photography of Scion vehicles in compelling layouts that speak directly to the target audience. The publication includes standard brochure content, including technical specs, accessories, and information about the purchase process, financing, and insurance. It also features lifestyle content—including music, fashion, art, nightlife, film, technology, and travel—to show readers that Scion understands their lives and interests. Some issues also include a three-dimensional cardboard pattern that folds into a toy-sized version of one of the Scion vehicles.

Let consumer passions dictate where and how the brand presents itself.

Rebel's under-the-radar Scion marketing includes sending "street teams" to events like Hot Import Nights, and supporting DJ contests, nightclub events, fringy art gallery showings, and car washes. The idea is to place Scion in the center of the action—where its brand community lives and plays.

Scion participates in over sixty events nationwide each month. The event marketing plan tailors the program to fit the spirit of the venue and then to create valuable interactions with target customers. If Scion decides it would be offputting to place an xB in the middle of a nightclub, for example, it won't happen. Instead, Toyota will sponsor the DJ, provide visual artists, and hand out free CDs and magazines.

Keeping it underground is not ***the same as stealth marketing.***

Keeping it underground means listening to consumers and giving them a voice. Stealth involves tricking people. Honest marketers oppose stealthy and deceptive tactics. They never pay people to say things, or ask people to misrepresent who they are or whom they're working for.

You want your consumers to talk openly and honestly with their communities. That's the whole point of keeping it underground. You should insist that any relationship between consumers and marketers is clearly disclosed right from the start. This open disclosure makes your messages even more powerful, because people know they're trustworthy (no other type of marketing demands this level of honesty).

Underground marketing gives consumers a powerful platform—and forces marketers to respect their needs. The goal is to empower consumers by engaging with them in blogs, message boards, communities, and the real world. You should give people the power to voice their dissatisfaction and expose dishonesty. It's about learning to listen, and it's the opposite of deception.

WORKBOOK

Get Started

1. **Great products fuel underground excitement.**

    Excellent products and services provide the foundation for any underground campaign. In today's vast marketplace, you have to really differentiate your brand with top-notch products to maintain the high standards of the underground. In short, you need to be worth talking about.
2. **Cultivate mutual respect.**

    You need to care about your customers' opinions and learn

what's important to them. Keeping it underground is not about stealth marketing, where you act like something you're not or, even worse, try to trick your customers. Honesty shows respect.

3. **Show diversity.**

   Don't choose actors or models whom you *think* represent the Connected Generation—you have to make sure you get a true cross-section. Variety is expected and diversity is a must in your staffing, marketing, and creative messages.

4. **Overdeliver in areas where your competitors are stingy.**

   Most competitors slug it out over the same few features and opportunities. Carve a new path and provide exciting options in the areas that your peers are ignoring.

Go for It.

Will you continue to spend the majority of your marketing budget on unpopular, message-based advertising, or will you shift considerable amounts of money to a more relevant, empathic, try-out approach? Identify two or three investments that are gobbling up your budget and could potentially be eliminated and redirected.

Who is your most powerful underground community? For Vespa, it was fashion leaders and designers. BMW turned to filmmakers, Scion to urban trendsetters. Select a group that represents your brand's core.

Now, leave your desk and take a walk, a drive, a subway ride; bring a notepad and a camera. Think through the places where your brand members spend time, go visit these spots, and build a portfolio of potentially underground spaces and communities. Consider locations, including bars, cafés, clubs, holiday resorts, sporting events, public transportation (buses, trams, subways, trains, taxis, ferries, waiting rooms), airports, lounges, cinemas, theaters, theme parks, concerts, beaches, parks, planes, shops, supermarkets, shopping malls, schools, universities, office spaces, gyms, conference venues, restaurants, and hotels.

SEVEN

BUILD IT TOGETHER

Connected Citizens Explore Their Creative Power and Influence Change

The Internet is an information free-for-all. Life-altering medical research, breaking news, and flawlessly crafted Web sites intermingle with explicit pornography, inane rantings, hate literature, and blogs that feature family photos of last night's macaroni-and-cheese dinner.

The Web is useful, flexible, and often extremely unreliable. Who could imagine it would be the right place to launch a free encyclopedia written by unpaid contributors? Jimmy Wales, for one.

Wales launched Wikipedia.com (later switched to Wikipedia.org) on January 15, 2001, as an open-forum complement to his experimental, expert- and academic-written Nupedia site. The former options trader was born August 7, 1966—a fact gleaned from the Wikipedia entry on him, no less—raised in Huntsville, Alabama, and now runs his indie knowledge source from St. Petersburg, Florida.[1]

A COMMUNALLY BUILT KNOWLEDGE SOURCE

At Wikipedia.org, anyone with a keyboard and an Internet connection can write or alter encyclopedia entries on everything from past presidents to *Star Trek*. Wikipedia has been called the free, people-powered library of the future. It's also been called brilliant and dangerous.

Wikipedia uses software called a "wiki"—named for the Hawaiian word *wiki wiki,* or "quick"—which allows anyone to edit and alter the articles. Wales designed the service as an "effort to create and distribute a free encyclopedia of the highest possible quality to every single

151

person on the planet in their own language." He also imagined that Wikipedia would surpass encyclopedias such as the venerable *Britannica* and would eventually be bound into print format.

Wikipedia debuted in 2001 with 200 articles in English. One year later, it had 18,000 entries. In 2005, Wikipedia had nearly 790,000 English-language entries and more than 13,000 active contributors toiling away on over 1.8 million articles in more than 100 different languages. At least ten of these multilingual editions—English, German, French, Italian, Japanese, Dutch, Polish, Swedish, Spanish, and Portuguese—boast more than 50,000 articles each.[2]

The site asks its volunteer contributors, or "Wikipedians," to follow a "neutral point of view" policy, in which ideas, opinions, and information presented by notable people or contained in literary works are summarized without personal commentary or analysis.

Wales is in demand as an open-source consultant for big business, but the nonprofit Wikimedia Foundation runs his free encyclopedia venture and all the material can be referenced under the terms of the GNU Free Documentation License.[3] Wikipedia has also branched out into a number of other free, multilingual, open-source projects such as Wikinews (a content news source), Wiktionary (dictionary and thesaurus), and Wikibooks (textbooks and manuals).

Wikipedia has gained global popularity for its simple editing, free distribution, and wide range of topics. It has also been criticized for systemic bias, deferring to consensus instead of credentials, and a potential lack of authority and accountability.

Part reference tool, part collaborative social experiment

It's no surprise that Wikipedia must constantly battle vandalism and inaccuracy. Anyone can edit the content, so there will always be people who post celebrity photos complete with devil horns.

What's remarkable is how well Wikipedia *can* work—vandals and all. Most Wikipedians are dedicated to their online community. They put great effort into their work, and a self-appointed team of referees ensures that everyone plays nice. Members can even create "watch lists" to monitor real-time site changes and article edits. These lists ensure that any wounds on Wikipedia are quickly patched and healed. For example, MIT's Fernanda Viégas and IBM's Kushal Dave and Martin Wattenburg found that mass deletions (one of the most common forms of Wikipedia sabotage) were corrected in a median time of 2.8 minutes. That time dropped to 1.7 minutes if an obscenity accompanied the deletion.[4]

Wikipedia has a structure that makes many users want to hang out and take care of their space. The encyclopedia works because the community works. This underlines the basic truth that brands don't solve problems—people do. In the same vein, Wikipedia itself doesn't write the articles; instead, its devoted members keep it running and evolving.

Wikipedia, like many other user-driven, open-source communities, is highly addictive. But the attraction can be difficult for outsiders to comprehend. Why would anyone spend hours online carefully editing and rewriting a free encyclopedia? There's a sense of instant gratification, for one thing. Wikipedia confers power. When a user logs on and makes a change, it has an immediate impact on millions and millions of people who use the site in their daily lives. For many users, it's the first taste of open-source software and its accompanying sense of empowerment.

Encyclopedias also feel official. Most people grew up cracking encyclopedia spines in their school or public libraries. These trusted books were the source for details on everything from river otters to the Ottoman Empire. You couldn't write a report or build a science fair project without those gleaming *Encyclopedia Britannica* or *World Book* sets.

To enter Wikipedia, therefore, is to set foot in hallowed territory. It makes the vast majority of users stand up a little straighter and try a little harder. Members feel a keen sense of responsibility. They want to uphold the tradition of excellence, and they know that someone might rely on their entry for an important project. And like any good community, the members want to keep it clean and functional. It works best when everyone cooperates.

Unlike a published, paper-and-ink encyclopedia, Wikipedia is also flexible and fast-moving. It tackles the random, eclectic pieces of pop culture that people are buzzing about. The tool is quirky and often quite surprising. The Web-based format is also richly hyperlinked. Wikipedia includes information in context and provides a map of other places to search, almost like having a built-in bibliography. The Connected Generation loves the tangent, and Wikipedia has endless rabbit trails to follow and explore.

Self-Government Rules

In an October 2005 issue of *Time* magazine, Esther Dyson—editor of the technology newsletter *Release 1.0* for CNET Networks—compared the Internet to alcohol: "It accentuates what you would do anyway. If you want to be a loner, you can be more alone. If you want to connect, it makes it easier to connect."[5]

Wikipedia is a self-governing knowledge-sharing community. It attracts people who enjoy details, facts, and spreading the word about the subjects they love most. There's a benevolent spirit that drives people to spend inordinate amounts of time updating and improving a free information source.

Such online communities are one of the most important social and technological developments of the last several years. People are gathering together to achieve common goals and create tools, products, and movements that could not exist without the power of numbers and the abilities of open-source software. Wikipedia's members feel that good can triumph over vandalism and desecration. We simply cannot underestimate the impact of driven, dedicated communities— a growing market tidal wave that has only just begun.

THE CRAVING: BUILD IT TOGETHER

There are currently 1 billion people connecting online around the world. Now that we've all learned how to surf for our favorite topics and even ninety-year-olds are actively e-mailing their grandchildren, the focus has turned to cooperation. We're reaching critical mass. Now change is economical, fast, possible, fun, and prevalent. With so many people conducting large portions of their lives online, we've begun to tap into the power of Web-based networks. Internet users are sophisticated and connected, and the activity networks they bring to their computers have created a powerful cultural force and have led to a huge shift in the way business is conducted. In the new model, the market serves as a forum for consumers to unite, share information, and effect change.

At the same time, people are becoming intoxicated by their growing ability to spark change—both as consumer groups and end users. This awareness is spurring mass creativity and launching a power shift away from companies and into the hands of consumers. People are uniting around a specific goal or context to create a desired outcome. Whether they're reviewing hotels on Tripadvisor.com or adding new entries to Wikipedia, Internet users are feeling empowered to have their say and contribute to online communities. In some cases these people stay connected for the long term, but more often they will accomplish their goals and quickly reconfigure into new groups with a different target outcome. The online world is a fluid organism in which people move in and out of participation according to their own interests, needs, and networks.

From Passive to Active

Instead of passively surfing from site to site, Net users are becoming much more active. In fact, the most popular sites are based on engagement and user-driven activities. The names of these Web portals have even become verbs in our collective language. We "Google" and "blog" and "MySpace" throughout the day, or "eBay" that collection of snow globes in the basement. Now, the most effective sites invite us to participate in small ways (by posting a fifty-word product review, taking a quiz, or writing comments on a news story) or to make large contributions (by creating a profile page, writing a full article, or designing your own screen wallpaper). These sites are the stickiest and, in many cases, the most profitable ventures on the Web.

When the Internet first emerged, it was all about seeing what other people were doing. People still watch videos, read blogs, and surf news sites, but there's an even stronger drive to create and share elements of our own lives. Now we want people to see what *we're* doing.

New technologies are putting power in the hands of anyone with access to a computer. They're helping us to harness our talents, opinions, money, and connections in the name of personal passions, and as a result, no industry will look the same again. In the software world, programmers everywhere are volunteering their expertise for over 100,000 open-source projects and are collectively restructuring the entire industry.

Community Leaders

More than ten years after eBay launched its online garage sale, the company has over 68 million active users and expects its 2006 consolidated net revenues to reach over $5.7 billion.[6] The user and buyer rating system is one of the smartest features of eBay, allowing members to speak out if they've had a great experience, or to tell all if the disco-era platforms didn't quite live up to expectations.

Napster opened the floodgates, and now over 100 million people share music and films online through programs such as Kazaa and Bit-Torrent.[7] The entertainment industry has fought back with a series of lawsuits, but there are still about a billion songs available for file sharing. Today we're all songwriters, journalists, and broadcasters, with more than 53 million Americans contributing material to the Internet.[8] There are at least 10 million blogs read by 32 million Americans—some of which draw more traffic than mainstream news sites.[9]

The Net has clearly started to hit its stride. It's now (among other things) a tool that connects people who will collectively build everything from social networks to political campaigns to shopping centers and beyond.

WHY WE WANT TO BUILD IT TOGETHER

1. **Customers, technology, and broadband have evolved.**
   Technology and Web sites have advanced to the point where it's easy for people to get involved, offer feedback, and participate as lightly or as deeply as they want. At the same time, the widespread availability of broadband means that more people can successfully access these new technologies. The Connected Generation is already fluent in the language of technology.

They find it easy to learn new software and rarely struggle to get up to speed.

Applications that would have found acceptance only with a radical fringe three years ago are now palatable to a much larger group. In fact, many of today's most successful technologies and community concepts were actually introduced (in a less-sophisticated form) prior to the dot-com crash. These were often strong ideas that simply outpaced most users' technical comfort levels and were too robust for then-prevalent dial-up connections. With today's savvy citizens and supercharged computers, the Net can, like no other medium, connect millions of people on their own terms, in their own time frames.

2. **We are more comfortable with online strangers and communities.**

    Fear and suspicion of online strangers and Web-based communities has significantly decreased. We are now more comfortable mingling, buying products from, and even dating people we meet online. There are many success stories from people who have felt the sparks fly through their computer keyboards (and who, more important, formed lasting, mutual bonds). There are even more tales of people who have started social movements, built powerful networks, and accomplished enormous goals by working together on the Web.

    These stories cross every sector, industry, and personality type, and pique our curiosity. We are learning to trust and function in the ecosystem of virtual communities, and we're realizing that groups have an innate ability (given the proper architecture) to self-organize, self-repair, and innovate. We are seeing the Web as a place where people can come together to create and influence change.

3. **The power shift is intoxicating.**

    In the traditional industry structure, consumers were isolated from each other. In the new market-as-forum paradigm, networked consumer communities are a potent force. The proliferation of connected consumers has produced a fundamental shift in the way businesses connect with their customers.

    In the past, companies "targeted" customers and tried to build profiles to attract their desired markets. In today's economy, most often the customer initiates the relationship, learns about products (and brands) from his or her peer and online social community, and evaluates the products for relevance and value. It's a fundamental power shift.

Many consumers have an overarching desire to help each other and to share their experiences—and many people have greater trust in online advice from complete strangers than in a brand's official claims or advertising messages. We want to protect each other in the marketplace and, increasingly, we reject push advertising.

As a result, customers are embracing their growing power, demanding more respect, and creating a more honest, open dialogue with brands of every stripe. In September 2005, blogger and Cerado cofounder Christopher Carfi created "The Social Customer Manifesto" on his site (www.socialcustomer.com). Capturing the new voice and standards of today's connected customers, Carfi outlined eleven key directives:

- I want to have a say.
- I don't want to do business with idiots.
- I want to know when something is wrong, and what you're going to do to fix it.
- I want to help shape things that I'll find useful.
- I want to connect with others who are working on similar problems.
- I don't want to be called by another salesperson. Ever. (Unless they have something useful. Then I want it yesterday.)
- I want to buy things on my schedule, not yours. I don't care if it's the end of your quarter.
- I want to know your selling process.
- I want to tell you when you're screwing up. Conversely, I'm happy to tell you the things that you are doing well. I may even tell you what your competitors are doing.
- I want to do business with companies that act in a transparent and ethical manner.
- I want to know what's next. We're in partnership . . . where should we go?[10]

4. **We have increased access to information.**

With access to unprecedented volumes of information, knowledgeable consumers can make well-researched decisions and collectively challenge the traditions of industries from entertainment to financial services to health care. Überinformed and increasingly vocal, consumers are using new tools and their empowered positions to become cocreators and brand partners.

As C. K. Prahalad and Venkat Ramaswamy write in their 2004 book, *The Future of Competition,* "The most basic change has been a shift in the role of the consumer—from isolated to connected, from unaware to informed, from passive to active."[11]

5. **Consumers are willing to create content without "reward."**

Five years ago, a handful of product reviews or a group of friends sharing music files would barely cause a ripple. Today, the mass scale of online consumer activity is shifting business models and shaking up business as usual. Equipped with easy-to-use online tools and willing to give of their time, people are behaving differently—surprising marketers and brands alike. Millions of people happily participate in the new social economy, without incentives or monetary reward. Yale Law school professor Yochai Benkler refers to this mass online cooperation as "peer production."[12]

6. **There is accountability for all.**

Cooperative online activities have created a heightened level of accountability for everyone. Consumers now sniff out false claims, fake blogs, and products that don't stand up to advertised claims. Individuals must also walk their talk. Users rank and rate online reviews or classify eBay sellers—elevating those who are articulate, helpful, and sincere, and revealing unhelpful or dishonest people. Sites like Lemondate.com and Truedater.com allow people to post reviews of online dating candidates and expose false or misleading information in their personal profiles. User-driven sites post so quickly that consumers will expose in a flash any false claims and time- or money-wasting products, services, accessories, and add-ons. Customers who feel abused or fooled now have a voice—and in some cases, they've got a giant, virtual megaphone.

Case Study—McDonald's Fake Blog

In February 2005, McDonald's created a blog (http://lincolnfry. typepad.com/blog/) and a new flash Web site to promote a Super Bowl television ad featuring a French fry that resembled President Abraham Lincoln. While the television ad didn't ruffle any feathers, the blog—with fake bloggers and fictional posts from "readers"—set up on SixApart's TypePad sparked a loud debate in the blogosphere. The blog copy was so campy that bloggers immediately called it out as a fake. Comments from bloggers ranged from "I'm not lovin' it" to "McDonald's, shame, shame."

The vast majority of bloggers felt that the fake was an insult, especially when the company doesn't have its own blog. Few bloggers take issue with corporate blogs, but many were outraged at what they saw as an exploitation of the purpose and spirit of these online journals.

7. **Loose connections are formed around passion points.**
    The Connected Generation delights in loose connections— those brief conversations and encounters that are sandwiched between the more structured elements of the day. It all began with e-mail, which gave us a convenient way to simply say "hello" to our friends (regardless of location) and pass on small nuggets of information without the commitment of a long encounter. Now, text messaging, blogging, podcasts, and other technological innovations give us the ability to stay connected with our multiple communities, regardless of whether the encounter actually flows both ways. These connections are a manageable way to nurture our communities without joining groups or stealing evenings away from our families.

    Such loose connections can also be addictive. Receiving online attention can make people feel closely bonded to a virtual community and add new dimensions to their sense of self. These connections also provide an elevated level of control over social interactions. Just like getting e-mail in the morning, people will often check the posted comments on their blog, community or message board several times in a single day.

8. **There's a new form of volunteering and community contribution.**

   Epinions.com peer reviewers may not collect highway trash on the weekend or serve at the local soup kitchen, but they feel that they're giving back to the global community in a significant way. Providing insight and support to fellow consumers on Epinions, or suggesting great new books for like-minded Amazon users to read, is a new form of volunteering and a recognized way to contribute to the consumer and human marketplace.

9. **The learning curve usually proves worthwhile.**

   User-driven technologies have evolved beyond a basic cool factor. New software, Web sites, and gadgets are now becoming increasingly practical, which gives us added motivation to use and adopt them in our daily lives. The learning curves can be substantial, but the payoff can be huge. When a new program really does make life a little easier, it's worth sweating through the instructions and messing around with all the options.

LESSONS FROM WIKIPEDIA

Create an architecture of participation.

Wikipedia and any other online sites that go beyond first-generation technology have a canny way of turning self-interest into social benefit—and real economic value. They have what tech-book publisher Tim O'Reilly calls an "architecture of participation," which makes it easy for people to do their own thing: define a word, create a link from their Web site to another site they like, rate a song, or simply show off their knowledge with an online product review.

Wikipedia can become a compulsive obsession because anyone can change an entry by clicking on the "edit this page" tab. The power is right at your own keyboard. Simple systems are critical for participation, because too many rules will keep people from being able to play and join the game. It's better to make it easy to participate and allow organic monitoring to emerge within the community. Although there are some risks and headaches involved, the benefits can often outweigh the hassle. As Amazon CEO Jeff Bezos explains: "You invite the community in, and you get all this help."[13]

Companies can no longer act autonomously.

Whether they're designing products, crafting marketing messages, or controlling sales channels, today's consumers seek to exercise their influence and provide commentary on nearly every part of the business process. Equipped with advanced tools and unsatisfied with the standard choices, consumers are demanding new status as brand cocreators. Increasingly, corporations will have to pay attention to customers who join forces online to get what they want and influence change.

Case Study—Lord of the Rings

Tens of millions of readers worldwide have long been enthralled by the epic novels of J. R. R. Tolkien, and his *Lord of the Rings* books have passionate fan communities—both online and off.

When the *Lord of the Rings* film trilogy went into production, there were already more than 400 unofficial Tolkien Web sites. Fans eagerly anticipated the big-screen adaptation of their favorite books, but they were also ready to pan the films if their concept of Middle Earth was poorly executed or the beloved story lines were compromised.

Instead of ignoring or overriding the vast global fan network, New Line Cinema wisely worked to include and engage them. New Line treated the most devoted Tolkien fans as early influencers—giving them insider tips and seeking their feedback on key film details.

Working closely with director Peter Jackson, the company created a Web site (www.LordoftheRings.net) that featured exclusive content, including rough costume sketches, handwritten production notes, and access to the production team. Millions of fans visited the Web site to offer their feedback, which also created a preprimed, passionate audience for the films' release dates.

Respecting fans and including them deeply in the cocreation

process builds a group that feels ownership in the final product and generates considerable respect for the creators.[14]

Alive and up-to-the-minute can triumph over "perfect."

Which is more important, precision or up-to-the-minute information? It depends on what you're doing, but increasingly people are choosing quick-moving, constantly updated sources. Wikipedia sits firmly between the open dice roll of Google and the slow formality of a traditional encyclopedia. You get context and richness, even if you do sacrifice some gravitas and precision—and no one can dispute that free is a good price.

Many users also love that Wikipedia is peer updated, which can make it feel more relevant and alive. The information is always fairly solid, heavily hyperlinked for added depth, and presented in the context of popular culture. You can't rely on it to the letter, but sites such as Wikipedia include additional references that traditional resources simply can't match. Literally thousands of new words and concepts that are too new to make the cut in a print encyclopedia will flourish and evolve in the medium of Wikipedia.

Case Study—Oh My News

"Citizen journalism" is thriving in South Korea, where the five-year-old online paper OhmyNews.com has 39,000 contributors writing up to two hundred stories each day on everything from the latest blockbuster to political demonstrations. According to a national magazine poll, the site is the sixth most influential media outlet in Korea, logging over 1 million visitors per day.

Founded by Oh Yeon Ho in February 2000, OhmyNews was the first open-source media site to accept, edit, and publish articles from its readers. A fifty-five-person staff creates about 20 percent of the paper's content, and the remaining stories come from nonprofessional freelance contributors who embrace the site's motto, "Every Citizen Is a Reporter."

OhmyNews was also an influential force in the 2002 South

Korean presidential elections, when winning candidate Roh Moo Hyun granted his first post-election interview to this citizen journalism site. An international English version also invites people to submit their stories at English.ohmynews.com.[15]

The rise of thematic communities

We're becoming increasingly selective and specific about where and with whom we spend our time. In response, the Web is splintering into thematic communities defined by interests. Traditionally, pre-Internet communities were defined by locations, such as "We all attend Notre Dame University" or "We all live in SoHo." But with the flexibility of the Web, thematic communities emerge around very specific needs and passions, such as "We're all diabetic" or "We all make our own microbrews." There's power in numbers, and while a single diabetic may not be able to catch the attention of Congress, a community of 2 million could trigger significant change.

Wikipedia has succeeded because it attracts people who want to contribute around their specific expertise and passion.

Case Study—Epinions.com

Themed interests are also the driving force behind product review Web site Epinions, which offers customer-written appraisals of thousands of products and services. Epinions.com is one of the strongest examples of a community that builds on collective personal interests. Billing itself as a "premier consumer reviews platform on the Web and a reliable source for valuable consumer insight, unbiased advice, in-depth product evaluations, and personalized recommendations," Epinions provides a forum where consumers share experiences and detailed opinions about products and services. The reviews cover a wide variety of categories (from where to stay on a Colorado ski trip to the best flat-screen televisions) and provide valuable advice from people who have no financial interest in the products themselves.

The Pew Internet & American Life project found that 33 million American Web surfers have reviewed or rated someone or something through an online rating system.[16] The Epinions community is divided into purchase categories such as Computers and Software, Electronics, Home and Garden, and Books. A core community of high-volume reviewers first organized themselves into these interest communities in order to enhance this prolific site. At Epinions, a video gamer in Kentucky will often find an active (and extremely well-informed) community of fellow gamers who take pride in contributing dozens of reviews and frequently post news and updates to the gamers' message boards.

Communities often have the ability to self-govern and self-repair.

Wikipedia and other open-source sites such as Epinions elicit a sense of pride and ownership among their participants. It's a community that everyone shares, so users are expected to keep it clean and in good repair—almost like members of a student government or a community group. No one wants negative material or subpar content to ruin their baby. A core vigilante group will naturally develop that voluntarily works to keep the neighborhood safe and clean. Even when verbal graffiti gets posted (as it inevitably will), it's quickly taken down. The watchdogs are always on duty.

Wikipedia has an innate capacity to heal itself. Those who truly care about the accuracy of submissions and the standards of the community will outnumber vandals with bad intentions. Volunteer Wikipedians monitor pages around topics they are passionate about, from religious entries such as "Islam" to controversial political topics. It's so easy to make changes that the fight for integrity is won by the person or the group that cares the most. At Wikipedia anyone can play, but for the most part, only the well-intentioned players stick it out. It's a lesson that anyone who feels nervous about creating loose, unstructured communities should take to heart.

Open-ended permission and loose power structure

Wikipedia is a social innovation, not a technological one. No one would stick around to play if the rules got too complex. With this in mind, Wikipedia is almost completely user driven and open ended. People don't have to get permission to do something useful. Think how often you see, for example, a business document with a grammatical error—a misspelled word or a run-on sentence that no one can correct without explicit permission. At Wikipedia, anyone can make simple changes.

Wikipedia also operates under two core principles. The first: neutrality. Wikipedians are directed to fairly represent all sides and to not take a stand on controversial subjects like politics, stem cell research, or assisted suicide. The second principle is good faith. All work should be approached with the assumption that the author is trying to help the project, not harm it. Of course, there's a margin for error, but considering the number of people participating and the volume of content they post, inaccuracies and poor quality are surprisingly uncommon.

Long-established business models are being dismantled.

Wikipedia has freed the encyclopedia from its shackles—making it a living, breathing organism of the people. For good or for bad, it has forever shifted how many people will access this type of information and radically stirred up the information industry in the process.

"Our work shows how quickly a traditional proprietary product can be overtaken by an open alternative," says Jimmy Wales. Unlike the creators of *Encyclopedia Britannica,* Wales is not aiming to generate much, if any, revenue. But "that doesn't mean that we won't destroy their business," he notes. *Britannica* spokesman Tom Panelas, however, says that the sheer number of articles isn't a measure of quality and may be information overload for most readers and researchers.[17]

Whatever your point of view, this potent new do-it-yourself trend is shaking up a raft of industries and challenging the status quo. It's also changing what and how people will pay for products and services. Long-established business models, from newspaper subscriptions to television advertising, are no longer the gold standard. Business as usual is not an option, and the bold new innovators may just run off with a lion's share of the customers.

Case Study—Skype

Skype is a free software download that lets you make free telephone calls with your computer. Calls from one Skype user to another are free, regardless of where they are in the world. People place calls with usernames instead of traditional phone numbers and the software includes an instant-messaging feature for chatting. Skype does not carry adware or spyware.

There are a number of paid add-ons: SkypeOut, for calling ordinary phones; SkypeIn, which allows users to post their real phone numbers so non-Skype users can call them; and Skype Voicemail, to take messages when subscribers are away from their computers.

To use Skype, you need a computer that runs Windows, Mac OS X, or Linux, or a PDA with Windows Pocket PC 2003. You also need an Internet connection, a computer headset or equivalent, and Skype software. For those people who don't like headsets, a number of manufacturers are making phones with a traditional look and feel that work with Skype.

Skype is a VoIP (voice over Internet protocol) program, which is simply a way to make telephone calls over a computer network, and it's not a new idea. While there are a number of other competitors on the market, Skype has had considerable success with home users, thanks to its ease-of-use, reliability, and word-of-mouth marketing. Just like instant messaging, computer-based VoIP programs rely on different data transmission methods, so people who use competing products can't call each other directly. This "lock-in" effect has helped snowball Skype's user base to more than 54 million members worldwide, and approximately 150,000 more join each day. It's also available in twenty-seven languages.

In fall 2005, eBay acquired Skype for a reported $2.6 billion in cash and stock, plus an additional $1.5 billion in rewards if targets are met by 2008.[18]

Case Study—Craigslist.com

Named for its founder, Craig Newmark, Craigslist.com was established in 1995 as a way to help people in the San Francisco Bay Area find a place to live, secure a job, sell their stuff, or even get a date for Friday night. More than ten years later, the site has expanded to at least seventy-five cities in the United States, Canada, the United Kingdom, Ireland, Europe, Australia, Asia, and Brazil. Craigslist is now a network for urban communities that features free classified ads and topic-based community forums—and is a household name for millions of people.

The site shuns banner ads and relies solely on paid job ads for its revenues. Craigslist logs more than 2 billion page views per month and over 8 million unique visitors. The company doesn't disclose financials, but some journalists have speculated that its annual revenues approached $10 million in 2004.

The big news is that experts believe the Craigslist site is shifting major revenues away from traditional advertisers. In one report compiled by the research group Classified Intelligence, sources estimated that Craigslist costs the Bay Area's traditional newspapers and their online divisions between $50 and $65 million annually from employment ads alone. Craigslist is a revealing example of how entire industry models and traditional revenues can shift virtually overnight.[19]

Peer-created content is gaining in importance.

The popularity of Wikipedia's peer-created model is also seen in the rise of consumer review sites. It's now common to consult product reviews from fellow consumers before making significant (and even minor) purchases. Customers have grown accustomed to getting the insider scoop and researching the pros and cons of hundreds of thousands of different products. Due diligence on online shopping reached critical mass in 2005, when several of the Net's largest comparison shopping sites acquired large consumer rating sites for major sums of cash.

Shopzilla.com and Shopping.com were acquired by the E. W. Scripps Co. and eBay, respectively. Scripps, the multimedia powerhouse, paid $525 million in cash for Shopzilla and its popular BizRate consumer review service. Similarly, eBay paid approximately $620 million in cash for Shopping.com and its consumer ratings site, Epinions.[20] Both Web businesses allow shoppers to locate virtually any product for sale online at the lowest price, and provide consumer ratings of merchandise and the e-tailers that sell them. With the leaders pairing shopping and peer reviews into a single site experience, brands need to realize that rich comparison content will soon become the standard for all companies that sell online.

Opening up channels of communication can mean free help and research.

If Wikipedia was written by an expert staff paid to keep it constantly updated, it could turn into one of the most expensive global projects on the Web. Instead, the site harnesses people's desire to participate and offer their knowledge and feedback for free. Wikipedia's simple architecture of participation unlocks the expertise of thousands and provides a forum for building knowledge together.

When you open up the channels of communication, the result can be a storehouse of new ideas and free support. Most brands have a gold mine of ideas embedded in their files, phone logs, CRM (customer relationship management) software, and call centers that they could easily mine for insight.

Case Study—Nestlé

When Beth Thomas-Kim, Nestlé's director of customer service, trolled through call logs from the company's toll-free customer comment line, her discoveries may have surprised more than a few top executives. Only 20 percent of the calls were complaints. The rest of the feedback focused on other topics, including marketing ideas, product suggestions, and opportunities for improvement (previously, Nestlé used its customer comment line chiefly to answer questions and to resolve customer complaints). Thomas-Kim had discovered a free customer insight pipeline right there in the call center.

Homing in on the Coffee-mate brand, Thomas-Kim launched a pilot program in which marketers called several hundred customers who had phoned in with ideas and suggestions. These one-on-one conversations yielded higher quality input than traditional focus groups, as customers felt free to express their detailed ideas and observations.

Some of these customer ideas have already made it onto store shelves. For example, many people said that Nestlé's eight-ounce Coffee-mate jar was too small. The company responded by increasing the size from eight to fifteen ounces. Sales increased immediately. Complaints that the pastel packaging made the product hard to find prompted new, brighter packaging.

Nestlé wisely tapped into existing customer feedback and has enjoyed the benefits of operating like a small firm that hears the daily ideas and concerns of its consumer base.[21]

Customers are building together during their offline time.

Working together online has changed the way customers operate in their offline activities as well. The Web is such a convenient meeting ground and scheduling mechanism that it's becoming economical to share more than just ideas or political beliefs.

Car sharing, for example, is growing quickly as brands including Zipcar and Flexcar let members use the Net to reserve cars from a fleet of available autos for an hourly fee. A hit in crowded cities, the cars can usually be secured almost on demand, whenever members need to get behind the wheel.

Case Study—Flexcar

Flexcar was the first and remains the largest car-sharing service in the United States. Members use the automated, self-service reservation and vehicle access systems to choose from dozens of new, fuel-efficient Flexcar cars, trucks, and minivans located across several metropolitan regions.

If you live in or near a major city and can commute by bus, carpool, bicycle, or foot, Flexcar might help you pocket some considerable cash by using its vehicle-sharing service for occasional driving trips. Personal memberships cost $40 a year, and the rates run from $7 to $10 an hour and $35 to $90 per day, including full insurance, fuel, maintenance, cleaning, parking, and a twenty-four-hour emergency service.[22]

In 2005, Revolution, the investment company run by AOL cofounder Steve Case, bought the controlling interest in Flexcar. This influx of new capital is fast-forwarding new changes, including more cars, more locations, improved technology (including Web site enhancements and reservations), plus fun additions such as iPod adapters for frequent use.

The future will unite companies and customers to cocreate.

Wikipedia tapped into a new market truth: Many people are highly motivated to improve treasured brands and offer their wisdom to simply boost the success of a project—even when they reap no financial rewards whatsoever. Customers are assuming a bold new role in the way products and services are developed among both start-ups and traditional corporations. Some companies are partnering in deeper ways with customers, and the result is a flurry of innovations and ideas. Corporations are creating stronger products and services by tapping into their customers' intellectual capital, unique perspectives, and diverse life experiences.

Case Study—Procter & Gamble's Connect + Develop

Procter & Gamble launched its Connect + Develop program in 2000, with a revolutionary goal of deriving at least 50 percent of its new products from ideas generated by nonemployee experts around the world. In addition to its own seven thousand-member staff research and development team, the company has

forged mutually beneficial relationships with best-in-class individuals and organizations around the world giving them access
to millions of potential innovators. The results so far? Everything
from Swiffer Wet Jet and Olay Daily Facials to Crest Whitestrips
& Night Effects, Mr. Clean Autodry, Kandoo baby wipes, and
Lipfinity cosmetics.[23]

WORKBOOK

Get Started

1. **Accommodate a range of participants.**
   Work to accommodate a varied group of consumers, from
   the active and highly sophisticated to the passive and less confident. Make a list of ways active people participate in your
   brand and the customer communication options for those who
   are less involved. How can you expand your range of options
   for involvement?

2. **Prepare your employees and managers.**
   Today, all managers must learn a new set of social skills—tools
   that will enable them to connect with individual consumers
   and thematic communities alike. The first step in designing
   your own "build it together" initiative is to train your people so
   they are open to educating customers, and to being educated by
   them in return. Who in your organization is an expert on connecting with your customers online? How are you equipping and
   training the rest of your staff to be equally effective?

3. **Context provides meaning for cocreators.**
   Customers are not interested in helping just any brand that
   comes along. Be sure to approach your customers when the
   brand experience has the greatest relevance and meaning for
   them. The most active participants are invested in the outcome
   because it will affect their lives or enhance their goals in some tangible way. What is motivating your current brand community to
   actively participate with your company? How can you fan their
   flame in a more direct way?

4. **Not everyone has come to play.**

Remember that not every consumer (including smart, active customers) will be interested in building new initiatives with you. Sometimes they just want to buy something and move on. Don't try to force a cocreative relationship on unreceptive customers; it will only alienate them.

Go for It.

What would it look like if your company developed a formal process for reaching out to customers and integrating their intellectual capital? Wikis, blogs, and peer reviews provide a way to support and encourage the stuff we love or simply feel curious about. In addition, "brand loyalists" offer advice, admonishment, and ideas to their favorite brands, all in an effort to make things better. Identify both a baby step and a big leap that your brand could take.

What department is most ready to test a "build it together"–style experiment and what could be its first inclusive project? Remember that people are interested in connecting with brands not just to create new products but also to solve existing problems. Many customers now interact with brands when they're pleased, as well as when they're disgruntled. The Connected Generation is filled with committed brand members who want the best for the company and the community, even if that means calling out the problems. What is a major challenge that your brand is facing that could benefit from your customers' input and ideas?

EIGHT

BRING IT TO LIFE

Everyday Activities Are Orchestrated
to Deliver a Dramatic Sense of Theater

I t's a little-known secret. Tom LaTour, chairman of Kimpton Hotels
and Restaurants (dubbed "the best hotel chain you've never heard
of" by *Money* magazine in 2004), deliberately spends some nights in
fleabag joints. We're talking places with uninvited guests of the
whiskered, long-tailed, and creepy-crawly variety. What would pos-
sess this award-winning CEO to give up the luxury of Missoni bed
throws, forty-two-inch flat-screen televisions, and famous restaurants for an uncomfortable night in the company of urban wildlife?
LaTour isn't experimenting with some wacky form of professional
rebellion—he's simply diligent. It's all in an effort to identify new
buildings for acquisition and to experience firsthand the plumbing,
heating, and electrical systems of the old buildings that Kimpton
transforms into their unique, character-driven properties.

Kimpton rescues historical treasures that have fallen into disrepair
and restores sites such as the 1795 Tariff Building in Washington,
D.C., into stunning properties. LaTour's personal due diligence in
checking out these diamonds-in-the-rough can make for some long
nights. Of the former incarnation of what is now the Hotel Monaco
Chicago, for example, LaTour says, "You couldn't take your shoes
off."[1] Once acquired, LaTour ensures that each property is renovated
to reflect the energy and personality of its distinct location, history,
and architectural style.

LaTour returns to spend a week in the rooms prior to each hotel's
grand opening—working through the details and troubleshooting
any last-minute issues, including bathroom stoppers that don't work
properly (his pet peeve). His hands-on approach is not limited just to

checking property acquisitions and openings. Once a year, Tom LaTour personally conducts the daily wine tasting in each of his forty hotels. While pouring the wine, he asks guests where else they travel on a regular basis and gains insight into new locations for expansion.

Why such attention to detail? According to LaTour, Kimpton strives to offer its guests an experience, not just a comfortable bed to sleep in. The company actively engages its clientele in a compelling form of brand theater, complete with luxurious details, surprising personal touches, innovative solutions to common challenges, and a strong sense of location. LaTour's team seeks to "create moments of truth—the points in time when guests experience the pinnacle of what they're seeking, in service, in hospitality, and in style."[2]

THE KIMPTON STORY

The Kimpton story began with Bill Kimpton, an investment banker-turned-hotelier, who conceived and developed the first "boutique" hotel in the United States. Kimpton sought to offer an alternative to the big-city hotels that most people had grown accustomed to by the early 1980s. Some industry insiders considered it a risky venture, but Kimpton persevered and created properties that were recognized for their personality, unique character, and distinct style.

The first property, the Clarion Bedford Hotel in San Francisco, opened its doors in 1981 and introduced guests to a new, more intimate experience complete with personalized service and a keen sense of adventure. Kimpton Hotels expanded throughout the Pacific Northwest by renovating historic buildings and bringing new life to their communities. Chef-driven restaurants added flavor to each property and helped secure Kimpton's reputation as the hospitality innovator. The company quickly developed a reputation for being the first to implement an extensive list of trendsetting hotel programs, services, and amenities, such as afternoon wine tastings in cozy living-room-style lobbies. Kimpton set the standard for the rest of the industry, and its forward-thinking tradition of brand theater has become the company's trademark.

LaTour, a twenty-year Kimpton veteran, took the helm when Bill Kimpton died in 2001. LaTour is responsible for guiding the company's strategic and operational direction. His careful attention to detail and creative vision have been pivotal in growing Kimpton Hotels from a regional boutique chain operating with separate property names to a national industry presence under the Kimpton brand umbrella.

Every Hotel Tells a Story

Each of Kimpton's hotels and restaurants shares five signature elements—care, comfort, style, flavor, and fun. At the same time, every hotel tells a different story. For example, Seattle's Hotel Vintage Park focuses on Washington state's wine country. Every guestroom is dedicated to a different Washington vineyard and displays artwork donated by each winery. In-room honor bars are stocked with local wines (some supplied and selected by the winemakers themselves). Hotel Vintage Park also offers branded amenities such as wineglasses, wine journals, and bottle openers. A nightly wine hour in the lobby allows guests to sample local wines by the glass, and the hotel hosts special wine events to entertain and educate guests, led by winemakers, experts, authors, and sommeliers. The hotel's chief concierge (affectionately nicknamed the "vine vixen") organizes the hotel's expanded wine program and sets up personal tours of Washington wine country, recommends special local vintages, and arranges preferred-guest access to high-profile wine and culinary events.

Seattle is also home to Kimpton's Alexis Hotel, which is famous for its Art Walk—a permanent and rotating collection of original artwork. Hotel guests are often found painting watercolor postcards in the lobby, and the Alexis has several celebrity suites that feature original artwork by Miles Davis and John Lennon, and a twelve-foot Dale Chihuly glass chandelier.

Kimpton's brand theater enriches everyday moments and common services to make them feel extra special and surprising. From its handsomely appointed rooms to the leopard-print guest robes and an endearing pet program, Kimpton infuses travel with romance, theater, and fun, and provides a welcome relief from the beige world of major hotel and hospitality chains. Kimpton delivers a unique experience that blends learning, connection, entertainment, and personal pampering.

Brand theater has definitely been good for business. Kimpton is on a roll and plans to double its hotel properties by 2010. But no matter how big Kimpton gets, the company pledges to remain true to its roots by personalizing guest experiences and enriching each and every stay with its luxurious and playful approach.[3]

THE CRAVING: BRAND THEATER

From beverages to designer fashions to dinnertime solutions, brand theater is popping up in virtually every industry as savvy companies deliver compelling and entertaining experiences.

Starbucks was the first to transform the simple act of drinking coffee into a full lifestyle statement. The coffee company masterfully created a rich, deeply textured experience by elevating an everyday activity to a special place and wrapping the entire brand in a cozy, upscale sort of cool. The drink names, graphics on the cups, furniture, and fixtures all contributed to carefully crafted brand theater.

The dressing rooms at high-fashion retailer Prada do not include bad lighting and mirrors with a decidedly unflattering perspective (when did my thighs slide into my knees?). In contrast, these IDEO-engineered masterpieces provide different lighting options that allow the customer to view the clothing in a warm evening glow or a cool blue daylight. The simple, eight-foot-square booth with Priva-lite glass walls can switch from transparent to translucent when a room is occupied. Once inside, the customer can flip the doors back to transparent at the touch of a switch, exposing themselves to onlookers or patient spouses waiting outside the room.

Still relying on coloring books to keep the kids busy while waiting for your table? Try Skeeball, Harley motorcycle simulators, and fighting video games—just some of the extracurricular offerings at Dave & Buster's (www.daveandbusters.com), a dining destination that has been described as a giant bar surrounded by eclectic games and a family-friendly restaurant. Brand theater is essential to Dave & Buster's bottom line, with nearly 46 percent of its $390 million 2004 sales coming from games and entertainment.[4] Themed restaurants are not innovations (Chuck E. Cheese led the charge years ago), but today there are more chains building brand theater with greater depth and savvy, according to Technomic, a Chicago restaurant consulting firm.

Dinner preparation, the bane of many busy women's existence, is getting a time-saving makeover. Meal preparation sessions at a Dream Dinners (www.dreamdinners.com) store blend the efficiency of a commercial kitchen with the comfortable atmosphere of a community gathering. Customers rotate through fully equipped, refrigerated recipe stations, complete with freshly chopped and prepared ingredients, to assemble preselected dinners tailored to their families' tastes. In less than two hours, customers leave with six or twelve ready-to-cook entrées. Just pop the assembled pans in the freezer and pull them out when you need dinner in a flash. Women often book meal sessions in groups and flock to this guilt-free, highly productive night out with friends.

Across the pond in Dublin, Ireland, the Guinness Storehouse had become the country's number one tourist attraction by combining live events with strong architecture, design, and advertising that create an imaginative brand experience. Thumping drums and Celtic dancing greet visitors below a roaring, man-made waterfall surging over slabs of suspended Lucite. Escalators and moving walkways whisk guests up a seven-story hive of glass and green I-beams to various exhibits and eventually to the 130-foot-high Gravity Bar, where bartenders serve an average of two thousand pints of Guinness beer on a single weekend day and twice as many on St. Patrick's Day.

Brand theater helps companies of all kinds to create emotional connections with their customers. It takes typical experiences a few steps forward by engaging the senses, the imagination, and the spirit, and turns routine experiences into entertainment. As companies such as Starbucks have clearly demonstrated, people will pay more to have a layer of fun wrapped around an ordinary task or destination. Why? Customers become part of the action. The theatrical experience evokes a fuller range of emotions—awe, surprise, delight, curiosity, sophistication, playfulness, danger, recklessness, and comfort—than we normally feel in our day-to-day routines. Brand theater taps into aspirations and reinforces who and what the brand is, and by extension, who the customer could be as well.

Personal connections are the beating heart of brand theater. Smart companies provide opportunities for their customers to connect with employees, loved ones, other customers, and friends. It also provides social currency—something fun to talk about at a dinner party. Rich, layered experiences can immediately make the competition seem sterile, cold, and flat. When there are so many choices at the same price point, brand theater tips the scales toward brands that offer compelling experiences. Whether it's business travel, grocery shopping, car repair, or dining, delivering great brand theater is an effective way to stand out in a competitive market.

WHY WE CRAVE BRAND THEATER

1. **We have abundant choices.**

   Never have consumers had so much choice. The Internet gives us the ability to quickly research competitors, compare features, and explore new options from bloggers and peer review sites. Customers have so much choice that they're starting to pick brands and products (and develop loyalty) not just based on the traditional elements of service, price, and quality, but also on the entire buying experience.

2. **Pioneers have raised the bar for everyone.**

   Customers are getting smarter and more sophisticated every year. It takes more to dazzle them these days. Early leaders such as Disney raised the brand experience stakes, and innovators in all industries are finding creative ways to design compelling, theatrical experiences. In return, customers are becoming much more discerning and demanding.

3. **Price is not the only factor.**

   CEOs in a variety of industries feel that they are emerging from a period of severe cost cutting—call it the Wal-Mart effect, if you will. Many brands are as lean as they can get without hurting performance. These trimmed-down companies are beginning to shift their focus away from price toward brand theater as a way to establish a competitive edge. According to former Dell CIO Jerry Gregorie, "The customer experience is the next competitive battleground."[5]

4. **We want an escape from everyday life.**

   A trip through Pottery Barn gets the decorating juices flowing faster than browsing through the average furniture store. It's now standard for bookstores such as Borders and Barnes & Noble to include cafés with wireless access. Jet Blue's leather chairs and personal movie screens make economy air travel a little bit more fun. Consumers of all kinds are embracing brand theater as an escape from the extraordinary stresses of modern life and feel magnetically drawn to brands that deliver emotionally satisfying experiences. Brand theater encourages us to slow down and breathe in life's simple pleasures.

5. **People are looking to brands for richer emotional experiences.**

   Brand theater is where goods and services intersect with emotions. When a consumer is "bored" with a category (say refrigerators), companies must take the opportunity to infuse the experience with fresh life—like Sub-Zero refrigerators (www.sub zero.com), some of which come with computer software that orders your groceries and monitors for spoiled items. Companies will benefit when they explore the service, entertainment, and luxury limits of their brands and consider what their products or services would look like if they fully engaged the customer.

6. **We long to feel special, to get royal treatment and exclusive privileges.**

   Consumers want to feel important. They crave exclusive treatment—the kind that gives them access to privileges that most others don't receive. They want to feel that a brand has anticipated their needs, sought to solve their problems, and attends to their every whim. The more access consumers have to high-quality goods and services, the more they crave a new level of status. They want tailored experiences that mirror their unique preferences and reflect a high degree of personal attention.

7. **We appreciate brands that go the extra mile.**

   Not all customer experience investments are created equal. Research shows that as brands invest in customer satisfaction, there is a period after the initial ramp-up where incremental improvements do not have significant impact on customer loyalty. At this stage, the brand has hit the mushy middle, where it simply resembles all the other competitors that are giving it a shot. At a certain point in the process, these small changes just don't have a noticeable impact. When companies step up the rate and quantity of innovation and stand out by creating a truly differentiated experience strategy, they will quickly attract a loyal following.

8. **We respond to the magnetic pull of brand theater.**

   In the words of Amazon.com CEO Jeff Bezos, "Customer experience is bigger than customer service."[6] In fact, Forum Research found that 80 percent of customers who switched suppliers expressed *satisfaction* with their previous vendor. What causes a happy customer to leave? It's usually because they can get the same level of customer service plus some exciting extras from someone else (remember the mushy middle?).[7] Companies with the most clearly differentiated experiences have turned their customers into loyal advocates and pulled new fans away from the competition. These brands manage the relationship to the point where customers can't imagine doing business with anyone else.

LESSONS FROM KIMPTON HOTELS

Employees create the experience—choose them carefully, support them fully.

Kimpton COO Niki Leondakis stresses that a company's culture of innovation and its ability to deliver unique experiences are only as good as its employees. Typically, a large portion of a brand's marketing investment and promotional promise is unwittingly undermined by ill-informed or demotivated staff behavior. The result is that many people who do intend to buy go away because of how they were treated. To address this challenge, Kimpton factors in personality and character when hiring. "In the selection process, we look at a number of attributes—not just the technical skill," she says. "It's more a matter of who they are as a person."[8] Kimpton employees feel passionate about working at a place where the brand's culture and value systems match their own.

Be an industry pioneer to stand out and generate buzz.

With a small marketing budget relative to the large chain hotels, Kimpton has to be savvy about spending its advertising dollars. Word-of-mouth referrals are critical to the company's marketing strategy, and many of Kimpton's programs are designed to generate buzz. As a result, the company has launched dozens of first-time industry programs and rolls out new or unusual efforts on a regular basis.

Kimpton's pet-friendly policies (any type of pet is welcome at all their properties, without a fee or special deposit) have been a great source of both PR and word-of-mouth interest. Every Kimpton hotel provides basic pet care supplies such as bowls, mats, beds, treats, pickup bags, and collar tags with the hotel's contact information, and each property offers a special pet package. For example, the 5th Avenue Suites Hotel in Portland, Oregon, has its own newsletter, *Dog Nose News,* and offers free psychic pet readings on the last Friday of every month. In Chicago, the Hotel Allegro welcomes felines with a personalized pouch containing bottled water, snacks, and a keepsake catnip toy. Their humans get a copy of *Cat Massage: A Whiskers-to-Tail Guide to Your Cat's Ultimate Petting Experience.* The $189 price tag includes overnight accommodations in a premier room and complimentary valet parking. Hotel Monaco's "Guppy Love" program delivers a complimentary companion goldfish to guest rooms upon request.

Transform ordinary areas into friendly spaces.

Founder Bill Kimpton was fond of saying that a hotel could overcome the loneliness of travel for its guests. To honor this tradition, Kimpton has rethought the lobby as a living room. The reception areas are relocated to one side, and oversized sandstone and lime fireplaces become the focal point. This contemporary hearth anchors the lobby and visually symbolizes comfort and relaxation. It also frames the complimentary wine receptions that have become a hallmark of Kimpton hotels. Specialty accommodations are designed to give guests a perfect environment in which to work, play, or just relax. Amenities include high-speed Internet access, wide-screen television sets, DVDs, video games, kitchen access, and mood lighting. The

Hotel Madera in Washington, D.C., features cardio, nosh, screening, and strength rooms.

Kimpton's friendly style is something distinctly different from the often hipper-than-thou sleekness of Ian Schrager's Morgans Hotel Group and Starwood's W Hotels. The Kimpton tradition encourages comfort and warmth. The goal is to create an all-inclusive atmosphere that makes travelers feel welcome and discourages any sort of snobbery or sterility.

Case Study—Apple Genius Bar

Creators of Apple Computer stores wanted their signature retail spaces to be a friendly place for Mac users and PC heathens alike. The team used the Ritz-Carlton hotels as an inspirational model. They watched Ritz managers put together new hotels in New York and New Orleans, and out of those visits came the Apple Genius Bar. The team observed that at the Ritz, the restaurant bar is a friendly gathering place. The bartender makes you feel welcome. They thought, "Wouldn't it be great if going to a computer store could be as welcoming?" Their vision is now a reality, with Apple's innovative Genius Bar help desk staffed with the friendly neighborhood "geniuses."

The idea was to create a space where perplexed customers could pull up a stool to share their technical glitches and random questions with a friendly expert. The concept has been such a success that the "pull up a stool" vision has been replaced by winding lineups of customers eager to take advantage of the free help (who doesn't want to talk tech-shop with a genius?). Online blogs have even called the Genius Bar—and its lengthy queues—a great place to meet girls.

Free, face-to-face neighborhood support is a critical differentiator between the Apple and Windows worlds. Dell and Hewlett-Packard, the dominant Windows PC manufacturers, charge $35 for telephone tech support after a warranty has expired. Even Apple bills $49 for postwarranty help. But problem solving with an in-store genius is always free. Some Apple outlets also have weekend DJs who spin tunes on their iPods, and all the stores have free workshops on Apple products. Some are even taught by high-profile names such as film director Spike Lee, singer Moby, and photographer Howard Bingham.[9]

Package customer experiences with flair and humor.

Kimpton understands that their guests are looking for more than just a home away from home—they're also eager to enjoy new experiences that go beyond their daily routine. In response, Kimpton upped the ante on their standard amenities and added dozens of playful, fun, romantic, and novel packages that express the hotels' themes, create opportunities to experience the city, and explore the edges of their guests' personalities.

Hotel Triton's "So Hip It Hurts" tattoo and piercing package promises guests the ultimate souvenir—a $65 tattoo or piercing credit at Mom's Body Shop on Haight Street in San Francisco. The general manager will escort guests to the tattoo parlor and provide smelling salts in case they faint. There's also a calendar of hip happenings each month.

Kimpton consistently adds racy offerings to enhance the now-standard mix of romantic weekends, spa getaways, and family play vacations. It's part of the company's charm. In Washington, D.C., Hotel Helix's "Twist and Shout" package is designed to keep the romance alive and laughing with Milton Bradley's iconic Twister game, champagne, massage oil, a pint of specialty ice cream (no spoons included), and a late, 3:00 P.M. checkout. Gay pride packages and romantic partners getaways are mixed with discreet retreats for men who want to maintain their air of masculinity but enjoy the odd manicure or exfoliation treatment of special metrosexual packages such as "Jethro Gets Metro" and "Metro Mojo."

Case Study—Destination Kohler

Any homeowner who has built a custom home or done serious remodeling knows the endless treks to the home improvement warehouse to pick out everything from sinks, tubs, and toilets to tile, molding, and paint. The process can be exhausting and the range of decisions positively overwhelming. Wisconsin-based Kohler Company has transformed the endless shopping trips into a rich, multisensory minishopping vacation with their weekend getaway package called Destination Kohler (www.destina tionkohler.com), an intriguing blend of accommodation, leisure, food, and of course Kohler products.

Destination Kohler includes accommodations at the American Club AAA five-diamond resort hotel in the village of Kohler, Wisconsin, a round of golf at the Whistling Straits golf course, a trip to the River Wildlife wilderness preserve, use of the Sports Core fitness and racquet center, and luxurious spa treatments at the 24,000 square foot Kohler Waters Spa.

Guests also get an appointment with a personal design consultant who reviews their house plans and walks them through the Kohler Design Center. Inside this 36,000-square-foot home design playground, customers browse through luxurious bath vignettes created by world-renowned designers, sample a huge array of kitchen and bath products, and gain an intimate understanding of how each item would work in their own homes. Just as Nike created sports supercenters with its Niketown retail complexes, Kohler is carefully controlling its own brand experience and creating engaging opportunities for customers and guests alike.[10]

Reflect your customers' values.

Kimpton understands the importance of protecting the environment and knows that many of its guests share this critical value. In the last decade, Kimpton has become the hospitality industry's undisputed green leader by pioneering environmentally responsible business practices. Kimpton's EarthCare program is a three-phase environmental plan that the company rolled out in early 2005.

The first phase involves conserving water, recycling, and using recycled paper with soy-based ink. The second phase includes organic products and introduces energy-efficient lighting. In the third phase, Kimpton takes it to a higher level with sustainable furnishings and eco-friendly paint materials. The program also ensures that company vendors uphold the same environmental standards. To guide this program, Kimpton has hired Danny Seo, an environmental advocate, bestselling author of *Conscious Style Home* and *Generation React,* and a leading eco-stylist, to serve as the company's environmental lifestyle consultant with a focus on style and design.

San Francisco's Hotel Triton has gone completely green, serving as a model for California's Green Lodging program. The Triton also offers a premium EcoFloor with organic and eco rooms, including everything from air and water filtration to organic linens and bedding and energy-efficient lighting. Kimpton is walking its environmental talk, matching the values of its guests, and inspiring a new group of people to live with greater environmental consciousness.[11]

Go deep with your most successful programs.

Attention to detail is the hallmark of Kimpton's success. The brand has made women a primary focus and developed new programs that address the way female guests operate when they stay at Kimpton properties. For example, many women feel unsafe doing their daily run or walk through an unfamiliar city, and guests were pulling the comforters off the bed and using them as cushions for impromptu yoga and stretching routines. No more. With the "Om Away from Home" program, guests just ring the front desk for a complimentary yoga basket, which includes a nonslip mat, foam bricks, straps, and the most recent issue of *Yoga Journal* magazine. Guests can also click on the television to watch Kimpton's closed-circuit yoga channel, available twenty-four hours a day. Each room includes an instructional guide by Judith Lasater, Ph.D., P.T., that outlines six restorative poses to help relieve travel fatigue.

The company knows a good thing when they see it, so Kimpton expanded this well-received program to include a new Mind. Body. Spa. wellness series that encourages guests to maintain healthy lifestyles on the road. The expanded program includes Pilates and guided meditations, plus in-room spa services.

Case Study—Whole Foods

Whole Foods has taken the mundane task of grocery shopping to an inspiring new level in an almost-as-big-as-Target, 80,000-

square-foot concept store near their home office in Austin, Texas. This culinary emporium is extremely interactive. Dip a fresh strawberry in a flowing, chocolate fountain. Watch while any one of 150 fresh seafood items are prepared before your eyes. Sip a glass of wine in the produce section. Enjoy roasted nuts or a fresh, made-to-order doughnut or pastry—with no artificial ingredients, of course.

For Whole Foods, brand theater has had a great impact on the bottom line. Other stores may be shrinking, but Whole Foods is bidding farewell to 31,000-square-foot stores in favor of 50,000-square-foot versions, with fifty-eight slated for construction by 2009. And according to a March 2005 *USA Today* story, Whole Foods grocery stores sell over $800 per square foot, twice what a typical supermarket sells. The chain's sales also jumped 15 percent in 2004 while the average supermarket grew just 1 percent.[12]

Be a telepathic problem solver.

Kimpton routinely addresses issues that other companies might consider inconsequential and creates full-service programs around them. Case in point—the Kimpton Tall Rooms, designed for lanky travelers who always have to duck their heads under doorways and showers, and rarely spend a night without their feet hanging off the bed. These special rooms have 96-inch-long beds specially built by Sealy (California King–size beds are only 84 inches), with Postulux Pillow-top mattresses and Italian-made, 100 percent cotton, 200-plus thread count sheets. The rooms also feature higher ceilings and doorframes, extra long bathrobes, raised showerheads, vanities, and toilets. The hotel also includes a local directory of stores that cater to tall people.

Case Study—Mini Cooper

Impatient Mini Cooper buyers don't have to wonder when their new wheels will be ready to drive. Instead, they can log on to Mini's Web site (www.miniusa.com) and use the "Where's My Baby?" tracking tool to follow their car from the factory in Britain to its ultimate delivery. For many owners, this interactive tool transforms the wait from endless to exciting, providing a sense of control and forging a deeper connection to this already beloved brand.

Mini USA buyers usually wait two to three months for their cars, so the savvy company created the tracking service (which is still fairly unusual) to acknowledge and soothe customers' anxiety. The Web site extends the nervous parent metaphor with excellent results. For example, during the "scheduled for production" phase, the tracking tool assures customers that their Mini "will begin to move through the 'birth canal' at our Oxford plant. . . . Rest well knowing that your baby is in the best of hands."

The Mini Web site does more than just provide information or sell products. It also keeps customers engaged, resulting in fewer complaints and a more positive brand experience. "Our ultimate goal was to make waiting fun," says Kerri Martin, Mini USA's marketing manager. Mini USA also keeps in touch with new owners in a fun, "you're part of the clan" way after their vehicle arrives. Owners receive an e-mail birthday card when their Mini is a year old and get updates when new features become available on the site.[13]

Mini Cooper's technology isn't groundbreaking, but it has a huge impact on the customer experience because it's integrated so smoothly with the brand. The delivery process is fun and individualized, and makes owners feel like they've joined a special club.

Partner to deliver greater value.

Locating world-class restaurants inside or next to the majority of Kimpton properties is yet another way that the company enhances their guests' experience. Not surprisingly, Kimpton also approaches the restaurant business from a different angle than most hoteliers.

The typical hotel food and beverage operation disappoints guests and loses money, but Kimpton restaurants are run as separate operations, with the restaurant manager reporting to the head of the restaurant group (not the hotel manager), and only 10 percent of revenues are expected to come from hotel guests. The majority of

Kimpton restaurants feature a "star" or up-and-coming chef who creates a destination where foodies want to gather.

The company allows these culinary masters to develop the restaurant style around their personalities and food passions, which fits Kimpton's diverse workforce and commitment to individuality. Partnering with famed chefs and independent restaurateurs is an essential element of Kimpton's brand theater and a smart way to provide some of the best dining experiences in the industry.

Case Study—Blue Star Jets Air Salon

Some commercial airlines may offer cashmere slippers and complimentary champagne, but frequent fliers still suffer from dry skin and sore muscles. Anyone who books private flights on Blue Star Jets' Air Salon (www.bluestarjets.com), however, can have all their grooming needs satisfied before landing. The award-winning private charter service has partnered with a plastic surgeon and a high-profile team of beauty experts to turn a cross-Atlantic flight into a full spa experience. The journey begins prior to takeoff with an antiaging meal custom designed by nutritionist Oz Garcia. A flying team from the Warren-Tricomi Salon administers beauty treatments such as haircuts, manicures, and massages. Plastic surgeon Paul Lrenc is even on hand to give Botox injections. This salon starts at $1,000 per service, not including charter costs.[14]

Prioritize your customers and deliver personalized rewards.

Instead of rewarding customer loyalty with a points program, Kimpton offers more immediate, personalized rewards for guests who frequent any of their properties. The company records customers' preferences with an online profile service, which is further embellished over time with small (and sometimes large) details. This makes the guest experience feel extra special and the service nearly telepathic. Based on the profile information and their travel frequency, Kimpton immediately rewards customers with their favorite things. For example, a running enthusiast might check in for her fourth visit and find a Diet Coke and a jogging magazine on the bed. Another guest might receive a package of Reese's peanut butter cups, a few lemon Luna bars, and the latest issue of *O* magazine.

The more often you stay, the better and more personalized the rewards become. Guests who check in fifteen times or stay forty-five nights during a calendar year receive Kimpton's elite Inner Circle membership. This status provides additional privileges, including custom room amenities, complimentary upgrades, preferred availability, special offers for new hotel openings, VIP status at partner restaurants, and a VIP reservation line, among other perks. Some Inner Circle guests will have a case of their favorite wine delivered to their homes, and on their fiftieth visit they can choose from a weekend in Napa Valley and private tastings at La Tour Vineyards, a weekend wellness retreat, a cocktail party or chef-hosted dinner, or shopping at the Kimpton Designers' Collection for home fixtures and furnishings.

Innovate programs for your target segments.

Kimpton homes in on the desires of underserved segments of the hospitality industry, including women and the homosexual community. Some of its most popular programs combine exploration with education. Sazerac, the restaurant adjacent to the Hotel Monaco Seattle, shares a "Little Bit of Lovin'" with a cooking class series in which guests learn to whip up a three-course, southern-inspired meal.

Kimpton's GLBT (gay, lesbian, bisexual, and transgender) travel program strives to meet the interests of gay and lesbian travelers through community outreach, incentive programs, and targeted advertising campaigns. Additionally, Kimpton has established K-GLEN, Kimpton Hotels' gay and lesbian employee network. K-GLEN representatives from every region of the country meet quarterly to advise the hotel group on serving the interests and needs of the gay and lesbian community.

In 2004, Kimpton was the only hospitality company to receive a 100 percent score on the Human Rights Campaign's Corporate Equality Index, which measures how major U.S. companies treat their homosexual, bisexual, and transgender staff, customers, and investors.

Nurture a corporate culture of innovation.

All the members of the Kimpton staff—from accountants to designers to housekeepers—work together to improve the customer experience. It's a culture that welcomes fresh thinking and quickly moves forward with changes, so hot new ideas can be implemented without too much fuss. Kimpton employees are expected to identify possibilities and take risks. "When you see an opportunity, you need to jump on it and own it," explains Leondakis. The company applauds all creative efforts, whether they're successful or not, to keep the self-empowerment ethic alive and thriving. By actively noticing, articulating, and acting on opportunity, the company creates a powerful culture of innovation. Programs grow stronger and staff members become bolder in their ideas and choices.

The Kimpton brand has weathered rough economic times, including two recessions and the sharp post-9/11 decline in the hospitality industry. By responding quickly to customers' changing preferences, the company can surpass top-heavy competitors who need longer time frames to meet new challenges.

Even the restaurants have developed a culture of innovation. Kimpton chefs across the country prepare miniature versions of menu items for less than full price—from starters to main courses—to meet the needs of dieters. At Scala's Bistro in San Francisco, pastry chef Mimi Young was tired of diners passing on dessert while following the latest diet, so she created one-third portions of her most popular desserts. Guests can indulge in a miniature version of the Chocolate IV; baby scoops of sorbet; a petite version of the Bostini (a modern take on Boston Cream Pie); and a mini crème brulee.

Circular organizational structures
promote communication.

Instead of the usual pyramid organization or a rigid hierarchy, Kimpton prefers a circular structure in which executives and employees are in constant communication. "It's all about collaboration and inclusion," says Leondakis. "As the COO, I talk to frontline employees regularly." Leondakis puts it simply: "There's this culture behind the scenes that manifests itself in a customer experience that is unique.

The care our employees show for our guests is the end result of the care that everyone shows for each other."

At Kimpton, serving the customer well is not enough. Kimpton's 5,500 employees are encouraged and even expected to have a genuine desire to understand and appreciate both customers and colleagues alike, as well as a dedication to team and personal development and the ability to adapt to change.

WORKBOOK

Get Started

1. **Go deeper into your brand experience.**

   Remember when car dealerships would hire clowns and offer free hot dogs and popcorn to attract buyers on the weekend? Buying a car did not offer enough excitement, so the dealership sought to entice customers through an unrelated source of entertainment. In contrast to this approach, brand theater takes you deeper into the experience. For example, a BMW car dealership could offer a race track to test drive their performance vehicles or provide a virtual reality simulator of the NASCAR racing experience.

2. **Learn from other industries.**

   Visit three brands in different industries and make note of all the small and large ways they deliver a sense of theater. Take note of the inexpensive extras that make the experience memorable. Next, get a fresh taste of your own brand's customer experience. For example, shop the stores, order something from the catalog, or call the customer service department. Use the fresh inspiration you gain from shopping in other industries to imagine five changes that will enhance your brand experience.

3. **Create vignettes and highly detailed displays.**

   Pottery Barn has nailed the concept of inspiring customers with their highly detailed displays. Customers may intend to dash in to replace a chipped espresso cup, but those room vignettes keep them browsing and lingering. Each scene is perfectly set; from the walnut table to the retro drink pitcher resting on a sky-blue serving tray, customers can imagine themselves serving lemonade with a fresh jolt of style.

4. **Boredom equals opportunity.**

Identify the boring and stale categories in your customers' lives. These are opportunities for innovation and compelling upgrades. Can you go deeper into the experience you are currently creating to make it more visual, fun, luxurious, sensual, memorable, and exclusive? For example, vitamins were formerly available only in capsules. Today, both adults and children can enjoy vitamins in new flavors and forms, including Yummi Bear's vitamin gummy bears, Vitaball's bubble gum, and Viactive's calcium soft chews in chocolate mint, caramel, French vanilla, and raspberry.

Go for It.

Don't just entertain your customers; engage them. How can your brand offer customers a more hands-on experience? Consider how Kimpton's celebrated chefs didn't just serve up great meals, but offered the ability to shop an open air market and cook with them in their restaurant kitchens.

Assemble your most creative staff members and think big. Forget about what is possible within your current budget, and instead think about crafting a customer experience that would bring your brand to life. Focus first on delighting your brand community and worry later about how to accomplish the goals. This way, the details won't stifle your creative process.

NINE

GO INWARD

Spiritual Hunger and Modern Media
Find Common Ground

Just off I-4 in Orlando, Florida, in a 10,000-square-foot office behind a carpet warehouse, are the headquarters of Relevant Media Group, a company that is revolutionizing how a new generation views faith and religion. Relevant isn't trying to hide its blossoming operations—they just love the high-ceiling building. A former warehouse for a major credit card company, there's a huge 34-x-14-foot bank vault in the middle of the space, and it's a gritty world away from suburban Orlando.

Relevant is a multimedia company that reaches young Christians with the message that "even though religion may be seen as irrelevant, a personal relationship with God is a relevant—and vital—aspect of a fulfilled life." It began with the Relevant online magazine (www.rele vantmagazine.com) and has grown to encompass a print magazine, *Relevant,* with a circulation of 80,000; a new magazine for women eighteen to thirty-four called *Radiant;* a broadband music video channel, Relevant.tv, streaming 24/7; a book division that has published titles, including *Walk On: The Spiritual Journey of U2* (which has sold more than 80,000 copies) and *The Gospel According to Tony Soprano;* and several other thriving divisions, including creative services and apparel.

This is no archaic, fire-and-brimstone venture. It's the brainchild of twenty-nine-year-old Cameron Strang, who started his company in June 2000 with two interns and one employee. He'd been working on the business plan since he was a nineteen-year-old student at Oral Roberts University in Tulsa, Oklahoma, and throughout his tenure as a managing editor of five magazines at Nashville publisher Vox Corporation. Relevant Media Group began as a creative services company to reach eighteen- to thirty-four-year-olds and launched a weekly e-mail newsletter in 2001. The books division came next, and in March 2002 Strang and his growing team launched the Relevant webzine, with daily articles and news from a progressive, faith-based perspective. By the end of the year, Relevantmagazine.com had over 100,000 unique visitors per month and nearly 5,000 readers who paid $10 each to reserve a subscription to the upcoming print magazine.

NEW GENERATION, NEW APPROACH

From the moment you step through the door, it's clear that Relevant is the wild child of the Christian community. The reception area has a black leather couch, three flat-screen televisions blasting music videos, and sharp track lighting. The walls are lined with *Relevant* magazine covers, including one featuring the rapper Mase, plus original illustrations and photographs. The production offices have sixteen-foot ceilings and open work spaces. At the back is a video production area: a 2,000-square-foot warehouse, a music studio, and a two-foot-high stage that hosts visiting bands (and was once put to good use by live bands at an office party for four hundred). The white metal vault, however, is the ultimate showpiece. The previous tenant used it to store credit cards before shipping them to customers. Relevant has taken the vault over as a conference room—complete with an air valve, should someone happen to get locked in.

The office is a direct reflection of the Relevant staff (who range in age from twenty-one to thirty-one), but it also provides a great analogy for the company's audience. All Relevant content is designed to reach young, twenty-something Christians (the target age is twenty-seven) who want authenticity and spiritual connections, and who move seamlessly between the secular and the sacred. Strang developed Relevant as a forum to discuss and explore the issues that matter to his generation—a group that questions religion and church, but doesn't question faith itself. "I wasn't finding the connection that I was looking for," says Strang, whose piercings and several-day-old stubble quickly obliterate religious stereotypes. "We needed to create a platform to have these conversations."

Where their parents equate the American church with truth, this new group of faith-seekers questions some of the church practices and perspectives and seeks unique ways to live out an ancient faith. This fundamental disconnect has turned many young worshippers of all faiths away from traditional religious venues and trappings. Some people believe that this generation hates church, says Strang, but that is simply not true. They're just looking for something deeper than the formal template of a traditional church service. They'd rather go down to a coffee shop and have an intimate conversation with their friends about their faith than attend a regular Sunday service. "They're not finding hunger and truth and authenticity in church."

While Relevant is not designed to replace church, it gives a new generation of Christians access to information through a faith-based lens about life, culture, society, entertainment, and relationships. Relevant knows that these people see their religion as a fluid and integral part of their lives—not something they pull out every Sunday for two hours—and it expects that they're tuned in to popular culture and mainstream media.

Whether it's a new book, article for the Web site, story, or streaming video, all Relevant media content falls into three categories—God, life, or progressive culture—and it all has to meet Strang's exacting standards. In 2005, Relevant had received over four hundred applications for a graphics-design job opening. "We might talk to *one* of those people," said Strang. "We're incredibly picky about who we hire." Relevant has always worked to be on par with any other market publication. Strang has no desire to be shuffled into a niche category, and maintains stringent high-quality standards to ensure that the organization's materials look hip and fun enough to appeal to its design-savvy, style-conscious audience.

Clearly, Relevant is on a roll. There are five divisions—Relevant Books, *Relevant* and *Radiant* magazines, Relevant Online (which encompasses the webzine and online community features), Relevant Network (a resource division for young adult pastors and ministers), Relevant Apparel (a line of T-shirts and accessories), and Relevant Solutions (the marketing arm of the company, providing online and offline branding advice and creative services). The new-media department is still in the works, and includes podcasts, videos, and Relevant.tv. But each and every division is united around the company's self-described mission to "create media for a generation of independent thinkers who were raised on pop culture and are hungry for God, but don't embrace dead religion."

Spiritually Hungry

Relevant is growing at lightning speed and forging deep connections with a young audience that embraces their faith, but has struggled to find a spiritually hungry yet forward-thinking community. While Relevant reaches a young, Christian demographic, there's a growing desire among many members of this generation to explore spirituality in some form—whether through Buddhism, Hinduism, or a mix-and-match style of self-awareness and mysticism. This generation craves deeper meaning in their lives, and they are actively searching for brands, media, products, and services to help them on this journey.

Strang began his company as a labor of love, which is the most important prerequisite for anyone who wants to tap into the craving for deeper meaning. He has also created a thriving architecture of participation that allows Relevant's brand members to write articles, dialogue on hot topics, and provide support and solutions to like-minded seekers within the global community.[1]

You'll see several other examples of smart, faith-centered endeavors throughout this chapter, but please understand that it does not cover the enormous range of belief systems, religions, and personal definitions of faith that exist and thrive around the globe.

THE CRAVING: GO INWARD

Increasingly, the meaningful life is defined as the spiritual life; spirituality has become a dominant value among today's consumers. In fact, the number of people who say they prayed to God during the previous week rose to 83 percent in 2004 from 77 percent in 1999, according to a poll by the Barna Research Group.[2] In general, this quest for meaning has fostered an increased focus on spirituality rather than on religion.

Entertainment and media with spiritual themes are thriving. Rick Warren's *The Purpose-Driven Life* and other bestsellers such as the *Left*

Behind series, *The Da Vinci Code, Life of Pi,* and *The Five People You Meet in Heaven* have helped to make spirituality the fastest-growing adult book category in the country, according to *Publishers Weekly.* A *TV Guide* cover story on the proliferation of television shows about God declared that "spiritual matters suddenly matter." In addition, the "spiritual cinema" category—a growing film genre whose movies ask the eternal questions "Who are we and why are we here?"—is suddenly winning audience choice awards at major U.S. film festivals, while sales from Mel Gibson's *The Passion of the Christ* passed the $600 million mark. Christian music sales now exceed those of classical, jazz, and new age music combined. Artistically, the Christian music genre is quite diverse, ranging from pop and acoustic folk to hardcore punk and heavy metal. Publications such as *Seventeen* magazine have also added new sections devoted to spirituality.

Celebrity-endorsed faith has become increasingly commonplace in newspapers and magazines. Tom Cruise and his well-known links to Scientology consistently make headlines, while Madonna, Demi Moore, Ashton Kutcher, and Britney Spears sport the $26 Red String bracelets as a visible symbol of kabbalah—the spiritual movement rooted in Jewish mysticism that's weaving through Hollywood in a way not seen since Scientology began attracting numerous converts and controversy over ten years ago.

"Religion and fashion are really becoming a big trend right now," asserted Jane Buckingham, president of the research and trend analysis firm The Intelligence Group, in an ABC News interview in 2005.[3] California clothing company Teenage Millionaire hit it big with shirts and hats featuring the slogan "Jesus is my homeboy" after several celebrities were sighted wearing the items. Since 2002, the company has sold more than a million of these shirts. They have since followed up their massive success with "Mary is my homegirl" merchandise.

In addition to making fashion statements, spirituality is also changing the way people connect and how families operate. Popular dating sites, such as JDate for Jewish singles around the world, are becoming the standard way for young people of similar faith to connect. JDate has even been adopted as a word in popular language, such as "I'm going on a JDate," or "We're JDating." More than 500,000 singles have filled out the site's exhaustive profile, which elicits information beyond the usual relationship histories, dietary habits, and favorite pastimes. In another spiritual realm, Mimi Doe, a parenting expert and author of *10 Principles to Spiritual Parenting: Nurturing Your Child's Soul,* has watched subscribers to her Web site, SpiritualParenting.com, swell from eight thousand in 1999 to fifty thousand in 2004.[4]

This growing emphasis on spiritual pursuits has not taken the form of increased religious attendance at mainstream houses of worship. Rather, it has seen people pursuing fundamentalism (such as born-again Christianity or Orthodox Judaism) or adopting a mix-and-match style of religious beliefs that blends eastern and western practices and spiritualism. At the same time, a growing debate about ethics and morality is affecting our attitudes toward business. Companies and media channels are introducing new products, services, and forums to support this spiritually hungry generation. Successful new brands and established companies alike are responding to spiritual values and working to hit the right notes with Gen X and Gen Y consumers in both creative advertising and brand messaging.

According to a recent survey for Reboot—a national network for young Jews—conducted by Greenberg Quinlan Rosner Research, the majority of eighteen-to-twenty-five-year-old Americans say religion and spirituality are important elements of their lives, but they're moving away from established religion to discover and experience their faith in informal, nontraditional, and highly personal ways.[5]

College students also show a strong level of interest in spirituality and religion, and have high expectations for the role their schools should play in their spiritual quest. According to a new study conducted by UCLA's Higher Education Research Institute (and funded by the John Templeton Foundation), four in five students say they have an interest in spirituality, three-quarters say they are "searching for meaning or purpose in life," and over three-quarters say they believe in God.

The same study explored how varying levels of spirituality translate into social and political attitudes, psychological and physical well-being, and religious preferences. The survey polled 112,232 freshmen at 236 colleges and universities and found that:

- 80 percent are interested in spirituality
- 76 percent are searching for meaning/purpose in life

- 74 percent have discussions about the meaning of life with friends
- 81 percent attend religious services
- 80 percent discuss religion or spirituality with friends
- 79 percent believe in God
- 69 percent pray

A summary report entitled "The Spiritual Life of College Students" found that students "are searching for deeper meaning in their lives, looking for ways to cultivate their inner selves, seeking to be compassionate and charitable, and determining what they think and feel about the many issues confronting their society and the global community."[6]

WHY WE CRAVE NONTRADITIONAL SPIRITUALITY AND FAITH-BASED COMMUNITY

1. **Many organized religions have forgotten or alienated this generation.**

   Organized to minister to families, most churches and religious groups have largely failed Gen X until recently. Teenagers have vibrant youth groups, but if you're an unmarried twenty-nine-year-old, you get stuck in a singles group—the church equivalent of a ghetto. This reality is changing some faith-based communities, but many twentysomethings prefer to explore spiritual connections in coffee shops and less traditional gathering places. This generation is used to controlling their media, communications, and experiences, so why should their faith be any different?

   "It seems like this is the one age group the church just doesn't understand," says Strang. "They have us through youth group, but then when we go to college, churches just don't seem to know what to do with us. It's like, 'Good luck, and we'll see you when you have some kids.'"

2. **Faith-based offerings often have a dated "dork factor."**

   My friend Chris is a musician who has always had a halo of "hip" floating over his head. He's now the father of two young children and a happily married guy who seamlessly mixes music and family. He's so happily married, in fact, that he finally gave in to his wife's request for a minivan. When they picked up the new wheels, Chris loaded the kids into the backseat, clicked on his seat belt, and adjusted the rearview mirror. As he started the vehicle, he turned around and said, "Hear that, kids? That's the last bit of cool draining out of me."

Church, religion, and the trappings of faith-based products and services often have the same unfortunate effect. Head into the Christian bookstore and just try to find something you'd actually want to be seen reading on the subway. This generation is hyperaware of the marketplace, and they don't want to compromise their sense of style in the interest of religion. It's not a question of vanity or a lack of commitment to their faith. Quite the opposite: Young believers are so eager to merge their private spirituality with their public lives that they want to wear it, listen to it, and talk about it without a sense of disconnect. The traditional trappings of religion—from formal services to corny figurines and needlepoint Bible verses—simply don't resonate with this group. "Cool" people aren't afraid to acknowledge their spiritual side, but for the most part, they are not being served by existing products, services, and media.

3. **We've glimpsed the possibility of less-formal venues for our faith.**

According to the Reboot survey, many eighteen-to-twenty-five-year-olds have highly informal, communal, or personal ways to express their faith, such as praying before meals (55 percent), talking with friends about religion and spirituality (38 percent), or reading religious magazines, books, and newspapers (33 percent).[7]

Faith doesn't always mean church services or a formal religious gathering. This group has blurred the lines between sacred and secular, finding spirituality in all aspects of their lives. They often feel a sharp disconnect with the traditional practices of their church, synagogue, or mosque—even as they appreciate the history behind these practices. While they respect tradition, to them it can feel forced in their modern, highly connected lives.

4. **We have nontraditional lifestyles and relationships.**

According to Margaret Feinberg, author of *Twentysomething: Surviving and Thriving in the Real World*—a book about navigating the decisions and changes of the postcollege years—the most important factor affecting her generation today is that people are getting married later in their lives or never marrying at all. From buying a house to making career plans and starting families, this shift affects almost everything in their lives. It also causes a greater gap between the traditional expectations of organized religion and the real-life realities of a young, changing generation.[8]

5. **Mainstream media shies away from spiritual content.**

Although the data clearly show a desire for faith-based media and information, Hollywood, publishing houses, and product manufacturers are generally hard-pressed to serve this need. There's a lot of fear around creating spiritual content for the mainstream. Remember the hoopla prior to the release of *The Passion of the Christ?* Some people said it would end Mel Gibson's career, but instead, by many accounts, it proved to be a massive success, both financially and artistically. Whether or not the religious theme and history resonated with viewers, many people applauded Gibson for making the film he was driven to make. On the other end of the pendulum, products and media created purely to capitalize on this market can exude insincerity and quickly backfire.

6. **We are seeking our own favorite blend.**

Generation Y is open and even excited about faith and spirituality. But when it comes to traditional religious organizations, most young people are saying, "What*ever*."

For many in the Connected Generation, the central spiritual tenets that provide substance to their faith are a custom blend of multiple-faith beliefs and religious practices. Their core values are the result of a cut-and-paste mosaic of feelings, facts, principles, experiences, and lessons. Their lifestyles represent an eclectic combination of traditional and alternative activities, so they're the first generation that will often choose a nonlinear style of thinking—a connect-the-dots-however-you-choose approach that has already been demonstrated in their relationships, which are much more racially integrated and culturally fluid than ever before.

7. **Traditional institutions' efforts to reach twentysomethings are all style and no substance.**

This is the flip side of stuffy, stodgy religious institutions.

There is a growing tendency among churches, products, and media to score high on style but low on substance. While this is a sincere gesture, it's also misguided. Many of these churches fail to realize that this group is completely unimpressed with flashy light shows and loud music. The Connected Generation is looking for something much deeper. Formality is unnecessary, but authenticity is critical.

8. **Marketers are out of touch with twentysomethings.**

   Much of the spiritual content and media created for twentysomethings is made in a generational vacuum by older marketers sitting around wondering "what those young people would like." Inevitably, the material hits the wrong notes and tends to meet the needs of someone much younger than the target market.

9. **We have diverse social circles.**

   Whereas older generations usually lived and socialized among members of their ethnic or religious groups, Generation Y sees their community membership as far more open and fluid. Only 7 percent of surveyed youths said that all of their friends are members of the same religion, and a mere 9 percent of the most religious respondents said that their friends come from the same religion.[9]

LESSONS FROM RELEVANT MEDIA GROUP

Take a peer-to-peer stance.

Relevant provides a forum that says, "You're not alone and there's a massive audience worldwide that is also seeking what you're seeking. Let's go on this journey together." Relevant rejects hierarchical structures and embraces a networked community of peers. While maintaining high standards in design and writing, the brand's tone and message has a clear sense of humility and takes a stance as a fellow seeker, not a top-down teaching perspective. This peer-to-peer posture is not only their authentic belief, but also a pitch-perfect attitude for a generation that doesn't want clear-cut rules or easy answers. As the Relevant team writes on its Web site:

Whether 20 years into it or just starting out, if you're at this web-
site you're probably on a spiritual journey. Christianity is not a destination. No one has it all figured out. And because of that you'll find
that the articles in Relevant probably ask more questions than give
answers, which is something we feel is vital to our spiritual growth.
We need to never stop pursuing Truth and authenticity with passion.

Provide a forum for open dialogue and tackle the juicy issues.

Above all, the Relevant brand community provides a space for free discussion and debate. The editorial staff doesn't raise controversial topics simply to stir up emotions, but they do cover what's happening in
their own lives and whatever else their community members are eager
to explore. And despite their faith-based perspective, the brand is
politically neutral. "The Conservatives think we're too Liberal, and the
Liberals think we're too Conservative," Strang says with a laugh. "We
think our members are smart enough to carve a path for themselves."

Relevant never takes an issue and says, "We're right. Here are the
answers." Instead, they show both sides of the argument. "We wres-
tle with the gray areas and infuse the biblical perspective," says
Strang. "Then we leave it at that."

Raw and real, not smooth or sanitized

Relevant mixes a Bible-based perspective on social issues with an of-
the-minute cultural sensibility. This generation wants things more
grassroots and more straightforward, and they want to see all sides—
the good, bad, and ugly. They don't want to be spoon-fed.

In the same way that Myspace.com is freeing music, Relevant is
freeing the Christian faith for a new generation and bringing it back
to its essential core—back to what matters. Even though this group is
high-tech and high-design, they reject anything that's too light, too
slick, and too packaged.

Market the brand like a rock band.

There's a fun, indie spirit at Relevant. The company has taken
deliberate steps to fuel word-of-mouth buzz and to generate viral mar-

keting among its members. They've even created volunteer "street teams," which distribute flyers, magazines, stickers, and posters in their communities through targeted hot spots such as music stores, concerts, college campuses, shops, festivals, and churches. There are currently 2,500 active members on the street and "Web teams" that promote the brand community and online magazine. Web team volunteers talk to people about Relevant in chat rooms and discussion forums, and on message boards. They're even equipped with buddy icons, desktop wallpaper, and banner ads.

Case Study—Rock the Vote

Rock the Vote is a nonprofit, nonpartisan organization that works to increase youth voter turnout through media campaigns and street team activities. Since its inception, the group has used typical rock band marketing methods to raise awareness with young adults. Rock the Vote coordinates voter registration drives, get-out-the-vote events, and voter education efforts, all to ensure that young people take advantage of their right to vote.

Rock the Vote was founded by members of the entertainment industry during the early 1990s, in response to a wave of political attacks on freedom of expression. The first members included Madonna, Iggy Pop, Red Hot Chili Peppers, and Woody Harrelson. Now entertainers ranging from Aerosmith to Steve Young work with young volunteers to support the organization. In addition to special concerts and tours, approximately thirty-five street teams are active in major cities across the United States during election season. These teams conduct peer-to-peer organizing and voter education activities, and attend numerous events to recruit more members and deliver knowledge to America's youth—all designed to tip the scales in a more progressive direction. In addition to registering over 3 million new young voters, Rock the Vote street teams have engaged young people as civic activists in their communities and contributors to the political process.[10]

Census numbers released in November 2005 showed a

groundswell of young voter participation in the 2004 election. Approximately 47 percent of eligible Americans ages 18 to 24 voted in 2004, up from 36 percent in 2000. No other age group increased its turnout by more than 5 percentage points.

Staff your company with passionate members of your brand community.

Brands that aim to "reach the young people" are often created from an outsider's perspective. No wonder they're out of touch. The staff of twenty-two at Relevant range in age from twenty-one to thirty-one. The company is constantly adding new, young talent and has a steady stream of about ten college interns to keep their perspective pitch perfect. "We believe it's critical that the products *for* the audience are made *by* the target audience," says Strang. "They know what matters to them. At Relevant, we keep fresh young blood coming into the company so we meet the needs of our readers."

Relevant doesn't have focus groups, either. "Our staff meeting is a focus group," explains Strang. If something is not on point, it won't fly with the Relevant staff. It's the simplest, most direct way to make sure that the content, voice, and perspective always hit the right demographic chords.

Create online tools to support community connections.

In 2005, Relevant dramatically expanded the established elements of its online community (member-written articles and message boards). The site now includes blogs from both staff and members; a searchable, user-driven event calendar for festivals, conferences, tours, and concerts; user profiles that enable members to list their favorite music, books, and interests, and to post photos and find local members in their area; an interactive, searchable gallery of user-submitted art and photography; a prayer room with prayer requests posted daily; a church directory with member comments and advice; premium content for *Relevant* magazine subscribers; a music section with videos, uploads, band profiles, and links to great indie groups; and a free, searchable version of *Today's New International Version* of the Bible.

Case Study—Ilkone i800 Mobile Phone

Dubai-based start-up IlkoneTel has developed the first handset designed for the Islamic community, called the Ilkone i800. The name *ilkone* is derived from an Arab word that means "universe," and the phone reflects the lifestyle and needs of a Muslim believer. While the phone itself isn't that visually interesting (it's even being promoted as "moderate looking"), the software provides some interesting and useful tools, including Hijri and Gregorian calendars (including date conversion), five-method Qibla direction (for determining the correct direction to face for prayer), English and Uthmanic versions of the Quran, and alarms (including the *azan* voice, an audible call to prayer) with prayer times for more than 5,000 cities. The i800 is available in Bangladesh, Indonesia, Malaysia, and India.[11]

Focus on daily applications of faith.

Engage in discussions and explorations that help people to live their lives. Relevant has thrived by putting topics of faith in a real-world, everyday context. It doesn't separate religion from reality, but understands that its members want to reflect their beliefs in their actions, choices, and relationships. In addition, Relevant covers topics that truly represent this generation's reality. Their parents faced different challenges and pressures, and the church may not be covering many vital topics. Relevant has stepped in to give voice to new mediums, new topics, and new pressures. Whether they're Muslim or Catholic, young believers today are living in a world that can be difficult to understand through a traditional, church-based lens.

Case Study—Beliefnet.com

Founded in 1999, Beliefnet.com is an independent, multifaith e-community designed to help people meet their religious and spiritual needs. The site provides tools such as prayer circles and kits for celebrating births, weddings, and other life milestones. The discussion and dialogue groups are among the most active elements of the site—created to help visitors learn from each other. Beliefnet aims to provide information and inspiration, but never to convert visitors to a particular religion or spiritual approach. It's a privately held company funded by individual investors, employees, and the Blue Chip Venture Company. The site connects seekers around topics of faith and spirituality, giving them a forum to explore the daily application of their beliefs. Beliefnet successfully navigated early financial trials in 2002 and today boasts over 2.5 million unique monthly visitors to their Web site and 5 million e-mail subscribers to their newsletters.

Position the brand for the older end of your target group.

We all know that tweens want to be like teens, teens aspire to lead the lives of college students, and college students dream of getting their first homes, jobs, and life partners. With that in mind, Relevant Media Group tailors their content to meet the needs of people five to seven years older than their average audience member. They knew that if they tried to target college students, they would end up reaching high-school students, so Strang and his team create content and design their services for a twenty-seven-year-old. They go deep into the realities of that person's life and reflect that twenty-seven-year-old experience in their topics, tone, voice, and perspective.

Their strategy has worked well. Only 3 percent of *Relevant* magazine's readers are under the age of eighteen. Strang is pleased with this low teenage membership. "We want to speak to someone whose worldview is more developed. I don't want to be a youth pastor. We want to cover and discuss issues with substance."

Relevant is a hit with college students, it's on-target for people in their midtwenties, and it's even pulling in a strong thirtysomething crowd who see themselves in a youthful light. Relevant's worldview creates a common thread that links these diverse groups together in conversation.

Don't skimp on product quality and design.

Like any other products, spiritual and faith-based products have to look good. Anything that's going to reach this generation needs to have quality design with a hip edge. The look and feel has to reflect the audience—their thoughts, values, directions, and style.

Strang wanted his magazine to hold its weight against top titles like *Paste, Fader, Rolling Stone,* and *Spin,* and the company's book division has the same high standards. He's adamant about the need for top-notch quality and an edgy look to satisfy younger readers. After all, the design and quality of the materials give customers their first indication that they've found an appealing brand and brand community.

Obviously, low-budget products make people think the brand is struggling, and as the old adage goes, you've only got one chance to make a first impression. From there, word-of-mouth excitement sustains sales and builds a support base. Good marketing begins with a solid product. People thought Strang was crazy to create such an expensive magazine right off the starting block, including a matte cover and high-quality paper. But Strang knew that design and visual style matter deeply to his young audience.

Evolve with your audience.

When Relevant magazine began, the focus was on "getting out of the faith ghetto." Strang and his team worked hard to normalize an audience that believed that they were on the fringe and often felt isolated from their church and faith community. Many of the articles validated how readers were feeling. They gave voice to a group that didn't have a voice. It was the right fit, because that's what Strang and his peers were experiencing. It was an authentic message that sprang from real-life questions and discoveries. Those same topics just wouldn't fly today, six years later, says Strang, because the Relevant worldview has become widely accepted. In fact, when the staff attends Christian publishing conferences that used to eye them with a mix of fear, suspicion, and curiosity, they're now the hit of the party. The company is on a journey, so there's a clear sense of growth and a progression to their content.

***Add new tools to support the community
and build connections.***

Relevantmagazine.com is growing in two primary areas—encouraging community through its user-driven components (blogs, photos, member profiles) and providing more dynamic features (video, premium content, podcasts, an expanded music section, a searchable Bible). Their audience is quick to adopt new media such as podcasts and blogs and is eager to interact with Relevant through these technologies. In response, Relevant aims to provide the latest online community tools and media channels for sharing spiritual content. Many other faith-based organizations are slower to embrace new technology and media, but Relevant has found that their connected community requests these new tools almost the moment they become available.

Case Study—Tickle.com

Tickle is the leading interpersonal media company, providing self-discovery and social networking services to more than 18 million active members in its worldwide community. Tickle's entertaining quizzes are a popular way for the Connected Generation to learn about themselves and share who they are with their network of friends. In the past few years, Tickle's traffic on spiritually based quizzes has grown and the site has responded with a lineup of tests from varied spiritual perspectives. Spiritually themed quizzes include the Chakra test, Discover your past life, What is your divine inspiration?, the Enneagram test, the ancient tarot, Do you have a sixth sense?, the Feng Shui test, and How sinful are you? The results are designed to be shared and can be easily e-mailed to friends—sparking new insights and deepening conversations.

***Provide up-to-the-minute access to the community
and its views.***

The Relevant Web site is user driven, so readers submit articles, photos, and comments that keep it fresh, current, and in touch with the beating pulse of this generation. All the articles also have convenient discussion boards in the right-hand margins to encourage feedback and interaction and to create a dynamic layer of new content. In many cases, these discussion threads are more interesting than the article itself, says Strang. "We can watch when certain hot buttons are hit—gay marriage, election, social justice, the church. We can see it first-hand and it influences the articles we plan for the magazine. Through our member-created content, we have a lifeline that tells us what matters to our community."

Tap into the brand community for ideas, course corrections, and opportunities.

Relevant magazine has two editorial meetings each week. At most of these meetings, the director of the online magazine will bring a Web site printout with a sizzling discussion thread or a new issue that the community is rallying around. In addition, there are hundreds of writers pitching magazine articles and new book concepts every month. Relevant is literally bombarded with ideas that clearly represent what matters to this community.

Leverage your international connections.

Because of its global reach, the Relevant brand doesn't feel like it's based in any specific region of the United States or even the world, but has a fully developed brand personality influenced by community members in the United Kingdom, Canada, and Australia. This helps to broaden the brand's outlook and the ideas reflected in its content. For example, U.K. and Canadian members can offer a different perspective on the war in Iraq and other international concerns—all through a spiritual lens. Relevant actively solicits articles and books from several international authors to ensure that the brand has fresh voices and global perspectives.

Crawl, walk, run.

The Relevant team is extremely careful about its marketing. According to Strang, the company simply can't throw money at brand awareness. Instead, they leverage existing assets and ensure that each media property supports the others. Rather than diving headfirst into a new venture, Relevant takes a crawl, walk, then run approach. They scope out the opportunity; find a way to try it out; dive in to a specific, measurable project; and test on the fly, then course correct.

Using the crawl, walk, run method allows Relevant to stay responsive without investing too much time or money in an ill-fitting direction. The company recently built a small studio in their offices for filming videos and recording broadcasts. They have the talent, so they can do unusual things such as market book titles with online videos, ask authors to read aloud and record a downloadable chapter, and use a viral approach to spread the word.

The studio has also made it simple for the company to create podcasts. The cost is relatively low, but Relevant takes the time to make them sound good. Strang and his team created the first podcast as an experiment, and were surprised when their show immediately hit the Top 100 Podcasts on Apple's iTunes site. Assured of a decent return on their investment, they now record a weekly podcast that covers entertainment news, discusses current events and content covered in upcoming issues of the magazine, and provides a behind-the-scenes update on what's happening at Relevant.

Don't be afraid of the beta version.

In the spirit of Google and Amazon, Relevant took the leap and launched a new version of their Web site in beta form. The team's ambitious plans for the sophomore version of the Web site resulted in several delays in the launch date. Meanwhile, the brand community was getting restless, sending e-mails and comments expressing their impatience and frustration. Relevant decided to launch before all the pieces were in place and to receive feedback on the core site. Every month they would add a few new features, and the members helped them to work out the bugs. In the end, this process became a great way to build loyal community members. The new features were highly anticipated—almost like a new gift each month. Now Relevant embraces beta launches because they engage the community at a deeper level.

If rolled out properly, a beta program can invite productive dialogue between customers, opinion makers, outside software developers, and the organization developing the software or service. Launching a new service as a beta program communicates to your customers that you want their input and care about their feedback. That's a powerful message.

WORKBOOK

Get Started

1. **Do a social and moral audit of your company.**
   At no other time has a company's ethical/moral stance toward its employees, its customers, and society as a whole been more important. What is your brand communicating through its actions and words to the marketplace? Go outside your company and talk to members of your brand community (customers, board members, employees, prospects) to learn what message is really being translated.
2. **Use spiritual themes in your creative messaging.**
   Tap into values such as spirituality, personal growth, and going inward in your creative messaging. Make a list of three brands that you feel have successfully reflected the "going inward" spirit in their advertising and messaging. Analyze the wording they use, the context and storylines they draw from, and the emotions they elicit. Use this exercise as a launch point for creating new taglines, themes, and storylines for your own brand.
3. **Use modern media to build community.**
   The Connected Generation is hungry for content, media, entertainment, and community with a spiritual bent. Clarify what segment of this passionate core you want to serve, get to know these people well by visiting as many Web sites and reading as many magazines as you can, and create a powerful and specific architecture for participation.
4. **Hit the right notes.**
   In general, this movement does not reflect an outward display of religion, but rather an inner spiritual hunger. Be sure to

work with members of the brand community to learn what is important to them, and don't rely on tired and false stereotypes. Make a list of what you think you know about the spiritual interests of your customers and what you need to learn in order to create materials and messages that resonate. Dive deep into these areas through existing and new research channels.

Go for It.

As a creative challenge, make it your goal to envision a new product, service, or media offering in your industry that would powerfully attract and meet the needs of today's spiritually hungry twenty- to thirtysomethings. Think of how Ilkone i800 expanded the role of a typical cell phone to be spiritually relevant and efficient for the Islamic community. The goal here is to go beyond the surface and to truly address the needs and desires of your spiritually hungry audience.

Identify one area of your brand (or a competitor's brand) that's already tapping into the craving of this generation to go inward. Take this initial effort and envision what it would look like if you expanded and stretched into multiple forms of media. For example, Relevant Media Group might consider creating daily content such as quotes or spiritually based questions that could be downloaded onto cell phones or by designing journals and daily Bible studies that integrate music.

TEN

GIVE BACK

Redefining Volunteerism and
the Meaning of Contribution

It was a case of working smarter, not harder. Community Awareness and Treatment Services (CATS)—a San Francisco–based nonprofit that had served the area's most at-risk homeless populations for over twenty-five years—was scrambling. Government funding cuts had dwindled their revenues and CATS was fighting just to keep the doors open. There were many questions and few answers: Should they solicit volunteers to help raise more funds? Recruit additional substance abuse counselors to donate their time and expertise?

The cavalry arrived in the form of a high-tech quintet of newbie volunteers courtesy of the Taproot Foundation, an organization that matches willing volunteers with nonprofits in need. These five experienced marketing professionals were drawn from some of the city's top firms and were brought together to provide graphic design, photography, copywriting, marketing strategy, and planning. Together they were ready to provide what CATS needed most—a well-branded marketing brochure to make their fund-raising efforts more effective.

With government dollars shrinking, CATS needed to reach out to new funding sources, including foundations and individual donors. But the organization desperately lacked clear, compelling marketing collateral for fund-raising and community education purposes. Their existing marketing materials were terribly outdated and didn't reflect their mission or explain their comprehensive network of treatment services. CATS asked the Taproot Foundation for help.

Taproot awarded CATS with a print brochure service grant (worth approximately $15,000) to jump-start the organization's marketing efforts. The five-member volunteer service grant team worked closely with CATS to create a compelling, professional brochure, beginning with three potential creative directions and messaging treatments.

CATS chose the new slogan "We reach farther to reach more," which succinctly explains the breadth of the organization's treatment services, including alcohol and substance abuse outreach, HIV/AIDS counseling, and much more.

The volunteers collaborated to further develop the layout, imagery, and copy. They also conducted a series of in-depth interviews with CATS' clients and staff to build a testimonial library that the organization could use for future marketing and fund-raising projects. The team's volunteer photographer produced a stunning photographic series that lends a poignant human face to homelessness—and captures the spirit of CATS' clients.

Over three months, team members each contributed five or six hours a week to the project and developed a persuasive brochure that told the CATS story with clear language and compelling design. The volunteers even worked closely with CATS throughout the revision process and helped to select a top-quality local printer.

The results were dramatic. After the brochure was released, individual donations to CATS surged a full 50 percent over the course of a year. Staff members were thrilled. "Our Taproot Foundation service grant provided us with much more than a brochure," said Teri Sideikas, development director at CATS. "It taught us how to tell our story and gave us the confidence to promote our organization in the community."

The new brochure also generated some unexpected results. Many local homeless people who had never visited CATS arrived at the center with the brochure in hand. Clearly, the marketing message had reached more than just potential donors.

The volunteers were equally thrilled with the project results. "This has been the most rewarding experience of my ten-year marketing career," Rebecca Rozanski told the Taproot Foundation. "I was able to make an important and tangible contribution to a great nonprofit organization, meet amazing people and gain an understanding of core issues facing our community."[1]

The innovative nonprofit is funded primarily through financial grants from sources that recognize the remarkable value of human capital and how Taproot Foundation can stretch their dollars. Many top organizations, including the Robin Hood Foundation, Draper Richards Foundation, Peninsula Community Foundation, Cisco Systems, and United Way of New York City, are supporting Taproot's award winning model.

VOLUNTEERING REDEFINED

Welcome to volunteering redefined for a new generation. The Taproot Foundation is the brainchild of Aaron Hurst, grandson of J. E. Slater, who served in the Kennedy administration and wrote the original blueprint for the Peace Corps. At age thirty-one, Hurst has successfully engaged a new generation of young professionals in volunteer service projects. Hurst estimates that about 90 percent of Taproot's volunteers are in their twenties and thirties, and that at least 47 percent are donating their skills and work hours to a charity or nonprofit for the first time.

Hurst says Taproot's strategic, carefully structured format is the foundation's key to success for engaging a new generation of eager volunteers. Modeled after the pro bono service assignments that have become a core element of the legal profession, Taproot encourages nonprofits to apply for projects that meet their needs in order to be matched with teams of skilled volunteers from the corporate sector. Taproot then provides coordination, tracking, and translation services to ensure the project runs smoothly and successfully for everyone involved.

The Taproot Foundation provides a variety of service grants focused on three main needs: fund-raising and marketing, information technology, and talent management. For example, marketing grants include brand identity (naming and logos), annual reports, brochures, basic Web sites, and advanced Web site development. Each service grant has specific deliverables and will typically be completed in less than sixteen weeks. Each volunteer on the team donates about five hours per week.

The Taproot Foundation has three overarching goals:

1. To build the capacity of individual nonprofit agencies by helping to develop their infrastructure in such critical areas as

marketing/fund-raising, information technology, and human resources—infrastructure that is taken for granted in the private sector.

2. To redefine volunteering by giving business professionals the opportunity to apply their existing skills and expertise to deepen the impact of social change organizations.

3. To break down barriers between the business and nonprofit sectors.

Just like his grandfather, Hurst believes that by working together as peers, we can bridge seemingly insurmountable barriers. Collaboration between business and nonprofit professionals toward common goals not only strengthens communities but also helps to remove cross-sector discrimination. The prestigious Ashoka Fellowship has even named Hurst as one of the top social entrepreneurs in the world for his innovative vision of community-based social change and for engaging a new generation of volunteers.

Taproot has clearly struck a nerve. Since 2001, over 250 nonprofit organizations have received an estimated $12 million in pro bono work from eight hundred volunteer professionals through the Taproot Foundation. The foundation currently receives over two hundred applications a month from potential volunteers. Four in ten project veterans ask for a new assignment as soon as they wrap an existing project, and more than nine in ten say they'd like to participate again in the future. Many Taproot volunteers also go on to become trustees or to donate money to the nonprofit organizations that they have helped.[2]

THE CRAVING: TO GIVE BACK

There's a new spirit of volunteerism underfoot—led by a young, Connected Generation that has different ideas about how to give back. In 2004, approximately 65 million people performed volunteer work, according to the U.S. Bureau of Labor Statistics. In most cases, what motivates the under-forty set to give back is very different from what inspired their counterparts just a generation ago.

Today's volunteers want to give their time and talents instead of just writing a check. In a 2001 report, the United Way of America said that members of Generation X are demanding more information about organizations before providing a cash gift; they tend to distrust large organizations; and are more likely than their predecessors to choose volunteer activities that provide challenges and social connections.[3] Gen X has shifted the giving model away from hierarchical, corporate-backed organizations (think Red Cross and United Way) and toward grassroots, hands-on, episodic volunteering in their local communities. This could mean helping with a community literacy program, heading up a city recycling campaign, or organizing a Race for the Cure running team.

While members of Gen X are more likely to attend college than their parents, many people under forty are facing economic hardships that were not common in previous generations. Gen X is statistically more likely to carry student loan and credit card debt, which can make it difficult for them to give financially. The rocky economy has not been kind to this age group, either. The technology boom of the late 1990s turned some into millionaires, but many more have struggled through layoffs, relied on working spouses to help pay the bills, and in some cases even moved back home to live with parents for a while.[4] But despite the economic hardships, this group does want to give back. A poll released in January 2005 by Monster.com reported that 66 percent of its users planned to seek volunteer work in 2005, up from 54 percent in 2004.[5] And Ami Dar, director of Idealist.org, said that site traffic had doubled in two years to reach 35,000 visitors a day in early 2005.[6]

With a passion for social justice and a burning desire to make a difference, Generation Y is donating more of its time to charitable causes than perhaps any other generation in history. According to Leslie Lenkowsky, a professor at The Center on Philanthropy at Indiana University, 90 percent of college-bound high-school students volunteer. Recent University of California surveys of college freshmen show a rising interest in politics, public life, and citizenship for the first time in decades. The fifteen-year-old Teach for America program is receiving a record number of applications from top college graduates willing to bypass jobs in law firms and Fortune 500 companies to spend two years teaching in low-income public schools. About seven-teen thousand applied for two thousand jobs in 2005, four times the number that tried in 2000.

Gen Y's social conscience has often been attributed to self-esteem–based parenting from the Boomers, the focus on giving back in their school programs during the 1990s, and the strong message from schools, homes, and churches that individuals can truly make a difference. This group has heard community-minded messages throughout their young lives, and routinely participated in recycling programs, toy drives, and fund-raising activities. The terrorist attacks of September 11, the shootings at Columbine and other American schools, plus news of natural disasters from around the globe have further heightened this generation's resolve to contribute and give back.

Many U.S. high schools have also made volunteer service hours a requirement for graduation. Students at Columbia Junior-Senior High School in Columbia, Pennsylvania, for instance, must complete a total of forty service hours between seventh and twelfth grades. Counselor Peggy Woods says that some students reach as many as five hundred hours by graduation, whereas others wait to put in their required forty until it's almost too late. But for many, this early vol-unteer experience gives many young people a taste for contribution without financial or material reward.[7]

Volunteer vacations are also making their way into the headlines as people continue to seek innovative and meaningful ways to spend their free time. A new reality television show called *Voluntouring* is in the works, and new organizations such as Voluntours organizes "travel with purpose" for its service-oriented clients.

The Connected Generation is determined to make a difference. This group embraces organizations and missions that are close to their hearts and that provide highly interactive, potentially transfor-mative ways to participate. It's an attitude that is influencing their career choices and shaping how they spend their downtime and vacations. In many cases, this motivated generation is interweaving career aspirations and mission-driven desires in a highly synergistic way.

WHY WE WANT TO GIVE BACK

1. **We want a chance to make a difference.**

   The Connected Generation has a burning, growing desire to make a difference and to use their lives for the greater good. This group is finding ways to include service and passion-driven community action in both their free time and their careers. Globally aware, technologically fluent, and often well traveled, this generation is finding innovative and exciting new ways to make contributing more visible, tangible, and even more fun.

2. **We have a heightened awareness of the world.**

   The images and headlines say it all. Earthquake-ravaged nations, a tsunami that swept in without warning, poverty and AIDS in Africa, plus a vast range of problems right in our own backyards—it's impossible to ignore how much need exists in every corner of the globe. The vast range of media technologies and the speed at which we hear news of critical problems seem to accelerate each day. This generation is hyperaware of everything from environmental problems to social justice issues and natural disasters. Today, sitting back in the comfort of our material blessings and ignoring widespread need is simply not an option.

3. **People we admire are giving back and making a difference.**

   Giving back is more creative, high profile, and fashionable than ever. Oprah has turned her media empire into a force for global change, harnessing viewers to successfully capture pedophiles, expose global human rights issues, and send celebrities to help in the wake of Hurricane Katrina. U2 lead singer Bono has been active and outspoken through his DATA organization, and the Live 8 concerts connected many of today's most popular bands with important fund-raising initiatives. Celebrities are putting social contributions square in the spotlight. Their impassioned and authentic efforts are also demonstrating new ways to use media and entertainment in order to make a difference.

4. **We see a chance to lead and step into more skilled positions.**

   The Connected Generation rarely waits around for anything. They are starting their own businesses and morphing entire industries with their Internet-fueled habits (hello, Napster) and linking with like-minded people to create change. Corporate structures might prevent this group from immediately assuming influential positions, but the volunteer arena is ripe for young, inspired, and passionate people to innovate and take the lead, learning as they go and forging new paths along the way.

Volunteering can serve a dual purpose. It's a perfect chance to gain professional or business skills, enhance a sparse résumé, prepare for a new career, or learn applicable, on-the-job skills. A U.S. Conference Board survey found that most executives believe volunteer participation builds skills and changes attitudes, including respect for diversity and a willingness to take risks. Many people have starry-eyed visions of a dream job or a particular industry without ever tasting the day-to-day reality. Volunteer work, however, can provide instant access to these areas and help people decide whether the fantasy will really match their skills, talents and expectations.

5. **We want to connect to our communities in meaningful (and contemporary) ways.**

    Traditional, community-based clubs often have aging members, a dated focus, and rigid structures that instantly spell turn-off for this Connected Generation. But just because they're not joining the Shriners or the Kiwanis Club doesn't mean that they don't want to feel connected to the community and to contribute to its health and success. Modern volunteer associations often combine fresh structures with fun people and a chance to make meaningful, direct connections with the community. This group wants to give back—they just don't want to do it the old way.

6. **There are opportunities for new friendships and professional connections.**

    Today's typical twenty- or thirtysomething stays in a job for only three years, maximum. That means there's a whole lot of moving from one city to another and reshuffling of social lives. Without the built-in networks that used to come from college communities and hometowns, this group looks for significant ways to meet kindred spirits. "A lot of folks, especially in our generation, don't have the social structure that once existed," says Taproot's Hurst. "This generation is so much more mobile than any other generation. They're very hungry and looking to connect with people who share their same values. They want to feel at home and are looking for social networks." Creating a way for volunteers to regularly connect and build bonds is becoming a prerequisite for modern social action groups.

Volunteering can often also put the candidate in pretty good professional company. A community's best-known movers and shakers often lead nonprofit boards and control corporate purse strings. In short, volunteering can provide invaluable networks, professional recommendations, and even on-the-job promotions.

7. **We seek meaningful adventure.**

Fulfillment and transformation drive the mythology of social contribution, not to mention many bestselling novels and box office hits. This generation believes that if you give your time and effort in a selfless way, not only will you make a difference, but you will return from the journey—literal or otherwise—changed in some important way. A season of service can present a unique sort of inner and outer personal adventure. The Connected Generation is eager to embark on this meaningful journey.

8. **We have more free time and resources to give.**

Time, or the perceived lack of those precious hours, is often the main reason why people don't volunteer. When children enter the picture, it can be even more difficult to devote the time and energy to projects outside the home. Some parents feel like they're neglecting their families if they spend evenings or weekends volunteering. Instead, many parents focus their volunteer hours on projects that support their children, such as coaching the soccer team or working in the school library for a day. But the Connected Generation is marrying and having children later in life, so they have more opportunities to enjoy volunteer activities without a complex layer of guilt.

9. **We are desperate to find meaning before transitions such as grad school or a new career.**

The "gap year" is a tradition that has long been popular overseas. This British term refers to an extended absence (usually one year) from full-time education, which high-school students take after graduation but before beginning college or university. The details vary, but some students travel, others work, and many combine both pursuits into an international working holiday. More U.S. youth are beginning to embrace this tradition, and international volunteering is one of the most popular options for gap year students, also known as "gappers." After the 2004 tsunami disaster in South Asia, many volunteers there were students on a gap year.[8]

This trend has also expanded past college-age students. The career gap refers to people twenty-five years or older who want to change careers or explore a vastly different path before they wake up fifteen years later and realize that they weren't satisfying their passions and using their gifts.

10. **We hope to find our true calling.**

Youth and idealism seem to go hand in hand—a good thing, by most accounts. Many people believe that they were put on this planet to make a difference, and the Connected Generation is searching for meaning a lot earlier than their parents (remember the recently defined "quarter life crisis" phenomenon?). There's a growing hunger among younger generations to identify their unique role in this world and to make a life-altering contribution. At the center of this generation beats a heart that desperately longs to make a difference. They will continue to find fresh ways to fulfill that vision.

LESSONS FROM THE TAPROOT FOUNDATION

Understand the players before you design the game.

The Taproot model thrives because Aaron Hurst deeply understands the people and the volunteers that he targets. He felt it was critical to know not just the needs of the nonprofit organizations but also of the volunteers he wanted to engage beyond their day-to-day careers.

Hurst began laying the groundwork for the Taproot Foundation during college and then spent nearly ten years conducting due diligence. He designed his own community service–based learning major at the University of Michigan at Ann Arbor, and created a program in which he and his fellow students taught creative writing to local prison inmates. After graduation, he worked for the DePaul Center for Education, documenting best practices in education, and later for the Chicago Education Foundation, a group that provides small grants to teachers.

It was in Chicago that Hurst got up close and personal with the serious constraints facing nonprofits of every sort, and where he developed the idea for Taproot. As this initial spark of inspiration grew, he realized that a deeper understanding of the business world would be imperative to Taproot's success. So Hurst spent the next five years in the private sector learning the subtleties of project management and figuring out what it takes to effectively run a business. His for-profit business experiences only affirmed his gnawing belief that corporate executives want to give back to their communities but often lack opportunities or entry points. His suit-and-tie days also gave him a firm grasp of the structured, yet independent, work environment that his volunteers would thrive in.

See unmet needs and determine why they remain unaddressed.

People who give money to the homeless, natural disaster victims, or environmental preservationists often wonder what their dollars are actually funding. They hope that the money will reach the intended recipients, but many worry that it will be squandered on administrative costs and unnecessary spending. There's an unspoken assumption that nonprofits will not spend donated money on salaries, cushy offices, or slick marketing materials.

Hurst decided that there was a major problem with aspects of this assumption. He saw cohesive, professional marketing materials as an essential tool for connecting nonprofits with potential backers. Organizations that lacked professional brochures and had foggy mission statements or confusing, poorly designed Web sites might never hit the radar of prospective donors. "Marketing equals fund-raising," explains Hurst.

Taproot focuses the bulk of its service grants on helping nonprofits create slick logos, Web sites, and information brochures that stand up against for-profit businesses and savvy mainstream brands. In today's crowded market, clear and attractive communications materials are a necessity, not a luxury. Nonprofits that receive Tap-root grants often say that the main strength of the program is how it provides "talent" grants rather than dollars, freeing the organizations from scrutiny about how they spend each and every cent. One recipient commented, "We had so many needs that we never would have taken $25,000 in cash and used it on a branding project."

The Taproot model bypasses the politics, instead delivering skills, talents, and expertise that create high-impact solutions to often pro-duce generous increases in giving.

Harness technology to connect and organize people and projects.

Taproot works hard to make volunteering easy, and its Web site is central to that mission. Well organized and highly detailed, the site provides nonprofits and volunteers with a complete picture of the opportunity, answers their questions, and provides everything they need to sign up.

Taproot isn't the only organization that embraces technology to reach a new generation of volunteers. Charities and local govern-ments from New York City to Fort Collins, Colorado, are using twenty-first–century tools to sustain volunteer projects. Many now list their activities on interactive Web sites and databases, update the information daily, and send regular e-mail messages to stay in touch with a growing cadre of volunteers. Effective use of the Web is expanding how charitable organizations can serve and provide a smooth point of entry for new volunteers.

Case Study—DonorsChoose.org

What if giving money to a specific charitable need were as easy as buying a first-edition Hemingway novel on eBay? You could simply pick what you wanted to fund based on the description, send your money electronically, and instead of a box arriving with yellowing pages, you would get a feedback pack-age brimming with student photos and thank-you notes, a letter from their teacher, and an expenditure report confirming that the tax-deductible gift was spent as directed.

DonorsChoose.org redefines traditional charitable giving by connecting teachers directly with donors. Teachers often spend their own money for supplies or abandon their creative plans due to lack of resources. With DonorsChoose, they can appeal to citizen philanthropists to fund their learning projects. The model is equally attractive to donors who, instead of blindly writing checks, can choose from a variety of worthy projects (small and large) to bankroll.

In Alameda, California, a middle-school newspaper and yearbook adviser is asking for a computer that would enable students to type their stories. Cost: around $1,300. In Winston-Salem, North Carolina, a first-grade teacher wants the technology to let her young readers listen to books on tape. Cost: under $700. And in Flushing, New York, a fifth-grade teacher at Public School 165 is trying to scare up five beanbag chairs for her library. Cost: under $200.

DonorsChoose launched in 2000, and as of January 24, 2006, over eight thousand individuals from fifty different states had donated more than $5 million dollars to 306,017 students. Nearly 70 percent of all requests are funded within two months. The most popular donations include classroom supplies, books, technology, and field trips, and a full 80 percent of these resources are reused by the following year's students. The organization's "citizen philanthropists" come from all walks of life, and at least 75 percent of donors have never given before to public schools.

DonorsChoose is the brainchild of former public high-school teacher Charles Best. This twenty-nine-year-old Yale University grad envisioned this innovative charity during his first year teaching at Wings Academy in the Bronx, New York. He and his colleagues often sat around the staff lounge dreaming up school projects that they couldn't afford. Best figured that there were probably plenty of people who would rather fork over a bit of cash for a specific classroom project than write a check to a traditional charity. It seems he was right.[9]

Help people "give what they know."

Taproot is built on the proven pro bono model because Hurst understood that the Connected Generation often finds it more satisfying to apply their well-honed skills to a service project instead of chopping vegetables or answering phones. Giving back with personal talents can make volunteers feel like they're contributing something valuable, rather than just filling a slot. Naming experts, for instance, are enlisted to create new business names and ID systems that clearly communicate the nonprofit's mission while graphic designers volunteer to create annual reports and fund-raising materials. "It's amazing how many of them want to be involved in the community, but they don't want their time to be wasted," says Hurst.

This savvy generation wants to use their skills to produce tangible results for deserving nonprofits. There's still a group that seeks a change of pace from the cubicle jungle by serving soup or building a habitat house on the weekend, but Taproot gathers volunteers who see great value in offering their professional talents and expertise.

Appeal to highly skilled and educated potential volunteers.

If you take the most talented business professionals and ask them to volunteer their well-honed talents to aid nonprofits, everyone benefits. The Taproot Foundation staffs their service grants with some of the best marketing talent available in their communities, including VP-level professionals. Taproot is not afraid to recruit from a highly skilled pool, and shows other organizations that it's worth exploring the deepest levels of their volunteers' abilities and experience.

Case Study—Teach for America

Teaching is a notoriously low-paying profession, and according to a report by the National Council on Teacher Quality, the profession attracts a "disproportionately high number of candidates from the lower end of the distribution of academic ability." Enter Teach for America, whose members typically have an

average G.P.A. of 3.5, top credentials, experience with children, and a strong determination to get results. For a surprisingly
large number of bright young people, Teach for America has
become a natural next step after college graduation. This popular organization sends recent college graduates into poor rural
and urban schools for two years with the same pay and benefits
as other beginning teachers at those schools. The nation's top
college talent is practically lining up to participate. In 2005,
Teach for America drew applications from 12 percent of Yale's
graduates and 11 percent of Dartmouth's graduating class, and
attracted 8 percent from both Harvard and Princeton. The
organization also recruits for diversity, receiving applications
from 12 percent of the graduates at Spelman College, a historically black women's college in Atlanta. In total, a record 17,350
recent college graduates applied to Teach for America 2005, and
the organization accepted about a third of the year's Ivy League
applicants and about a sixth of all applications.[10]

Structure the volunteer process using proven business practices and models.

The Taproot Foundation combines the efficiencies of traditional vol-
unteer-matching services with the quality management practices of
leading business consulting firms. This enables the foundation to
assign volunteers to the most appropriate projects for their skills and
to ensure the timely delivery of quality professional services.

The Taproot process is detailed yet streamlined, and above all, well
executed. Volunteer involvement begins after completing a straightforward online application form and a simple interview with a Taproot staff member. The interview is designed to ensure that the
applicant's volunteering experience will be a good match with his or
her skills, available time, and interests. Next, the applicant attends one
of the monthly two-hour orientation sessions. At this point, the volunteer is logged into the database. Taproot then notifies volunteers
when there's a team opening that matches their skill set, and volunteers can choose whether or not to participate. A seasoned volunteer
leader supports each assembled group throughout the five-to-six-

month project, with a final client presentation meeting. Finally, Taproot receives project evaluations from all team members and nonprofit contacts. Next up, celebration for a job well done.

Build in management systems for accountability.

Strategic due diligence is a hallmark of the Taproot program. Each volunteer team includes appropriate creative talent and an experienced volunteer project manager who serves as a liaison between clients and volunteers—making sure that expectations are reasonable and the work proceeds on schedule. Taproot grants come with firm deadlines, typically about six months from the project launch. Individual workloads ebb and flow throughout the process, but the project manager ensures that it doesn't fall into pro bono never-never land.

All the volunteers know exactly what is expected at the outset, thanks to a clear project blueprint that helps them schedule the work around family life, full-time jobs or planned vacations. In return, Taproot's structure delivers results that often surpass the private sector. Since 2001, volunteer managers and their teams have delivered 85 percent of the pro bono projects on schedule. Of these projects, 95 percent of grant recipients rated the value of the deliverable as "high."

Tap into established communities to find talent.

To build a capable volunteer pool, Taproot has homed in on twenty- and thirtysomethings who have marketing, project management, and high-tech career experience. As veteran volunteers discuss their projects and positive experiences, they naturally recruit others from both their professional and personal networks. Monthly gatherings and social events keep the connections strong and continually expand the volunteer base.

Case Study—Chill by Burton Snowboards

Burton Snowboards has found a similar hotbed of talent in colleges and universities for their nonprofit organization. Chill is an international intervention program that takes disadvantaged inner-city kids snowboarding once a week for six weeks and provides them with everything they need to have an incredible experience on the slopes, including lift tickets, instruction, bus transportation, and head-to-toe gear. Launched by Burton Snowboards, Chill is a nonprofit organization that recruits a passionate group of volunteer snowboard instructors from colleges.

When the Chill bus pulls into the parking lot, forty-five or fifty very excited kids pour out, ready to conquer the hill. Most are unfamiliar with their surroundings and their equipment, but they're eager to become snowboarders and catch air on the half-pipe.

Chill has fourteen program sites that attract reliable and enthusiastic volunteers. The college students are eager to help because they love to snowboard and want to share their expertise with others—to have a personal and direct impact. Chill gives these student volunteers the chance to work directly with the most enthusiastic of learners, disadvantaged inner-city kids. It's an incredible source of personal fulfillment, plus Chill offers free lift tickets to volunteers and gives them the chance to ride before and after the kids arrive. It's an attractive opportunity to indulge their passion for snowboarding and give back to the community in a single shot.

The formal structure of postsecondary education offers additional incentives for organizations like Chill. Many colleges now make it a pregraduation requirement that students "give back" to their communities, so they are already involved in clubs that organize dances, concerts, and other events to raise money for nonprofits. This spirit of contribution has a powerful ripple effect. For example, Chill increasingly sees college students who want to organize benefit events on behalf of the program.

Students from New York University's snowboarding club have successfully held a spring dance during the last three years that raised between $5,000 and $8,000 annually for the Chill organization. Many colleges also require students to get hands-on work experience through an internship or coop program. Chill has worked with many students who have made significant time contributions in exchange for college credit and professional experience.[11]

Clearly define the tasks and expectations.

Time is our most valuable currency. Taproot understands that many would-be volunteers shy away from projects or organizations because they feel that their time will be wasted or they simply don't have enough free hours to contribute. The Taproot Web site provides a detailed description of each role that team members will play, including key benefits, related skills, and alternate titles. Volunteers begin their experience with a clear understanding of how they fit into the project and what is expected of them. This limits the possibility of ballooning job descriptions or unmanageable expectations. Instead, volunteers feel confident about their work and can openly express any potential fears or concerns.

Leverage best practices.

At Taproot, volunteers can access customized project blueprints designed by executives from top consulting agencies. Each type of service grant has a step-by-step roadmap for organizing the team, executing the project, and providing the deliverable in the most effective way possible. These proven strategies give shape to the projects, get all the team members on the same page, and eliminate the confusion and leadership issues often associated with bringing new groups together for the first time to accomplish a task.

Streamline live and virtual group communications
for maximum efficiency.

Although the Taproot teams do occasionally meet to collaborate and connect with the client, a good portion of their volunteer work can be done independently from home. The bulk of the work is accomplished virtually through Yahoo groups, phone calls, and e-mail. This structure creates a more flexible volunteer experience and helps team members to seamlessly integrate the work with career, family and free time.

Lower the financial barriers to giving back.

Cash flow can prevent many people from giving back. "In the first ten or fifteen years of a career, people have limited money-giving ability, but they can offer a relatively significant donation of time and skills," says Hurst. "The average Taproot volunteer donates five to seven thousand dollars in work, and they could never have given that much in cash." Taproot overcomes financial limitations by accessing professional talents.

Support the desire to build relationships and forge ongoing social connections.

No matter where you are in your career, volunteering is a great way to build a solid network of friends and colleagues. From planned get-togethers to informal relationships and friendships, the social aspect of volunteering has never been so important. Taproot has noticed a grassroots social network forming within its organization, where groups will naturally cluster around their skill sets. For example, a large group of Web site designers might meet to discuss how they could improve the Taproot business model (Hurst says even he has been surprised by volunteers' passion for improving the process), then follow up the "official" business with conversations, drinks, or dinner.

Case Study—One Brick

One Brick is bringing a social-networking element to volunteering, providing a fun and rewarding way to give back to the community. Their concept of casual volunteering fits people's busy lives, and rather than requiring an ongoing commitment, it enables volunteers to join only the events that suit their schedules and interests—turning volunteer work into a choice rather than a chore.

Volunteers simply RSVP to the events they can, and want to, attend, arriving ready to work and meet new people. Examples of One Brick projects include sorting food for the community food banks, cleaning up neighborhood parks, building and cleaning children's playground facilities, and providing staff-power for athletic events, marathons, and fund-raisers.

One Brick provides San Francisco–area nonprofit organizations with the labor and sweat equity they need to achieve their goals. The organization also encourages its volunteers to meet and mingle. After each event, volunteers gather at a local restaurant or bar to eat, drink, and keep the conversations flowing. One Brick also organizes social activities such as happy hours, hikes, camping trips, cooking classes, wine tastings, and rock climbing. These "extracurricular" events help volunteers to strengthen the relationships they've developed at the community projects and develop a stronger social network in their own lives.

WORKBOOK

Get Started

1. **Identify a cause that stirs your staff and customers.**
   The pressure for brands to differentiate themselves from competitors is more intense than ever, and finding a cause that customers can embrace is one way to leap ahead. "There are people who will travel further and pay a bit more if they'll feel better about their purchasing decision," says Joe Marconi, consultant and author of a book on cause marketing. *The IEG Sponsorship Report,* a Chicago trade publication, also estimates that companies spent $991 million on cause marketing in 2004, up 57 percent from 1999.[12]

2. **Avoid being overt or too commercial in your cause marketing.**
   Cause marketers have to keep the overt brand building to a whisper, or they risk turning off the very people that they're trying to woo. Teenagers and twentysomethings, especially, can smell advertising a mile away, says Carol Cone, CEO of the marketing consultancy Cone Inc. There's no swoosh on Nike's yellow band, for example, just the word "LiveStrong." According to Nike's Burns, "It's what Lance believes in." This subtle approach is an admirable turn from the shameless self-promotion of many charity sponsors. And for Nike, it's profitable as well.

3. **Attract young talent through skill-building opportunities.**

   Train younger volunteers in the skills and competencies that will not only help your organization but truly interest them. They love win-win contractual relationships.

4. **Make it simple to give your charity's projects as a gift.**

   DonorsChoose makes it easy for philanthropists to give school projects as gifts. The donor can recognize someone special by funding a project in his or her honor. The donor gets the tax deduction and the classroom acknowledges the recipient. In many cases, parents use this tool to introduce their children to philanthropy.

Go for It.

What are the core concerns of your target audience, and how can you connect your cause to these concerns? Consider how Burton's Chill program linked passionate young snowboarders with underprivileged kids who were eager to try the sport.

Taproot Foundation and DonorsChoose.org are powerful because their innovative business models link volunteers and donors to deserving recipients in meaningful and efficient ways. How can you create an online business model for your current charitable project that fully leverages the ease, simplicity, and instant gratification available through the Internet?

THE NEW PLAYERS
YOU NEED TO KNOW

"What's next?"

This is the question that always stumps people. By now, you probably have a strong, real-world understanding of the values and cravings that drive this brave new marketplace. But when it's time to move forward, there may still be a lot of questions lingering in your mind: Should we hire a consultant? Build a new division? Whom do we give this project to? Can I tackle this on my own, and, if yes, how?

To set out on a plan of action, here are the new key players you simply must have—or have access to—in your organization, regardless of size or budget. No matter what industry you're in, no matter the size of your organization, and no matter the actual job descriptions, you want at least one person on your staff who has the following five sets of talents and skills—you simply can't build compelling brands for the Connected Generation without them. Even if you're a solo entrepreneur, these are the people you will need to find as strategic partners.

1. **Content strategists**

    Born storytellers and communicators, content strategists explore how company content intersects with user- and community-driven content. Strategists understand what people want to know, what they want to share, and how to connect the dots to build a clear roadmap for participants. Content strategists tend to work with everyone in the organization but must collaborate closely with tech experts and high-level managers.

Content strategists assess all existing communication channels and materials (including Web sites, blogs, brochures, ads, podcasts, white papers, and video files), work with internal managers to envision new directions and possibilities (technologies, language, tone, new approaches), and create a workable plan to develop content that will cut through the clutter and deliver the brand messages in a compelling, authentic manner.

These new professionals are not just repurposed PR specialists. They do not build brand profiles or work to get messages into the news media. Content strategists are more like internal auditors—analyzing, planning and often creating the content from the inside out in a way that defines the organization. Strategists see patterns and they know how to match big picture brand goals with specific content possibilities. They ask the hard questions and cut through the spin.

Content strategists' core competencies include:

- clustering
- observing
- planning
- distilling
- storytelling
- writing
- assessing
- creating

As children, content strategists were:

- Finishers and doers with concrete, specific solutions
- Listeners who synthesized ideas and made them work
- Creative types who wrote the scripts, built the stories, and figured out how to make the school play better
- Diplomats who could move in and out of different social groups with ease
- A quiet voice of reason when people were yelling and overflowing with ideas
- Imaginative dreamers who still had their feet on the ground
- Dangerously inconspicuous

Content strategists' three-question tool kit:

- What do we want to say?
- How are we going to say it?
- In what formats will we say it?

2. **Community connectors**

Community connectors are the nurturers who maintain diverse personal and professional circles and always get the inside scoop. Community connectors have razor-sharp social instincts. They know how to work with people from a wide range of interests and backgrounds, and they naturally put everyone at ease.

Connectors move between the company and the brand community to learn what each group wants, and then figure out how to satisfy their different interests. They listen to the community, making them feel heard and valued, and convey their desires back to the organization. Connectors anticipate social needs and suggest new things that will support the community. They understand what makes Epinions reviewers tick, for example, or what the DJs at a Scion event will think is utterly cool.

As communities work closely with brands to refine products and develop new services, the community connector is a critical team member with a 24/7 lifeline to the brand population. One caveat: Community connectors must always be insiders. They can't be outsiders who are "trying to see what the young people want," or fiftysomething men aiming to connect with new moms. Outsiders won't be embraced. Connectors must be members of a community in which they are known, respected, supported and trusted.

Community connectors' core competencies include:

- nurturing
- speaking
- communicating
- facilitating
- listening
- understanding
- anticipating

As children, community connectors were:

- Social conveners who organized the parties, brought people together, mixed different groups, and moved between circles
- Community-minded activists who wanted to see people treated well, wrote issue-based editorials for the local newspaper, and planned rallies around social causes
- Facilitators who were liked by teachers, but were also respected by students
- Not watchdogs, but justice-minded optimists who had a sense of right and wrong
- Trusted insiders who wanted to make the school better and remembered everyone's name at the class reunion

Community connectors' three-question tool kit:

- Who is our core community?
- What do they want and need?
- How can we make things better for them?

3. Change agents

Explorers who constantly push the limits, change agents are maverick thinkers who listen from both the inside and outside and chart a brave new course for success. They tend to have interesting, unusual networks and instinctively know what's going on at the fringes. Change agents love to take risks and take notice of the underground rumblings. They're also expert code-breakers who see parallels in divergent places.

Change agents will ensure that your organization stays fresh and evolves with the brand community. They take a highly strategic view of the operations and dream up new ways to work smarter and more effectively, and to do just about anything more creatively. Their job description may be difficult to pin down, but they are a critical source of intuitive, investigative brand intelligence.

Change agents move smoothly between customers, entry-level workers, and top executives. They develop great relationships and partnerships that always seem to pay off in the most surprising, serendipitous ways. Sometimes these "undercover" thinkers may not have the hard-and-fast facts to back up their plans, but their ideas are always worth exploring. Change agents will notice and make inspired connections that are right on target—and ahead of the competition.

Change agents' core competencies include:

- noticing
- feeling
- understanding
- exploring
- trying
- influencing
- risk taking
- connecting

As children, change agents were:

- Not the most popular kids, but able to infiltrate any group
- Always blazing new trails, so they preferred to work on the side rather than the center
- Treasure hunters and decoders of secrets
- Influencers who started new trends or whose quirky activities or ideas built a loyal following
- Chameleons who were equally at home with grandparents, siblings, the corner store owner, and the babysitter down the street

Change agents' three-question tool kit:
- What is happening that no one else is seeing?
- How could we push the edges and the limits?
- What are people not telling us?

4. Visionary leaders

When it's time to generate excitement, you need visionary leaders: not paper figureheads pushing nothing but carnival smoke and mirrors, but talented, driven motivators who can visualize the finish line in the distance and how to get there. These strong people will attract funding, launch challenging projects, and inspire everyone to give their very best.

Visionary leaders are most effective when they know what's on the table. They have a clear sense of where the brand should go and what it means to succeed. These compelling professionals will clearly and effectively communicate the vision and stand firm, even in the face of criticism or tricky obstacles.

Visionaries can be animated or reserved, but they are magnetic and tend to naturally convince people to buy into their dreams and their ability to execute. Projects may come and go, but everyone follows as these charismatic people navigate the twists and turns. Visionary leaders ooze confidence and move forward with an unshakable belief that "this will work."

The core competencies of visionary leaders include:

- leading
- supporting
- encouraging
- continuing
- believing
- motivating
- provoking
- inspiring

As children, visionary leaders were:

- The popular leaders of the pack who attracted a following and commanded the whole group
- Exciting influencers whose absence was sharply apparent if they moved, missed a day of school, or left the group
- Big thinkers with good (but not the most original) ideas, who loved to manage other people as they sold the chocolates, ran the lemonade stand, or built the snow fort
- Social boosters who made other kids feel good, smart, fun, and better than they normally would feel about themselves
- Quietly compelling or loud and outrageous. Either way, people listened and followed their lead

- Stand-out personalities who attracted attention (and project funding) from parents and teachers alike
- Known for their poise and polished social skills, and often called the "ones to watch," who might become CEOs, celebrities, and politicians

Visionary leaders' three-question tool kit:

- How and why will this work?
- Who needs to know about it?
- Why is this the best way to proceed?

5. **Architects**

These essential players build structures and environments that encourage participation. Architects make sure that everything is simple, clean, easy, useful, and fun. In many cases, architects are brilliant with new media or technology, but they are never mere server room hobbits. They create innovative ways for people to enjoy the new marketplace.

Architects need to work with every team member at some stage in the game. Their guiding purpose is to make sure that things actually function as planned. They suggest adjustments and ways to improve the brand at every juncture. These logical thinkers are specific and highly detail oriented—nothing is too small or insignificant to tackle.

Rarely do architects crave the spotlight, but they are wonderful at bringing out the best in others and love to teach new skills. They think carefully about what will enable their friends and colleagues to perform with maximum results. Architects are usually not out to change the world (or the brand), but they know how to put the pieces together. For them, it's all about coordination.

Architects' core competencies include:

- teaching
- training
- adjusting

- tweaking
- coordinating
- planning
- helping
- developing
- fixing

As children, architects were:

- Behind-the-scenes organizers who figured out how to pull off the Halloween costume dance or make the cafeteria food better
- Not the public face of get-togethers or projects, but the ones who called everyone, put the teams together, and organized the baseball games on Saturday afternoon
- Planners who created environments that would help people achieve their goals. If four girls arrived at the ball diamond, the architect decided how to involve them, and still keep the boys happy.
- Calm realists who showed you how to play tether ball or explained the double Dutch jump rope game
- Imaginative problem solvers who turned the abandoned lot into a skateboard park
- Masters of course correction and restructuring who figured out why the tree house was sagging and mobilized both parents and kids to fix the problem

Architects' three-question tool kit:

- What will make this work even better?
- How can we bridge all these different worlds?
- What will be the best way to help people thrive?

I recently saw a movie that helped me visualize the discovery process I experienced while writing this book. The camera angle started in tight, near the ground. All textured and pixilated, it was difficult to even see what the object was. Slowly the camera backed away, exposing a park bench, and as it reached higher, it became obvious we were above New York City's famous Central Park. As the camera lifted, the island of Manhattan came into view and eventually I was staring at the earth suspended in space. Ah, perspective. Sometimes perspective and insight are all about where the lens is focused and how high you're positioned.

This book started with a vague notion that the landscape was shifting as I noticed the rumblings in my own network. You might be sensing change in your organization, too. I suggest you get your latte and napkin out and begin to scribble down what you're seeing. I assure you, the shift is real and you're probably taking in more information and subconscious details than you realize. Take time to bring all these peripheral thoughts to the surface. Scribbling them down is the equivalent of lifting the camera up a good ten feet to gain some initial perspective.

Next, you need to look strategically at what you're noticing. Perhaps you're seeing in action some of the ten cravings discussed in this book (Is your audience primarily interested in making discoveries for themselves? In adventure? In beautiful design?), and certainly you're observing how the five essential criteria (experience, transparency, reinvention, connection, and expression) are alive in your brand community. Make note of the most powerful craving in your industry and the form it takes. At this point, you might want to select a few maverick brands or examples from the appropriate chapter and use them as learning models.

This book provides a framework for putting that insight into practical, profitable use, but it still requires a leap on your part. This is a time of unprecedented change and your challenge is not to blindly take action, but to assemble the puzzle pieces and move forward with clarity and intention.

The Connected Generation has left the building. They're not there to heed the obvious ads or to passively accept what brands dish up, or to settle for the old, impersonal models. Instead, they have entered a wide-open space and created a dynamic consumer playground.

Get out there and participate.

ACKNOWLEDGMENTS

My faith, family, and friends make my life and business such a fun and meaningful adventure.

This book is the culmination of some of the most heartfelt and brilliant help around. First and foremost to the incomparable Cheri Hanson, who is hands down the finest writer, thinker, and partner I could ever have dreamed of working with. Researching and writing this book with you was an amazing adventure—we cracked a code and built a great friendship. When we work together everything feels possible.

Huge thanks to the team at Free Press and especially my editor Wylie O'Sullivan, who championed this book from the beginning and brought her insight and talent to every step of the process. I am grateful to my literary agent Kim Goldstein for her encouragement and hard work.

For my husband Dave, who is the definition of support and belief. Thank you for jumping off cliffs with me and standing together during the hard and the good. Thanks to my parents Larry and Joyce Fisher (the ultimate grandparents!) whose eyes always light up for me. My sister Kris Harris, who has the best laugh, and sweet Cooper, my fellow book fan, who makes me smile. Levi, Hannah, and Micah, who have character to match their assignments. You are all three quite "magical." My assistant, Katie Lilly, who "gets me" and has made my life so much easier. Nicole Williams, whose candid conversations, timely introductions, and genuine friendship have helped me navigate my life and career in new directions.

A heartfelt thanks to my legendary friends who have been a source of great belief, growth, adventure and laughter: Robyn Knox, Tutti McCormick, Jami York, Kalen Lee, Marcie Whittier, Danita Hamel, Rachel Johnson, Amy Smith, Evie Poole, Christy Curtis, Katie Haynes, Scott and Darcy Penzer, Katie Leonard, Molly Barry, and Mary Lou Davis.

NOTES

INTRODUCTION

1. As this generation gets older, Gen Y will probably refer to everyone born from 1980 to 1999. According to common usage as reflected in most dictionaries, Gen X includes all those in the United States born in the 1960s or 1970s (from 1960 to 1979), but for marketing purposes, it is common to segment out those born from 1960 to 1964 as members of the tail end of the postwar Baby Boom. Thus, Gen X is confined to those born from 1965 to 1979, and the Baby Boomers represent those born from 1945 to 1964.

CHAPTER 1: SHINE THE SPOTLIGHT

1. Chris Murphy is a fictional athlete.
2. Interview with Deryk Gilmore and the University of Oregon Sports Marketing intern staff. Deryk Gilmore left his position as director of player development on March 15, 2005, and is currently working as a sports agent.
3. "Gravanity," *Trend Watching,* January 2005, www.trendwatching.com/trends/.
4. Allen Wallace, "More Details on Classes Six Through Ten," *Superprep* magazine, February 23, 2004.
5. NCAA Rules and Bylaws, www.ncaa.org.
6. Ryan Underwood, "Jones Soda's Secret," *Fast Company* magazine, March 2005.
7. Sarah Sennott, "Customer Placement Advertising: The Latest Marketing Trend Makes the Consumer a Player Inside the Commercial," *Newsweek International Edition,* November 29, 2005, www.msnbc.msn.com/id/3037881/site/newsweek/.
8. Amazon.com, "The Playstation #2 itoy," Amazon.com review.
9. University of Oregon football staff, *Oregon Recruiting Guide,* 2004.
10. Rob Moseley, "Ducks Crank up the Cool Factor with Comic Relief," *Register-Guard,* January 26, 2005, www.registerguard.com.
11. Steve Rogers, "ESPN Announces 'Dream Job 2' and '3' Casting Calls, Moves Second Series Premiere up to September," *Reality TV World,* June 23, 2004, www.realitytvworld.com.
12. Douglas Atkin, *The Culting of Brands* (New York: Penguin, 2004), page 76, www.cultingofbrands.com.

CHAPTER 2: RAISE MY PULSE

1. Interview with Jack Elmer of JaCiva's.
2. Interview with Brian Kurth of Vocation Vacations, www.vocationvacations.com.
3. Mark Romeo, "Experience Club," *The Experience Economist Blog,* May 25, 2004, blog.brandexperiencelab.org.
4. See "About the Academy," www.scratch.com.
5. Lorrie Grant, "Maytag Stores Let Shoppers Try Before They Buy," *USA Today,* June 6, 2004, www.usatoday.com.
6. Excerpt from Lisa Johnson, "Rutabaga Water Divas—Boosting Profits and Participation with a 'Visible' Marketing Approach," *Reaching Women,* February 2005, www.reachwomen.com/articles.php.
7. See Nike operations 6453, Trend Watching, www.trendwatching.com.
8. See "Company Info," www.thrillseekersunlimited.com.

CHAPTER 3: MAKE LOOSE CONNECTIONS

1. Anick Jesdanun, "MySpace Looks Like Everybody's Hot Spot on the Net," *Associated Press,* February 19, 2006.
2. Interview with Natasha Duprey.
3. Lydia Polgreen, "The Pen Is Mightier than the Lock," *The New York Times,* September 17, 2004, www.nytimes.com.
4. Caroline Hsu, "Tribal Culture: Single But Not Alone, These Urbanites Are Redefining the 'Adultescent' Years," *U.S. News & World Report,* October 13, 2003, www.usnews.com.
5. Robert Wuthnow, *Loose Connections: Joining Together in America's Fragmented Communities* (Cambridge, MA: Harvard University Press, 2002).
6. Nancy Hass, "In Your Facebook," *The New York Times,* January 8, 2006, www.nytimes.com.
7. *Trend Letter* quote referenced by Myra Stark, *"2004: The Consumer Context Report,"* Saatchi & Saatchi Web site, www.saatchikevin.com.
8. Katharine Mieszkowski, "Steal This Bookmark! Tagging, the Web's Newest Game, Lets You See What Other People Are Reading and Thinking. Welcome to the Key-Worded Universe," *Salon,* February 8, 2005, www.salon.com.
9. Jim McClellan, "Tag Team: An Innovative Photo Organizing Service Is Taking the Web by Storm," *The Guardian,* February 3, 2005, www.guardian.co.uk.

Additional Reading

Associated Press, "MySpace Source of New Fears," *Boston Herald,* February 20, 2006, www.bostonherald.com.

Comments

All popular Internet sites come with inherent risks and controversies, and MySpace is no exception. Police, parents, and school administrators have urged caution and taken steps to protect children and teenagers from online predators. For example, in March 2006 a federal grand jury indicted two men who prosecutors say used MySpace.com to set up sexual encounters with two underage Connecticut girls, ages eleven and fourteen. Online bullies have used MySpace profiles to threaten fellow students and mock staff members. In response, some schools have restricted Internet access from school computers or even ordered students to take down personal Web logs, regardless of where they are updated and accessed.

CHAPTER 4: GIVE ME BRAND CANDY

1. Motorola Press Release, "Introducing the Motorola Razr V3," July 27, 2004, www.motorola.com.
2. Roger Jellicoe quoted in Scott D. Anthony, "Motorola's Bet on the Razr's Edge," *Harvard Business School Working Knowledge,* September 12, 2005, http://hbswk.hbs.edu/index.jhtml.
3. Roger Jellicoe quoted in Anthony, "Motorola's Bet on the Razr's Edge."
4. Bruce Nussbaum, "Get Creative," *BusinessWeek,* August 1, 2005, www.businessweek.com.
5. Norio Ohga quoted in David Polcaro, "Design and Usability—Bridging the Gap," *Pixel Bridge,* February 2002, www.pixelbridge.com/index.php.
6. Bill Moggridge quoted in "What Is Design," *Design Council,* www.design-council.org.uk.
7. Virginia Postrel, *The Substance of Style* (New York: HarperCollins, 2003), www.vpostrel.com.
8. David Danielson, B. J. Fogg, Leslie Marable, Cathy Soohoo, Julianne Stanford, and Ellen R. Tauber, "How Do People Evaluate a Web Site's Credibility?," *Consumer Reports,* October 29, 2002, www.consumerwebwatch.org/index.cfm.
9. Interview with Nancy Lafferty-Wellott of Habits & Habitats, www.habitsandhabitats.com.
10. Site editor, "Case Study, Oxo International—Good Grips Kitchen Tools," *Design Council,* March 2, 2004, www.design-council.org.uk.
11. Site editor, "Design Index," *Design Council,* January 8, 2005, www.design-council.org.uk.
12. Brandon Schauer, "Interview: John Zapolski: Design as a Core Strategy," *Institute of Design,* www.id.iit.edu.
13. Roger Jellicoe quoted in Anthony, "Motorola's Bet on the Razr's Edge."
14. Phil Schiller quoted in Lev Grossman, "Stevie's Little Wonder," *Time* magazine, September 19, 2005, www.time.com.
15. Roger Jellicoe quoted in Anthony, "Motorola's Bet on the Razr's Edge."
16. Interview with Moni Wolf, director of design for Motorola iDEN, www.motorola.com.
17. Rick Lingle, "Go-Gurt: An Updated View," *Packaging World* magazine (Web exclusive), August 1, 2002, www.packworld.com.
18. Tina Zinter-Chahin quoted in Stanley Holmes, Christopher Palmeri, and Joseph Weber, "Mosh Pit's of Creativity," *BusinessWeek,* November 7, 2005, www.businessweek.com.
19. Site editor, "Case Study, Almus-drug Packaging," *Design Council,* March 8, 2004, www.design-council.org.uk.

20. Jay Ihlenfeld quoted in Michael Arndt, "3M: Reading Between the Lines," *Business-Week,* August 1, 2005, www.businessweek.com.
21. IDEO quoted on www.tompeters.com.
22. Site editor, "Case Study, Oxo International–Good Grips Kitchen Tools."
23. Motorola/Burton Snowboards press release, "Motorola and Burton Snowboards Announce Relationship and Unveil State-of-the-Art Snowboarding Products," July 25, 2005.

CHAPTER 5: SIFT THROUGH THE CLUTTER

1. Interview with Stuart Hunter, roll: Bicycles.
2. "Twinsumer," *Trend Watching,* www.trendwatching.com/trends/.
3. Jeffery Zaslow, "If Your TiVo Thinks You Are Gay, Here's How to Set It Straight," *The Wall Street Journal,* November 29, 2002, www.wsj.com.
4. Steven Gray and Ethan Smith, "New Grind at Starbucks, a Blend of Coffee and Music Create a Potent Mix," *The Wall Street Journal,* July 19, 2005, www.wsj.com. Also see www.hearmusic.com.
5. Katharine Mieszkowski, "Steal This Bookmark! Tagging, the Web's Newest Game, Lets You See What Other People Are Reading and Thinking. Welcome to the Key-Worded Universe."
6. See "Steve Ells Founder and CEO Story," www.chipotle.com.
7. Polly La Barre, Melinda Davis, and Glen Senk, "Do You Offer Your Customers What They Really Want?," *Fast Company RealTime Blog,* June 3, 2003, www.fastcompany.com.
8. Vicki Iovine and Peg Rosen, *Girlfriends' Guide to Baby Gear* (New York: Perigee, 2003).

CHAPTER 6: KEEP IT UNDERGROUND

1. Interview with Brett Riepma, Toyota Scion owner.
2. See the Rebel Organization, "Scion Case Study," www.rebelorganization.com.
3. Jeri Yoshizu quoted in the Rebel Organization, "Scion Case Study."
4. Cited in Brett Clanton, "DaimlerChrysler Explores Brand for Younger Buyers," *The Detroit News,* July 26, 2004, www.detnews.com.
5. Todd Lassa quoted in Jonathan Cunningham, "Underground Highway: Toyota's Scion Uses Urban Marketing," *Metro Times,* January 12, 2005, www.metrotimes.com.
6. Malcolm Gladwell, *The Tipping Point* (New York: Little, Brown, 2000), www.gladwell.com.
7. Cited in Andy Cutler, "The Need for Customer-Centric Marketing," iMedia Connection, August 17, 2005, www.imediaconnection.com.
8. See "Media Relations," www.harley-davidson.com.
9. Jamie Allen, "This 'Witch' Boasting Wicked Marketing Brew," *CNN Interactive,* www.cnn.com.
10. Cited in Word of Mouth Marketing Association, "Research and Metrics," www.womma.org/research.htm.

11. Cited in Word of Mouth Marketing Association, "Research and Metrics."

12. Cited in Word of Mouth Marketing Association, "Research and Metrics."

13. J. Walker Smith, "Re-engaging Resistant Consumers: The Practice of Compelling Marketing," live presentation at the Advertising Research Foundation's 51st Annual Trade Show and Convention, April 18, 2005. See also www.yankelovich.com.

14. Josh Levine quoted in the Rebel Organization, "Scion Case Study."

15. Interview with Jackie Huba, coauthor of *Creating Customer Evangelists,* www.creating customerevangelists.com.

16. Jack Morton, "2003 Worldwide Experiential Marketing Survey," October 22, 2003, www.jackmorton.com.

17. Jennifer Vilaga, "Profitable Player: Kiehl's," *Fast Company,* October 2005, www.fast company.com.

18. BMW USA press release, "The Hire—the Acclaimed Film Series by BMW—Will End a Four and a Half Year Internet Run October 21st," October 11, 2005, www.bmwusa.com/bmwexperience/filmspr.htm.

19. Kerry A. Dolan, "The Soda with Buzz," *Forbes,* March 28, 2005, www.forbes.com.

20. "Parsons Students to Develop Fashion and Product Design Concepts for the Vespa," *Dexinger.com,* December 8, 2004. See also www.vespausa.com.

21. Reuters, "Grass-roots Marketing for Napoleon Dynamite," *MSNBC,* July 21, 2004, www.msnbc.com.

22. Cited in Chris Woodyard, "Outside-the-Box Scion Scores with Young Drivers," *USA Today,* May 2, 2005, www.usatoday.com.

23. Darren Seeman quoted in Chris Woodyard, "Outside-the-Box Scion Scores With Young Drivers."

Additional Reading

Fara Warner, "Learning How to Speak to Gen Y: Toyota's Quest to Woo Younger Consumers Is a Drive Toward Companywide Innovation," *Fast Company,* July 2003, www.fastcompany.com.

Linda Tischler, "The Good Brand," *Fast Company,* August 1, 2004, www.fastcom pany.com.

Anni Layne Rodgers, "Traditional Car Companies Are Courting a New Group of Consumers with Hard-driving Innovation," *Fast Company,* June 1, 2002, www.fast company.com.

CHAPTER 7: BUILD IT TOGETHER

1. Wikipedia.org, Jimmy Wales profile.

2. Wikipedia.org, Wikipedia profile.

3. Gnu.org, Preamble, November 2002.
   According to www.gnu.org, "the purpose of the GNU Free Documentation License is to make a manual, textbook, or other functional and useful document 'free' in the sense of freedom: to assure everyone the effective freedom to copy and redistribute it, with or without modifying it, either commercially or noncommercially. Secondarily, this License preserves for the author and publisher a way to get credit for their work, while not being considered responsible for modifications made by others."

4. Daniel H. Pink, "The Book Stops Here," *Wired* magazine, March 2005.
5. Esther Dyson quoted in group interview transcript, "The Road Ahead," *Time* magazine, October 24, 2005.
6. Cited in Amanda Cantrell, "eBay Tumbles on Reduced Guidance," *CNN Money,* October 19, 2005, www.cnnmoney.com.
7. Cited in Robert D. Hof, "The Future of Tech: The Power of Us," *BusinessWeek,* June 20, 2005.
8. Cited in Robert D. Hof, "The Future of Tech: The Power of Us."
9. Cited in Robert D. Hof, "The Future of Tech: The Power of Us."
10. Christopher Carfi, "The Social Customer Manifesto," *The Social Customer Manifesto Blog,* September 2005, www.socialcustomer.com.
11. C. K. Prahalad and Venkat Ramaswamy, *The Future of Competition* (Boston: Harvard Business School Press, 2004), page 2.
12. Yochai Benkler, "Coase's Penguin, or, Linux and the Nature of the Firm," *Yale Law Journal,* 112: 2002.
13. Jeff Bezos quoted in Robert D. Hof, "The Future of Tech: The Power of Us."
14. C. K. Prahalad and Venkat Ramaswamy, *The Future of Competition,* pages 129–30.
15. Christopher M. Schroeder, "Is This the Future of Journalism?," *Newsweek* (Web exclusive), June 18, 2004, www.newsweek.com.
16. Press release, "33 Million American Internet Users Have Reviewed or Rated Someone or Something as Part of an Online Rating System," Pew Internet & American Life project, October 20, 2004, www.pewinternet.org.
17. Jimmy Wales and Tom Panelas quoted in Robert D. Hof, "The Future of Tech: The Power of Us."
18. John Blau, "eBay Buys Skype for $2.6 Billion," *PC World,* September 12, 2005, www.pcworld.com. See also www.skype.com.
19. Pamela Parker, "Study: Craigslist Costs Bay Area Newspapers $50M/Year," *ClickZ,* December 27, 2004, www.clickz.com.
20. Stephanie Olsen, "Scripps to Buy Shopzilla for $525 million," *CNET News.com* June 6, 2005, www.news.com.
21. Deborah Ball, "Toll-Free Tips: Nestlé Hotlines Yield Big Ideas," *The Wall Street Journal,* September 3, 2004, page A7.
22. Flexcar press release, "Steve Case's Revolution Acquires Flexcar," August 31, 2005, www.flexcar.com.
23. John Teresko, "Technology Leader of the Year–P & G's Secret: Innovating Innovation," *Industry Week,* December 1, 2004. See also www.pgconnectdevelop.com.

Additional Reading

John Seigenthaler, "A False Wikipedia 'Biography,'" *USA Today,* November 29, 2005, www.usatoday.com.

knowledge@Wharton, "Can Wikipedia Survive Its Own Success?" *Managing Technology Wharton,* January 27, 2006, www.knowledge.wharton.upenn.edu/article/1361.cfm.

Comments

The open-source nature of Wikipedia is not without its casualties and controversies. On November 29, 2005, journalist John Seigenthaler, Sr., once a member of Robert

Kennedy's staff, wrote an op-ed piece in *USA Today* noting that an article on Wikipedia had incorrectly linked him to the assassinations of Robert Kennedy and John F. Kennedy. The Wikipedia article, which was live on the Web site for four months, stated that "John Seigenthaler, Sr. was the assistant to Attorney General Robert Kennedy in the early 1960s. For a brief time, he was thought to have been directly involved in the Kennedy assassinations of both John and his brother Bobby. Nothing was ever proven." After being contacted by Seigenthaler, Wikipedia eventually deleted the inaccurate information, and today contains an entry entitled, "John Seigenthaler, Sr. Wikipedia biography controversy" explaining the history of the false entry.

In another example of controversial editing, former MTV VJ and podcasting pioneer Adam Curry was accused of deleting Wikipedia's references to Kevin Marks, another early podcasting pioneer. In a December 2, 2005, blog entry, Curry took ownership of the deletion and apologized.

Some entries require ongoing diligence. Potentially controversial Wikipedia entries, such as one on George W. Bush, welcome readers with the following: "In response to recent vandalism, editing of this page by new or anonymous users has been temporarily disabled. Please discuss possible changes or request unprotection."

CHAPTER 8: BRING IT TO LIFE

1. Amy Gunderson, "26 Most Fascinating Entrepreneurs: Tom LaTour Kimpton Hotels and Restaurants," *Inc.*, April 2005, www.inc.com.
2. Kimpton press kit, "Kimpton Hotels and Restaurants Overview."
3. Interview with Vanessa Bortnick, Kimpton Hotels Media Relations.
4. Eric Wahlgren, "That's Entertainment!," *BusinessWeek,* June 2, 2005, www.business week.com.
5. Jerry Gregorie quoted in Jena McGregor, "2004 Customer First Awards: Experiencing the Next Competitive Battleground," *Fast Company,* www.fastcompany.com.
6. Jeff Bezos quoted in Jena McGregor, "2004 Customer First Awards: Experiencing the Next Competitive Battleground."
7. Cited in Shaun Smith, "Profiting from the Customer Experience Economy," 2001, www.customerserviceworld.com.
8. Niki Leondakis quoted in Philip Hayward and Jessica Downey, "Good Thinking: How the Hotel Industry Innovates and the Cultures That Drive It," *Lodging Hospitality* magazine, December 2004.
9. Joe Wilcox, "Moseying up to Apple's Genius Bar," *CNET News.com,* May 16, 2001, www.news.com.
10. See www.destinationkohler.com.
11. Carlo Wolff, "Environmental Evangelism," *Lodging Hospitality* magazine, March 2005.
12. Bruce Horovitz, "A Whole New Ballgame in Grocery Shopping: Whole Foods Turns Drudgery into Entertainment," *USA Today,* March 8, 2005, www .usatoday.com.
13. Jena McGregor, "High Tech Achiever: Mini USA," *Fast Company,* October 2004, www.fastcompany.com.
14. Liz Krieger, "T&L Reports: Plane Pampering," *Travel & Leisure* magazine, August 2004, www.travelandleisure.com.

Additional Reading

Gene Sloan, "Let the Pillow Fights Begin," *USA Today,* Friday, August 27, 2004, www.usatoday.com.

Jill Rose, "Feel the Beat," *American Executive* magazine, June 2005, www.redcoat publishing.com.

Ryan Tate, "Kimpton Hotels Remakes Its Beds," *San Francisco Business Times,* January 28–February 3, 2005, http://sanfrancisco.bizjournals.com/sanfrancisco.

Liz French, "Corporate Spotlight: Kimpton Hotels," *American Executive* magazine, December 2004, www.redcoatpublishing.com.

CHAPTER 9: GO INWARD

1. Interview with Cameron Strang of Relevant Media Group, www.relevant-magazine.com.
2. Barna Research Group, "Religious Activity Increasing in the West," *Barna Update,* March 1, 2004, www.barna.org.
3. Jane Buckingham quoted in Barbara Pinto, "Christian-Themed Apparel Sees Popularity Surge," *ABC World News Tonight,* May 5, 2005, www.abcnews.go.com.
4. Cited in S. Johanna Robledo, "Big Story: Top 5 Parenting Trends of 2004," www.babycenter.com.
5. Reboot press release, "Study: Most Young Adults Value Faith, But Shun Organized Religion," April 11, 2005, www.rebooters.net/poll.html.
6. Higher Education Research Institute UCLA, "College Students Show High Levels of Spiritual and Religious Engagement," November 21, 2003, part of an ongoing research study titled "Spirituality in Higher Education: A National Study of College Students' Search for Meaning and Purpose," www.spirituality.ucla.edu.
7. Reboot press release, "Study: Most Young Adults Value Faith, But Shun Organized Religion."
8. Margaret Feinberg, *Twentysomething: Surviving and Thriving in the Real World* (Nashville: W Publishing Group, 2004), www.margaretfeinberg.com.
9. Reboot press release, "Study: Most Young Adults Value Faith, But Shun Organized Religion."
10. Paul Chavez, "Rock the Vote in Debt, Hopes to Keep Rolling," *Chicago Sun-Times,* February 15, 2006. See also www.rockthevote.org.

Rock the Vote turned sixteen in 2006, after celebrating a successful young voter turnout in the 2004 election. However, the birthday milestone marked a tough year, as the nonprofit group founded in Los Angeles in 1990 is $500,000 in debt and down to just two employees, from twenty in 2002, according to tax documents and Hans Riemer, the organization's political director. The organization, which is in the process of restructuring, provided a letter to the *Los Angeles Times* in February 2006 that said Rock the Vote has a "modest debt" that is typical after a presidential election. "While no organization wants to deficit finance, elections are important enough to require hard choices," the letter said in response to a recent article on its financial struggle. "So when we sensed the surge of youth participation in 2004, we used all the credit at our disposal. This is something organizations do routinely." Rock the Vote registered 1.4 million voters for the 2004 election at college campuses.

11. IlkoneTel press release, "Islamic Mobile Phone Launched," August 14, 2004, www.ilkonetel.com.

CHAPTER 10: GIVE BACK

1. Andrea Orr, "Attracting Attention: The Taproot Foundation Provides Organized Volunteers Who Deliver Marketing Expertise," *Stanford Social Innovation Review*, Spring 2005.
2. Interview with Aaron Hurst, president and founder of the Taproot Foundation, www.taprootfoundation.org.
3. Anne Fisher, "Do Gen Xers Balance Work and Life Differently?," *Fortune*, August 10, 2004, www.money.cnn.com/magazines/fortune/.
4. Peter Panepento, "Connecting with Generation X," *Chronicle of Philanthropy*, March 31, 2005, www.philanthropy.com.
5. Cited in "Doing Well in Your Career by Doing Good Outside It," *The New York Times*, February 27, 2005, www.nytimes.com.
6. Penelope Trunk, "Grassroots Volunteering Draws Young People," *The Boston Globe*, May 29, 2005, www.boston.com.
7. Peggy Woods quoted in Sharon Jayson, "Building on Volunteerism: Young People Increasingly Are Giving of Themselves," *One Star Foundation*, December 9, 2004, www.onestarfoundation.org.
8. Lisa O'Donnell, "Gap vs. Grind: Authors Say 'Gap Year' Break Helps Students Focus, Grow," *The Wall Street Journal*, September 9, 2005, www.wsj.com.
9. See www.donorschoose.org.
10. Tamar Lewin, "Top Graduates Line up to Teach the Poor," *The New York Times*, October 2, 2005, www.nytimes.com.
11. Interview with Chill director Jenn Davis. See also www.burton.com/chill.
12. Joe Marconi quoted in Lauren Gard, "We're Good Guys, Buy from Us," *Business-Week*, November 22, 2004, www.businessweek.com.

INDEX

ABOUT THE AUTHORS

LISA JOHNSON is the coauthor of *Don't Think Pink* and CEO of The Reach Group, an international marketing consultancy which helps companies create more compelling brand experiences for women (ReachWomen.com) and the Connected Generation (ReachXandY .com). A sought-after corporate trainer and brand consultant, Lisa has worked with top companies nationwide and has up-to-the-minute knowledge of market forces, trends, and consumers' buying minds. Her marketing concepts have appeared in Harvard Business School's Working Knowledge, the *New York Times Magazine,* the *Chicago Tribune,* and on NPR's *Marketplace.* SoundViews named her first book *Don't Think Pink* one of the top thirty business books of 2004.

CHERI HANSON is a writer, journalist, and content strategist based in Vancouver, Canada. Her work appears in a variety of national magazines and newspapers, and she is the coauthor of *Earn What You're Worth* (Penguin Group). As a copywriter and content strategist, Cheri has collaborated with award-winning companies in a diverse range of industries including tourism, technology, marketing, publishing, and sporting goods. Visit her Web site, www.cherihanson.com.